INDEX

TO THE

DOCUMENTS OF THE LEGISLATURE OF NEW-YORK,

FROM THE YEAR 1842 TO THE YEAR 1854, INCLUSIVE.

PREPARED BY THE DIRECTION OF THE SENATE OF NEW-YORK.

BY WILLIAM H. BOGART.

"A MIGHTY MAZE, BUT NOT WITHOUT A PLAN."

ALBANY:
C. VAN BENTHUYSEN, PRINTER TO THE LEGISLATURE.
1855.

State of New-York.

No. 33.

IN SENATE, JAN. 3, 1855.

INDEX

Of Senate and Assembly documents, pursuant to resolution of March 1854.

In conformity with the direction of the Senate, contained in their resolution of 21st March, 1854, the accompanying index is submitted.

If the object of the compiler has been attained, there will be found in this catalogue, such an obvious arrangement of the subjects, that what the State has placed upon record, can be easily ascertained.

The index prepared by Philander B. Prindle, Esq., closed in 1841. This one now prepared, includes the period of 1842 and 1854.

It has been my effort to make this something more than a mere list of titles; and rather to present a classified guide to these archives.

Only in these documents, and their predecessors can be found a truthful history of the action and progress of New-York, in all that belongs to its greatness.

INDEX.

Mr. McCarty's report, claims; Doc. 84, vol. 3, Ass'y Docs. 1848.

ADJUTANT GENERAL.

Annual report, Rufus King; Doc. 41, vol. 2, Ass'y Docs. 1842.

Letter from (Rufus King) to Gov. Seward, with return of appointments; Doc. 157, vol. 7, Ass'y Docs. 1842.

Annual report (Rufus King); Doc. 24, vol. 2, Ass'y Docs. 1843.

Annual report (A. C. Niven); Doc. 5, vol. 1, Senate Docs. 1844.

Annual report (A. C. Niven); Doc. 3, vol. 1, Ass'y Docs. 1845.

Annual report (Thomas Farrington); Doc. 6, vol. 1, Ass'y Docs. 1846.

Report as to the number of uniform companies; Doc. 184, vol. 5, Ass'y Docs. 1846.

Annual report (R. E. Temple); Doc. 39, vol. 1, Ass'y Docs. 1847.

Annual report (Samuel Stevens); Doc. 54, vol. 2, Ass'y Docs. 1848.

Report of Samuel Stevens in relation to resolution of enquiry as to first division of militia; Doc. 45, vol. 2, Ass'y Docs. 1849.

Annual report (Samuel Stevens); Doc. 88, vol. 2, Ass'y Docs. 1849.

Annual report (Samuel Stevens); Doc. 51, vol. 3, Ass'y Docs. 1850.

Annual report (Samuel Stevens); Doc. 7, vol. 2, Ass'y Docs. 1851.

Annual report (L. Ward Smith); Doc. 7, vol. 1, Ass'y Docs. 1852.

Annual report (L. Ward Smith); Doc. 28, vol. 1, Senate Docs. 1853.

Report (L. Ward Smith) as to clerical force in office; Doc. 47, vol. 2, Senate Docs. 1853.

Report (R. E. Temple) as to military commutation moneys in city of New-York; Doc. 72, vol. 2, Senate Docs. 1854.

Annual report (R. E. Temple); Doc. 17, vol. 1, Ass'y Docs. 1854.

ADOPTED CITIZENS.

Report of Adjutant General Niven as to the adopted citizens forming portion of the military guard of the city of Hudson, in 1845; Doc. 16, vol. 1, Ass'y Docs. 1845.

Judiciary committee's report on petitions relative to the naturalization of foreigners; Doc. 245, vol. 7, Ass'y Docs. 1845.

ARUNAH M. ADSIT.

Report of committee on greivances, on loss of boat in canal; Doc. 136, vol. 4, Ass'y Docs. 1845.

AGRICULTURE.

Report of the American Institute, on subject; Doc. 101, vol. 4, Senate Docs. 1842.

Mr. Dickinson's report; Doc. 46, vol. 1, Senate Docs. 1843.

Mr. Daniel Lee's report; Doc. 115, vol. 5, Ass'y Docs. 1844.

Mr. Abbott's report; Doc. 198, vol 7, Ass'y Docs. 1844.

Mr. J. B. Smith's report; Doc. 60, vol. 2, Senate Docs. 1845.

Mr. Daniel Lee's report; Doc. 200, vol. 6, Ass'y Docs. 1845.

Mr. Kinne's report; Doc. 148, vol. 5, Ass'y Docs. 1846.

Mr. Beckwith's report; Doc. 150, vol. 5, Ass'y Docs. 1847.

Mr. Burchard's report on agricultural farming; Doc. 151 & 153, vol. 6, Ass'y Docs. 1847. (In same Document as report of American Institute.)

Mr. Beckwith's report on same subject; Doc. 169, vol. 6, Ass'y Docs. 1847.

Mr. R. B. Watson's report on same; Doc. 187, vol. 7, Ass'y Docs. 1847.

Mr. Tuthill's report on agricultural department in connexion with Rensselaer Institute; Doc. 192, vol. 6, Ass'y Docs. 1848.

Mr. Crispel's report on agricultural farm and college; Doc. 212, vol. 5, Ass'y Docs. 1849.

Draft Bill and testimonials in relation to Russell Comstock's discovery in agricultural science; Doc. 23, vol. 3, Ass'y Docs. 1850.

Mr. Joseph Blunt's report (commissioners J. Blunt, A. J. Downing, William Risley, Samuel Cheever, John Greig, E. C. Frost, Henry Wager, J. P. Beekman,) on the subject of an agricultural college and experimental farm; Doc. 30, vol. 3, Ass'y Docs. 1853.

Mr. W. Graham's report on appropriation to library and museum; Doc. 56, vol. 4, Ass'y Docs. 1850.

Memorial of Genesee college in relation to an agricultural farm; Doc. 86, vol. 5, Ass'y Docs. 1850.

Mr. Leavenworth's report on same subject; Doc. 104, vol. 5, Ass'y Docs. 1850.

Memorial of T. C. Peters and William Buel on the subject of an agricultural college and experimental farm; Doc. 158, vol. 6, Ass'y Docs. 1850.

Mr. G. Brayton's report on agricultural college and mechanical school; Doc. 33, vol. 2, Ass'y Docs, 1851.

Mr. Stillwell's minority report against an agricultural college, Doc. 116, vol. 4, Ass'y Docs. 1851.

Resolutions of the State of Florida in relation to a board of agriculture at Washington; Doc. 126. vol. 4, Ass'y Docs. 1851.

Mr. J. W. Babcock's report on agricultural college; Doc. 100, Ass'y Docs. 1852.

Mr. McElwain's report in relation to the agricultural society of Rensselaer county; Doc. 4, vol. 1, Senate Docs. 1853.

Mr. S. S. Smith's report in relation to an agricultural college; Doc. 36, vol. 2, Ass'y Docs. 1853.

AGRICULTURAL SOCIETY, STATE.

Transactions for 1841: Doc. 131, vol. 6, Ass'y Docs. 1842.
do 1842: Doc. 63, vol. 2, Senate Docs. 1843.
do 1843: Doc. 100, vol. 5, Ass'y Docs. 1844.
do 1844: Doc. 85, vol. 3, Senate Docs. 1845.
do 1845: Doc. 105, vol. 4, Senate Docs. 1846.
do 1846: Doc. 150, vol. 5, Ass'y Docs. 1847.
do 1847: Doc. 125, vol. 2, Ass'y Docs. 1848.

Memorial in relation to agricultural school; Doc. 65, vol. 2, Ass'y Docs. 1849.

Transactions for 1848: Doc. 200, vol. 4, Ass'y Docs. 1849.
do 1849: Doc. 175, vol. 7, Ass'y Docs. 1850.
do 1850: Doc. 120, vol. 6, Ass'y Docs. 1851.
do 1851: Doc. 126, vol. 6, Ass'y Docs. 1852.
do 1852: Doc. 112, vol. 5, Ass'y Docs. 1853.
do 1853: Doc. 151, vol. 6, Ass'y Docs. 1854.

ABRAHAM AKER.

Mr. Niven's report; privileges and elections, on claim to seat occupied by George J. J. Barber of Cortland county; Doc. 21, vol. 1, Ass'y Docs. 1845.

ALABAMA STATE.

Resolutions of, concerning national domain; Doc. 19, vol. 1, Senate Docs. 1842; Doc. 43, vol. 2, Ass'y Docs. 1842.

Resolutions of, concerning the admission of Texas; Doc. 25, vol. 2, Senate Docs. 1842; Doc. 48, vol. 2, Ass'y Docs. 1842.

Resolutions on subject of assumption of State debts, and in regard to the controversy between New-York and Virginia; Doc. 88, vol. 3, Senate Docs. 1843.

ALABAMA TOWN.

Report of Canal Board in relation to damages occasioned by overflow of canal; Doc. 136, vol. 4, Ass'y Docs. 1846.

Mr. McCarty's report; Doc. 26, vol. 2, Ass'y Docs. 1848.

Attorney General Jordan's report; Doc. 52, vol. 2, Ass'y Docs. 1848.

ALBANY.

Mr. Eli Perry's minority report on the bill concerning the election of certain officers, and the combination into one act of several acts; Doc. 114, vol. 4, Ass'y Docs. 1851.

ALBANY HOSPITAL.

Annual report of Governors; Doc. 71, vol. 3, Ass'y Docs. 1853.

ALBANY PENITENTIARY.

Mr. Finch's report; Doc. 52, vol. 2, Ass'y Docs. 1853.

ALBANY AND SCHENECTADY TURNPIKE CO.

Mr. Hopkins' report on application to abandon a portion of their road; Doc. 110, vol. 5, Ass'y Docs. 1852.

JOHN ALBERTY AND JOHN W. ALBEBTY.

Mr. Barrow's report, claims; Doc. 99, vol. 3, Ass'y Docs. 1854.

ALEXANDRIA, DISTRICT OF COLUMBIA.

Proceedings of municipal council, in relation to retrocession to Virginia; Doc. 53, vol. 4, Ass'y Docs. 1842.

HENRY P. ALEXANDER, DAVID TOMLINSON.

Mr. Fitzhugh's report; Doc. 63, vol. 2, Ass'y Docs. 1849.

SAMUEL ALEXANDER, HIRAM DICKSON.

Report of Commissioners of Land Office; Doc. 106, vol. 3, Senate Docs. 1843.

ALLEGANY COUNTY.

Mr. Wheeler's report in relation to the erection of a jail; Doc. 108, vol. 2, Ass'y Docs. 1848.

ALMS HOUSE OF NEW-YORK.

Memorial of commissioners; Doc. 57, vol. 2, Senate Docs. 1845.

AMERICAN ATLANTIC STEAM NAVIGATION COMPANY.

Mr. Titus' report on renewal of charter; Doc. 232, vol. 6. Ass'y Docs. 1845.

JACOB C. ANTHONY, ROBERT FEN.

Report of Canal Board; Doc. 43, vol. 3, Ass'y Docs. 1850.

APPEALS—COURT OF.

Report of Clerk, C. S. Benton, as to funds and securities; Doc. 110, vol. 3, Ass'y Docs. 1849.

Report of clerk, Charles S. Benton, as to funds and securities; Doc. 85, vol. 3, Senate Docs. 1849.

Report, C. S. Benton, in relation to funds and securities; Doc. 43, vol. 2, Senate Docs. 1849.

Communication from George T. Comstock, reporter, Doc. 96, vol. 5, Ass'y Docs. 1850.

Mr. Vanderbilt's report relative to the submission of the constitutionality of the Canal law of 1851: Doc. 15, vol. 1, Senate Docs. 1852.

APPOINTMENTS BY GOVERNOR AND SENATE.

List of civil officers appointed by the Governor with the consent of the Senate, Doc. 4, vol. 1, Senate Docs. 1845.

Mr. A. C. Hand's (majority) report, as to power to appoint, under new Constitution; Doc. 61, vol. 2, Senate Docs. 1847.

Mr. Joshua A. Spencer's (minority) report on same subject; Doc. 62, vol. 2, Senate Docs. 1847.

APPORTIONMENT OF REPRESENTATIVES IN CONGRESS.

Act of Congress concerning, June 25, 1842. Document A., accompanying Governor Seward's message, extra session; Doc. 106, vol. 4, Senate Docs. 1842. Doc. A., accompanying Doc. 195, vol. 7, Ass'y Docs. 1842.

Report of select committee, Mr. Ruger; Doc. 107, vol. 4, Senate Docs. 1842.

Report of committee of conference, Mr. Foster; Doc. 109, vol. 4, Senate Docs. 1842.

Report of majority select committee; Doc. 196, vol. 7, Ass'y Docs. 1842.

Report of minority; Doc. 197, vol. 7, Ass'y Docs. 1842.

Further report of select committee, Mr. S. E. Church; Doc. 198, vol. 7, Ass'y Docs. 1842.

Mr. C. D. Robinson's report, with plan of districting; Doc. 87, vol. 3, Senate Docs. 1851.

Communication from Alex. H. H. Stuart, secretary of the interior, in relation to returns of population, under census of 1820; Doc. 63, vol. 2, Senate Doc. 1821.

Majority report upon districts; Doc. 131, vol. 6, Ass'y Docs. 1851.

Mr. T. H. Benedict's minority report on division; Doc. 122, vol. 6, Ass'y Docs. 1821.

Mr. Higbie's minority report against considering the subject at the extra session; Doc. 153, vol. 6, Ass'y Docs. 1831.

APPRAISERS—CANAL.

Report and rule of appraisement; Doc. 101, vol. 5, Ass'y Docs. 1844.

Comptroller Flagg's report as to compensation; Doc. 74, vol. 2, Senate Docs. 1845.

Report in case of Joseph Demont, Orrin Tyler, Edward Myndese; Doc. 46, vol. 3, Ass'y Docs. 1845.

Report in case of Packard Bruce; Doc. 51, vol. 2, Ass'y Docs. 1847.

Report of claims allowed appraisers; Doc. 14, vol. 1, Senate Docs. 1849.

Report on Auditor of books and records; Doc. 28, vol. 1, Senate Docs. 1849.

Annual report; Doc. 69, vol. 2, Senate Docs. 1850.

Annual report; Doc. 41, vol. 2, Senate Docs. 1851.

Mr. Upham's report on the bill authorising the Canal Appraisers to award damages in certain cases; Doc. 73, vol. 3, Senate Docs. 1851.

Annual report; Doc. 60, vol. 2, Senate Docs. 1852.

Report in relation to calendar of business; Doc. 47, vol. 2, Ass'y Docs. 1853.

Annual report; Doc. 40, vol. 2, Senate Docs. 1853.

JAMES H. ARMSBY.

Address to the Albany Medical Society as its President; Doc. 85, vol. 2, Assem. Docs. 1852. (This contains the history of foreign hospitals.)

Address to the same, Nov. 1852; Doc. 67, (page 137) vol. 3; Ass'y Docs., 1833. (This contains a history of American hospitals.)

ARSENAL, STATE, CITY OF NEW-YORK.

Mr. Oakley's resolution; Doc. 62, vol. 3, Ass'y Docs. 1845.

Report of Commissioners of Land Office, Doc. 54, vol. 2 Senate Docs. 1848.

Further report on same subject; Doc. 55, vol. 2, Senate Doc. 1848.

Further report; Doc. 29, vol. 1, Ass'y Docs. 1849.

Mr. Bowen's report; Doc. 137, vol. 3, Ass'y Docs 1849.

Attorney General Jordan's report in relation to the sale of old lot to corporation of New-York; Doc. 211, Ass'y Docs. 1849.

Report in Campbell & Hood's case of claim; Doc. 43, vol. 2, Senate Doc. 1851.

ARSENALS OF THE STATE.

Report of Commissary General John Stewart; Doc. 238, vol. 5, Ass'y Docs. 1849.

ART UNION.

Mr. D. B. Taylor's report, ; Doc. 115, vol. 6, Ass'y Docs. 1853

ASSEMBLY OF 1842.

Official list; Doc. 3, vol. 1, Ass'y Docs. 1842.

Rules and orders; Doc. 6, vol. 1, Ass'y Docs. 1842.

Standing committees; Doc. 8, vol. 1, Ass'y Docs. 1842.

List of members and officers, and residences. Doc. 9, vol. 1, Ass'y Docs. 1842.

Additional rules; Doc. 10, vol. 1, Ass'y Docs. 1842.

ASSEMBLY OF 1843.

Official list; Doc. 1, vol. 1, Ass'y Docs. 1843.

Standing committees; Doc. 5, vol. 1, Ass'y Doc. 1843.

Rules and Orders; Doc. 8, vol. 1, Ass'y Doc. 1843.

ASSEMBLY OF 1844.

Official list; Doc. 1, vol. 1, Ass'y Docs. 1844.

Rules and orders; Doc. 5, vol. 1, Ass'y Docs. 1844.

Standing committees; Doc. 8, vol. 1, Ass'y Docs. 1844.

Members, Officers and residence; Doc. 11, vol. 1, Ass'y Docs. 1844.

ASSEMBLY OF 1845.

Official list; Doc. 1, vol. 1, Ass'y Docs. 1845.

Rules and orders; Doc. 5, vol. 1, Ass'y Docs. 1845.

Standing committees; Doc. 13, vol. 1, Ass'y Docs. 1845.

Residence list, of members and officers; Doc. 15, vol. 1, Ass'y Docs. 1845.

Statistical list; Doc. 205, vol. 6, Ass'y Docs. 1845.

ASSEMBLY OF 1846.

Official list; Doc. 1, vol. 1, Ass'y Docs. 1846.

Rules and orders; Doc. 2, vol. 1, Ass'y Docs. 1846.

Standing committees; Doc. 11, vol. 1, Ass'y Docs. 1846.

Residence list; Doc. 15, vol. 1, Ass'y Docs. 1846.

Statistical list; Doc. 205, vol. 6, Ass'y Docs. 1846.

ASSEMBLY OF 1847.

Official list; Doc. 1, vol, 1, Ass'y Docs. 1847.

Rules and orders; Doc. 2, vol. 1, Ass'y Docs. 1847.

Mr. Burnell's report on rules and orders; Doc. 6, vol, 1. Ass'y Docs. 1847.

Standing committees: Doc. 7, vol. 1, Ass'y Docs. 1847.

Residence list; Doc. 8, vol. 1, Ass'y Docs. 1847.

Statistical list; Doc. 161, vol. 6, Ass'y Docs. 1847.

Residence list at extra session; Doc. 193, vol. 7, Ass'y Docs. 1847.

ASSEMBLY OF 1848.

Official list; Doc. 1, vol. 1, Ass'y Doc. 1848.

Reprint of rules of 1847; Doc. 2, vol. 1, Ass'y Docs. 1848.

Rules and orders; Doc. 6, vol. 1, Ass'y Docs., 1848.

Standing committee; Doc. 8, vol. 1, Ass'y Docs. 1848.

Residence list; Doc. 9, vol. 1, Ass'y Docs. 1848.

Report in relation to an assault in the House; Doc. 213, vol. 6, Ass'y Docs. 1848.

Statistical list; Doc. 188, vol. 5, Ass'y Docs. 1848.

ASSEMBLY OF 1849.

Official list; Doc. 1, vol. 1, Ass'y Docs. 1849.

Rules and orders; Doc. 4, vol. 1, Ass'y Docs. 1849.

Standing committees; Doc. 9, vol. 1, Ass'y Docs. 1849.

List of members and officers; Doc. 11, vol. 2, Ass'y Docs. 1849.

Statistical list of do; Doc. 126, vol. 3, Ass'y Docs. 1849.

ASSEMBLY OF 1850.

Rules and orders; Doc. 2, vol. 1, Ass'y Docs. 1850.

District list; Doc. 3, vol. 1, Ass'y Docs. 1850.

Standing committees; Doc. 4, vol. 1, Ass'y Docs. 1850.

Residence list; Doc. 10, vol. 1, Ass'y Docs. 1850.

Rules and orders adopted; Doc. 12, vol. 1, Ass'y Docs. 1850.

Select committees; Doc. 21, vol. 3, Ass'y Docs. 1850.

Joint rules; Doc. 38, vol. 3, Ass'y Docs. 1850.

ASSEMBLY OF 1851.

Joint rules; Doc. 4, vol. 1, Senate Docs. 1851.

Joint rules, Mr. E. D. Morgan's report from committee of conference; Doc. 36, vol. 2, Senate Docs. 1851.

Official list; Doc. 1, vol. 1, Ass'y Docs. 1851.

Rules and orders of last Assembly; Doc. 3, vol. 1, Ass'y Docs. 1851.

Standing committees; Doc. 6, vol. 1, Ass'y Docs. 1851.

Residence list; Doc. 13, vol. 1, Ass'y Docs. 1851.

Rules and orders of the Assembly; Doc. 14, vol. 1, Ass'y Docs. 1851.

Report in relation to the purchase of the Revised Statutes; Doc. 16, vol. 1, Ass'y Docs. 1851.

ASSEMBLY OF 1851, 2D.

District list; Doc. 138, vol. 5, Ass'y Docs. 1851.

Standing commitees extra session; Doc. 141, vol. 5, Ass'y Docs. 1851.

Resolutions and rules, extra session, Doc. 142, vol. 5, Ass'y Docs. 1851.

Statistical list; Doc. 85, vol. 3, Ass'y Docs. 1851.

ASSEMBLY OF 1852.

District List; Doc. 2, vol 1, Ass'y Docs. 1852.

Rules and orders of 1851; (reprinted) Doc. 3, vol 1, Ass'y Docs. 1852.

Standing committees; Doc. 5, vol. 1, Ass'y Docs. 1852.

Rules and orders; Doc. 12, vol. 1, Ass'y Docs. 1852.

Residence list; Doc. 13, vol. 1, Ass'y Docs. 1852.

Statistical list; Doc. 128, vol. 7, Ass'y Docs. 1852.

Joint rules; Doc. 36, vol. 2, Ass'y Docs. 1852.

ASSEMBLY OF 1853.

Official list; Doc. 2, vol. 1, Ass'y Docs. 1853.

Rules and orders; Doc. 3, vol. 1, Ass'y Docs. 1853.

Amended rules and order; Doc. 7, vol. 1, Ass'y Docs. 1853.

Residence list; Doc. 9, vol. 1, Ass'y Docs. 1853.

Standing committees; Doc. 11, vol. 1, Ass'y Docs. 1853.

Rules and orders as finally adopted; Doc. 12, vol. 1, Ass'y Docs. 1853.

Joint rules; Doc. 17, vol. 2, Ass'y Docs. 1853.

Statistical list; Doc. 41, vol. 2, Ass'y Docs. 1853.

ASSEMBLY OF 1854.

Official list; Doc. 1, vol, 1, Ass'y Docs. 1854.

Reprint of rules of 1853; Doc. 2, vol. 1, Ass'y Docs. 1854.

Rules as adopted; Doc. 6, vol. 1, Ass'y Docs. 1854.

Standing committees; Doc. 8, vol. 1, Ass'y Docs. 1854.

Joint rules; Doc. 11, vol. 1, Ass'y Docs. 1854.

Residence list; Doc. 13, vol. 1, Ass'y Docs. 1854.

Statistical list; Doc. 124, vol. 3, Ass'y Docs. 1854.

ASSEMBLY CHAMBER.

Report as to printing the report of a select committee on the arrangement of seats; Doc. 27, vol. 2, Ass'y Docs. 1843.

Mr. Williams' majority report, on such arrangement; Doc. 55, vol. 3, Ass'y Docs. 1843.

Mr. M. L. Lee's report on ventilation and heating ; Doc. 29, vol. 2, Ass'y Docs. 1848.

Mr. John A. Cross' report on ventilation ; Doc. 44, vol. 2, Ass'y Docs. 1849.

State Engineer H. S. Seymours' report on ventilation; Doc. 63, vol. 4, Ass'y Docs. 1850.

Mr. L. Ward Smith's report on allowing the use of the Hall to Gerrit Smith, to deliver a lecture on Slavery, and on the question of the use of the Hall for purposes disconnected with legislation; Doc. 112, vol. 5, Ass'y Docs. 1850.

ASSEMBLY DISTRICTS.

Mr. N. K. Hall's report; Doc. 203, vol. 6, Ass'y Docs. 1846.

Report of the Secretary of State, N. S. Benton, in relation to the failure of the Board of Supervisors of Niagara county to fix the Assembly districts; Doc. 171, vol. 6, Ass'y Docs. 1847.

ASSEMBLY.

Statistical list of those persons who have represented the several counties of this State in the House of Assembly from 1777 to 1852; Doc. 128, vol. 7, Ass'y Docs. 1850.

Mr. Weeks' report relative to the impeaching power; Doc. 123, vol. 6, Ass'y Docs. 1853.

Assessments in the city of New-York for opening streets and avenues, and their incidents.

Report of Senators Furnam, Verplanck and Scott, with testimony; Doc. 100, vol. 4, Senate Docs. 1842.

Mr. J. W. Beekman's report from a select committee of investigation, with testimony; Doc. 100, vol. 5, Ass'y Docs. 1850.

ASTOR LIBRARY.

Mr. George J. Cornell's report on the memorial of the Mayor, Aldermen and Commonalty of New-York, Washington Irving and others,in relation to incorporation; Doc. 10,vol. 1, Ass'y Docs. 1849.

Annual report of trustees; Doc. 43, vol. 3, Ass'y Docs. 1850.

Annual report of trustees; Doc. 36, vol. 2, Ass'y Docs. 1854.

Annual report of trustees; Doc. 20, vol. 1, Senate Docs. 1852.

ATHENEUM AT PARIS.

Communication from the U. S. charge des affaires at Paris; H. Ledyard and consul at Paris, and Draper, in relation to the establishment of an American Atheneum at Paris; Doc. 119, vol. 4, Ass'y Docs. 1843.

ATOMIC THEORY OF LIFE.

Thomas Spencer's treatise; Doc. 67, (page 193,) vol. 3, Ass'y Docs. 1853.

ATTORNEY GENERAL.

Report of Comptroller Flagg, as to sums paid for extra services to Greene C. Bronson, Samuel Beardsley, Willis Hall, George P. Barker; Doc. 102, vol 3, Senate Docs. 1846.

Report of Comptroller Flagg, as to moneys paid John Van Buren, from Sept. 30, 1845, to Jan'y 1, 1847, other than for salary; Doc. 47, vol. 2, Ass'y Docs. 1847.

AUBURN STATE PRISON.

Annual report of Inspectors; Doc. 31, vol. 2, Ass'y Docs. 1842.

Manufacture of silk, in Document I, in Doc. 2, vol. 1, Senate Docs. 1842. Same, vol, 1, Ass'y Docs. 1842.

Annual report; Doc. 9, vol. 1, Senate Docs. 1843.

Communication from Inspectors respecting condition; Doc. 97, vol. 3, Senate Docs. 1843.

Annual report; Doc. 18, vol. 1, Senate Docs. 1844.

M. Bartlett's report; Doc. 57, vol. 2, Senate Docs. 1844.

Annual report of Inspectors; Doc. 8, vol. 1, Senate Docs. 1845.

Annual report of Inspectors; Doc. 46, vol. 2, Senate Docs. 1846.

Report of Agent, Russell Chappel, as to earnings of convicts; Doc. 87, vol. 3, Senate Docs. 1846.

Report of Inspectors in relation to the punishment of the convict Plumb; Doc. 83, vol. 3, Ass'y Docs. 1846.

Report of Inspectors in relation to their regulations of punishment; Doc. 137, vol. 4, Ass'y Docs. 1846.

Further report on same subject; Doc. 226, vol. 6, Ass'y Docs. 1846.

Annual report; Doc. 11, vol. 1, Senate Docs. 1847.

Report of Luman Sherwood, an Inspector; Doc. 12, vol. 1, Senate Docs. 1847.

Annual report of Inspectors; Doc. 30, vol. 1, Senate Docs. 1848.

Report of committee on claims on the account of Christopher Morgan and T. M. Pomeroy, as counsel for the State in the examination of the charges against the Inspectors and Agent, made by Isaac Sisson; Doc. 17, Vol. 1, Senate Docs. 1853.

Inspector Darius Clark's report on indebtedness; Doc. 62, vol. 2, Senate Docs. 1854.

AUCTION DUTIES.

Comptroller Flagg's report, as to amount of such duties paid into treasury, with statistical tables; Doc. 208, vol. 6, Ass'y Docs. 1845.

Mr. J. D. Stevens' report; Doc. 209, vol. 6, Ass'y Docs. 1846.

Mr. Whitney's report on restoration to city of New-York; Doc. 192, vol. 3, Ass'y Docs. 1849.

Mr. Bowen's report, with letters from New-York auctioneers; Doc. 218, vol. 5, Ass'y Docs. 1849.

Statement of duties paid, 1852; Doc. 5, (page 119) vol. 1, Ass'y Docs. 1853.

ORRIN AUSTIN.

Mr. Schoonmaker's report, claims; Doc. 14, vol. 1, Senate Docs. 1850.

HORATIO AVERILL, LEWIS AVERILL, JOSEPH BAUDER.

Report of Canal Commissioners; Doc. 114, vol. 4, Senate Docs. 1847.

THOMAS AVERILL.

Mr. S. E. Church's report; Doc. 136, vol. 7, Ass'y Docs. 1842.

AVON.

Report of Regents of the University in relation to consolidation of school districts in Avon, with the Avon academy; Doc. 105, vol. 3, Senate Docs. 1845.

ROBERT NIXON.

Mr. Schoonmaker's report, claims; Doc. 17, vol. 1, Senate Docs. 1851.

JOHN H. BABCOCK, LEANDER FOX, W. H. BENNETT.

Mr. Hale's report; Doc. 27, vol. 1, Ass'y Docs. 1849.

Mr. Fitzhugh's report; Doc. 121, vol. 3, Ass'y Docs. 1849.

JOHN H. BABCOCK, JOHN C. PHILIPS, LEWIS RANSOM.

Mr. Gilbert's report, claims; Doc. 47, vol. 2, Ass'y Docs, 1852.

LUKE P, BABCOCK, JACOB KEISTLER, CHARLES C. ELIOT, MAHITABLE ELIOT, HARRIET N. ELIOT, JOHN B. ELIOT, MARY L. STANFORD.

Mr. Schoonmaker's report, claims ; Doc. 65, vol. 3, Senate Docs. 1851.

Mr. S. Baldwin's report, claims; Doc. 79, vol. 3, Ass'y Docs. 1854.

VARNUM M. BABCOCK.

Mr. Joshua A. Spencer's report in relation to the entry of land: Doc. 126, vol. 4, Senate Docs. 1847.

Mr. S. G. Raymond's report; Doc. 39, vol. 2, Ass'y Docs. 1848.

ANTHONY T. BADGLEY, ANDREW BINGHAM.

Mr. Danforth's report, grievances; Doc. 179, vol. 5, Ass'y Docs. 1845.

HORACE BAILEY.

Mr. Manning's report; Doc. 29, vol. 2, Ass'y Docs. 1843.

BAKER, BRAYTON & Co., (Brayton & Cheesebro.)

Report of committee on claims, Mr. Ruger, on claims; Doc. 63, vol. 3, Senate Docs. 1842.

Report of Canal Board; Doc. 53, vol. 3, Ass'y Docs. 1844. Doc. 54, vol. 3, Ass'y Docs. 1844.

Mr. Alvord's report, claims; Doc. 84, vol. 3, Ass'y Docs. 1844.

Mr. Alvord's report, claims; Doc. 88, vol. 3, Ass'y Docs. 1844.

HENRY BAKER, (John G. Veeder, Administrator.)

Report of committee on claims; Doc. 64, vol. 2, Senate Docs. 1852.

Mr. Hopkins's report, claims; Doc. 53, vol. 1, Senate Docs. 1854.

BALDWINSVILLE DAM.

Mr. Lewis' report; Doc. 47, vol. 3, Ass'y Docs. 1850.

Report of Canal Board; Doc. 94, vol. 3, Senate Docs. 1850.

ALONZO C. BALDWIN, ELAM T. BALDWIN.

Report of Canal Board; Doc. 43, vol. 3, Ass'y Docs. 1844.

CHARLES BALDWIN, HALLOCK STILWELL.

Mr. J. A. Lott's report, as to marshal of court martial; Doc. 83, vol. 2, Senate Docs. 1844.

W. BALDWIN, A. P. McDONALD.

Mr. E. Ward's report, claims; Doc. 51, vol. 2, Senate Docs. 1851.

WILLIAM W. BALDWIN, CATHARINE V. S. BALDWIN.

Mr. W. A. Gilbert's report, claims; Doc. 79, vol. 2, Ass'y Docs. 1852.

THOMAS AND MARY BALL, AND THEIR SON, WILLIAM BALL.

Report of Commissioners of the Land Office; Doc. 112, vol. 5, Ass'y Docs. 1844.

BANKS AND BANKING.

Mr. Solomon Townsend's report; Doc. 148, vol. 7, Ass'y Docs. 1842.

Mr. Solomon Townsend's report Doc. 187, vol. 7, Ass'y Docs. 1842.

Memorial of citizens of Oswego county; Doc. 174, vol. 5, Ass'y Docs. 1843.

Mr. George B. Warren's report on the subject of compelling a redemption at the city of New-York; Doc. 127, vol. 5, Ass'y Docs. 1844.

Mr. Corning's report on the actual places of business of certain banks; Doc. 97, vol. 3, Senate Docs. 1845.

Report of Comptroller Flagg, of the agents for the redemption of bank notes, and the special agents to supply the place of Bank Commissioner; Doc. 100, vol. 3, Senate Docs. 1845.

Mr. Corning's report on the affairs of the Receivers of insolvent safety fund banks; Doc. 118, vol. 3, Senate Docs. 1845.

Report of Comptroller Flagg relative to the issue of registered bank notes; Doc. 161, vol. 5, Ass'y Docs. 1845.

Report of Comptroller Flagg as to stocks deposited in the banks; Doc. 31, vol. 2, Ass'y Docs. 1846.

Mr. N. K. Hall's report as to whether the annual statements of unclaimed dividends and deposites can advantageously be entered in a public book of record at the office of Secretary of State; Doc. 67, vol. 3, Ass'y Docs. 1846.

Mr. S. Lawrence's report as to redemption of bank notes in Troy; Doc. 131, vol. 4, Ass'y Docs. 1846.

Comptroller Flagg's report as to amount of canal stocks deposited as securities; Doc. 186, vol. 5, Ass'y Docs. 1846.

Further report on same subject; Doc. 202, vol. 6, Ass'y Docs. 1846.

Mr. S. Lawrence's report (bank of Dansville,) discussing the question whether the Legislature possesses the power of investigation over the banks formed under the general law; Doc. 224, vol. 6, Ass'y Docs. 1846.

Mr. H. Z. Hayner's report on same subject; Doc. 225, vol. 6 Ass'y Docs. 1846.

Attorney General Van Buren's opinion on same subject; Doc. 106, vol. 4, Ass'y Docs. 1847.

Comptroller Flagg's report as to registers; Doc. 135, vol. 4, Ass'y Docs. 1847.

Comptroller Flagg's report relative to an increase of the circulation of incorporated banks; Doc. 123, vol. 4, Senate Docs. 1847.

Comptroller Flagg's report in relation to payments to the Bank Fund; Doc. 145, vol. 4, Senate Docs. 1847.

Report of number of free banks as securities; Doc. 199, vol. 7, Ass'y Docs. 1857.

Comptroller Fillmore's report on allowances to be made to Safety Fund banks, on payments in advance; Doc. 56, vol. 2, Senate Doc. 1848.

Comptroller Fillmore's report of bank fund stock; Doc. 44 vol. 2, Senate Docs. 1848.

Mr. Ayrault's report on so much of Gov. Young's message as relates to the subject of banks; Doc. 27, vol. 1, Senate Docs. 1848.

Mr. Ayrault's report on replenishing the Safety Fund; Doc. 65, vol. 2, Senate Docs. 1848.

Comptroller Fillmore's report on the registration and issue of bank notes; Doc. 91, vol. 3, Ass'y Docs. 1848.

Mr. Schermerhorn's report relative to circulation of Safety Fund banks; Doc. 116, vol. 3, Ass'y Docs. 1848.

Mr. Schermerhorn's report on so much of Gov. Young's message as relates to banks; Doc. 70, vol. 3, Ass'y Docs. 1848.

Comptroller Fillmore's report, on deposit of money in certain banks; Doc. 182, vol. 5, Ass'y Docs. 1848.

Mr. Campbell's report, on policy of re-incorporation; Doc. 141, vol. Ass'y Docs. 1849.

Mr. J. M. Cook's report on so much of Gov. Fish's message as relates to the constitutional requirement concerning individual liability of stockholders in monied corporations; Doc. 42, vol. 2, Senate Docs. 1849.

Report of Commissioners of Canal Fund, as to the propriety of keeping deposits of public moneys in banks, exceeding one-third of the capital of said bank; Doc. 31, vol. 1, Ass'y Docs. 1849.

Mr. J. M. Cook's report in relation to admitting United States stocks as a basis of circulation; Doc. 22. vol. 1, Senate Docs. 1849.

Mr. J. M. Cook's report, on so much of Gov. Fish's message as relates to currency and banking; Doc. 53, vol. 2, Senate Docs. 1850.

Mr. Upham's minority report on same subject; Doc. 54, vol. 2, Senate Docs. 1850.

Mr. J. M. Cook's report on so much of Gov. Fish's message as relates to banks; Doc. 25, vol. 1, Senate Docs. 1850.

Report of Comptroller, W. Hunt, as to expenses of Banking Department; Doc. 85, vol. 5, Ass'y Docs. 1850.

Mr. J. M. Cook's report as to the time when Safety Fund banks shall contribute; Doc. 39, vol. 2, Senate Docs. 1851.

Report of commissioners, O. L. Holley and L. Benedict, in relation to the destruction of certain plates and bank notes; Doc. 136, vol. 5, Ass'y Docs. 1851.

Report of Comptroller, Ph. C. Fuller, on taxation; Doc. 87, vol. 3, Ass'y Docs. 1851.

Annual report of Superintendent, D. B. St. John; Doc. 9, vol 1, Ass'y Docs. 1852.

Report of investigating committee in relation to State deposites; Doc. 98, vol. 3, Senate Docs. 1852.

Annual report of Superintendent, D. B. St. John; Doc. 6, vol. 1, Ass'y Docs. 1853.

Mr. Russell Smith's report on the enlargement of the basis of circulation; Doc. 46, vol. 2, Ass'y Docs. 1853.

Mr. Russell Smith's report, in relation to circulation of Safety Fund banks; Doc. 81, vol. 4, Ass'y Docs. 1853.

BANKS.

Gov. Seymour's message, returning, with objections, the bill in relation to admitting city stocks as basis for banking; Doc. 113, vol. 6, Ass'y Docs. 1853.

Proposed acts to authorise the forming of corporations for banking purposes; Doc. 128, vol. 4, Ass'y Docs. 1854.

BANK OF ALBANY.

Report of unclaimed dividends and deposites; Doc. 33, vol. 2, Ass'y Docs. 1842.

Report of same; Doc. 187, vol. 5, Ass'y Docs. 1843.

do do do 17, vol. 1, Ass'y Docs. 1845.

Report; Doc. 175, vol. 6, Ass'y Docs. 1847.

do 203, vol. 6, Ass'y Docs. 1848.

BANK OF AMERICA.

Annual report of unclaimed dividends and deposites; Doc. 36, vol. 2, Senate Docs. 1842.

Annual report of same; Doc. 8, vol. 1, Senate Docs. 1844.

ALBANY CITY BANK.

Annual report of unclaimed dividends and deposites; Doc. 14, vol. 1, Senate Docs. 1842.

BUTCHERS' AND DROVERS' BANK.

Annual report of unclaimed dividends and deposites; Doc. 12, vol. 1, Senate Docs. 1842.

Annual report as above; Doc. 10, vol. 1, Senate Docs. 1844.

CANAL BANK, ALBANY.

Annual report unclaimed dividends and deposites; Doc. 46, vol. 4, Ass'y Docs. 1842.

Annual report as above; Doc. 195, vol. 5, Ass'y Docs. 1843.

do do do 158, vol. 6, Ass'y Docs. 1844.

do do do 220, vol. 6, Ass'y Docs. 1845.

CATSKILL BANK.

Annual report, unclaimed dividends and deposites; Doc. 20, vol. 2, Ass'y Docs. 1842.

Report of condition; Doc. 117, vol. 4, Ass'y Docs. 1843.

Annual report, unclaimed dividends and deposites; Doc. 180, vol. 5, Ass'y Docs. 1843.

Annual report of same; Doc. 179, vol. 7, Ass'y Docs. 1844.

Annual report of same; Doc. 113, vol. 4, Ass'y Docs. 1845.

CAYUGA COUNTY BANK.

Annual report of unclaimed dividends and deposites; Doc. 38, vol 2, Senate Docs. 1842.

CENTRAL BANK, CHERRY VALLEY.

Comptroller Flagg's report on issue of registered notes in place of old circulation, believed to be destroyed; Doc. 141, vol. 4, Senate Docs. 1847.

CITY BANK OF BUFFALO.

Comptroller Flagg's report as to the assets; Doc. 120, vol. 4, Ass'y Docs. 1846.

COMMERCIAL BANK, ALBANY.

Annual report of unclaimed dividends and deposites; Doc. 90, vol. 5, Ass'y Docs. 1842.

Annual report of condition; Doc. 184, vol. 5, Ass'y Docs. 1843.

Annual report of condition; Doc. 163, vol. 5, Ass'y Docs. 1845.

COMMERCIAL BANK, NEW-YORK.

Report of R. M. Blatchford, receiver; Doc. 75, vol. 3, Ass'y Docs. 1843.

DRY DOCK COMPANY, NEW-YORK.

Annual report of condition; Doc. 52, vol. 4, Ass'y Docs. 1842.
Report of same; Doc. 189, vol. 5, Ass'y Docs. 1843.
do do 181, vol. 7, Ass'y Docs. 1844.
do do 171, vol. 5, Ass'y Docs. 1845.
do do 179, vol. 7, Ass'y Docs. 1847.
do do 210, vol. 6, Ass'y Docs. 1848.

BANK OF GENEVA.

Report of unclaimed dividends and deposites; Doc. 7, vol. 1, Senate Docs. 1842.
Report as above; Doc. 199, vol. 5, Ass'y Docs. 1843.
do do 104, vol. 4, Ass'y Docs. 1845.
do do 91, vol. 2, Ass'y Docs. 1847.
do do 205, vol. 6, Ass'y Docs. 1848.

GREENWICH BANK.

Annual report of unclaimed divividends and deposites; Doc 15, vol. 1, Senate Docs. 1842.
Annual report as above; Doc. 192, vol. 5, Ass'y Docs. 1843.

LA FAYETTE BANK.

Annual report of unclaimed dividends and deposites; Doc. 10, vol. 1, Senate Docs. 1842.

LEATHER MANUFACTURERS' BANK.

Report of unclaimed dividends and deposites; Doc. 34, vol. 2, Ass'y Docs. 1842.
Report as above; Doc. 198, vol. 5, Ass'y Docs. 1843.
do do 9, vol. 1, Ass'y Docs. 1845.
do do 21, vol. 1, Ass'y Docs. 1846.
do do 172, vol. 6, Ass'y Docs. 1847.
do do 209, vol. 6, Ass'y Docs. 1848.

MANHATTAN COMPANY.

Report in relation to unclaimed dividends and deposites; Doc. 40, vol. 2, Ass'y Docs. 1842.
Report as above; Doc. 179, vol. 5, Ass'y Docs. 1843.
do do 219, vol. 6, Ass'y Docs. 1845.
do do 18, vol. 1, Ass'y Docs. 1846.

Report of unclaimed dividends and deposites; Doc. 177, vol. 7, Ass'y Docs. 1847.

Report as above; Doc. 207, vol. 6, Ass'y Docs. 1848.

MECHANICS' BANK, NEW-YORK.

Report unclaimed dividends and deposites; Doc. 252, vol. 5, Ass'y Docs. 1843.

Report as above; Doc. 159, vol. 6, Ass'y Docs, 1844.

Report; Doc. 174, vol. 6, Ass'y Docs. 1847.

MECHANICS' AND FARMERS' BANK.

Report of unclaimed dividends and deposites; Doc. 35, vol. 2, Ass'y Docs. 1842.

Report as above; Doc. 194, vol. 5, Ass'y Docs. 1843.
do do 54, vol. 3, Ass'y Docs. 1845.
do do 16, vol. 1, Ass'y Docs. 1846.
do do 176, vol. 7, Ass'y Docs. 1847.
do do 204, vol. 6, Ass'y Docs. 1848.

MERCHANTS' EXCHANGE BANK NEW-YORK.

Annual report unclaimed dividends and deposites; Doc. 191, vol. 5, Ass'y Docs. 1843.

Report as above; Doc. 170, vol. 5, Ass'y Docs. 1845.
do do 17, vol. 1, Ass'y Docs. 1846.
do do 178, vol. 7, Ass'y Docs. 1847.
do do 208, vol. 6, Ass'y Docs. 1848.

MERCHANTS' BANK.

Annual report of unclaimed dividends and deposites; Doc. 167, vol. 7, Ass'y Docs. 1844.

Report as above; Doc. 184, vol. 5, Ass'y Docs. 1845.
do do 256, vol. 6, Ass'y Docs. 1848.

NATIONAL BANK.

Annual report of unclaimed dividends and deposites; Doc. 40, vol. 2, Senate Docs. 1842.

NEW-YORK, BANK OF.

Statement of deposites and dividends unclaimed; Doc. 185, vol. 5, Ass'y Docs. 4843.

NEW-YORK STATE BANK.

Annual report of unclaimed dividends and deposites; Doc. 75, vol. 4, Ass'y Docs. 1842.

Annual report as above; Doc. 193, vol. 5, Ass'y Docs. 1843.

NORTH RIVER BANK.

Mr. Solomon Townsend's report against the re-charter as a Safety Funk bank; Doc. 79, vol. 4, Ass'y Docs. 1842.

PHOENIX BANK.

Annual report of unclaimed dividends and deposites; Doc. 17, vol. 1, Senate Docs. 1842.

Annual report of same; Doc. 182, vol. 5, Ass'y Docs. 1843.
do do do 180, vol. 7, Ass'y Docs. 1844.

UNION BANK.

Annual report of unclaimed dividends and deposites; Doc. 13, vol. 1, Senate Docs. 1842.

Annual report as above; Doc. 201, vol. 5, Ass'y Docs. 1843.

WATERVLIET BANK.

Communication from George R. Davis, receiver; Doc. 204, vol. 5, Ass'y Docs. 1854.

Further report; Doc. 227, vol. 5, Ass'y Docs. 1849.

WESTCHESTER COUNTY BANK.

Annual report of unclaimed dividends and deposites; Doc. 49, vol. 2, Ass'y Docs. 1842.

BANK OF WHITEHALL.

Annual report of unclaimed dividends and deposites; Doc. 59, vol. 4, Ass'y Docs. 1842.

Annual report of same; Doc. 190, vol. 5, Ass'y Docs. 1843.
do do do 180, vol. 5, Ass'y Docs. 1845.

BANK COMMISSIONERS.

Annual report; Forbes, Cary, Starr, Averill; Doc. 29, vol. 2, Ass'y. Docs. 1842.

Message of Governor Seward, vetoing bill changing manner of appointment; Doc. 83, vol. 4, Senate Docs. 1842.

Annual report, same Commissioners; Doc. 34, vol. 2, Ass'y. Docs. 1843.

Willis Hall's report (Banks and Insurance companies) on abolition of office and registration of bank notes; Doc. 154, vol. 5, Ass. Doc's. 1843.

BAPTIST MISSIONARY CONVENTION.

Mr. O. Clark's report, on subject of devises to religious corporations; Doc. 67, vol. 2, Senate Docs. 1844.

PETER BARGY'S ESTATE,
(Peter Cagger, Administrator.)

Report of Canal Board; Doc. 135, vol. 5, Ass'y Docs. 1843.

Mr. Van Valkenburgh's report, claims, Doc. 75, vol 2, Ass'y Docs. 1852.

JOHN M. BARHYDT, JAMES. B. VAN VORST.

Mr. N. Jones' report, claims, Doc. 62, vol. 2, Senate Docs. 1852.

OLIVER BARKER.

Report of Canal Board; Doc. 115, vol. 4, Ass'y Docs. 1846.

Mr. J. G. Floyd's report; Doc. 16, vol. 1, Senate Docs. 1849,

AARON BARNES, JOHN E. HINMAN.

Report of Canal Board; Doc. 119, vol. 5, Ass'y Docs. 1842.

Report of Canal Board; Doc. 73, vol. 3, Ass. Docs. 1845.

Mr. Tefft's report, claims, Doc. 79, vol. 3, Ass. Docs. 1845.

WILLIAM GEORGE BARNHART AND ASSOCIATES.

Mr. W. A. Wheeler's report, claims, Doc. 160, vol. 6, Ass'y Docs. 1850.

Report of Bishop Perkins, George Reddington and John Fine, Commissioners, Doc. 8, vol, 1, Ass'y. Docs. 1851.

Mr. Amsbry's report; Doc. 58, vol. 3, Ass. Docs. 1853.

Report of Commissioners of Land Office; Doc. 34, vol. 2, Ass'y. Docs. 1853.

Mr. Robert Lansing's report: Doc. 32, vol. 1, Senate Docs. 1854.

T. R. BARTO.

Mr. Gleeson's report; Doc. 24, vol. 1, Ass'y Docs. 1854.

T. D. BARTON.

Report of Commissioners' of Canal Fund as to moneys paid at Syracuse; Doc. 101, vol. 3, Senate Docs. 1846.

DAVID BARRETT.

Proceedings of Canal Board, and testimony in investigation of his acts as Canal Superintendent; Doc. 71, vol. 3, Senate Docs. 1853.

BASIN AT ALBANY.

Mr. Willis Hall's report, select committee, in relation to relief of citizens of Albany from basin assessment; Doc. 177, vol. 5, Ass'y Docs. 1843.

Mr. Stevens' report, judiciary, in relation to the assessment; Doc. 192, vol. 7, Ass'y Docs. 1844.

Report of Canal Board; Doc. 83, vol. 2, Senate Docs. 1845.

Mr. Porter's report, finance; Doc. 106, vol. 4, Senate Docs. 1846.

Mr. J. E. Beer's report, claims; Doc. 136, vol. 4, Ass'y Docs. 1847.

Mr. McCarty's report, claims; Doc. 66, vol. 3, Ass'y Docs. 1848.

Report of Canal Commissioners on construction of basin near lock No. 2; Doc. 17, vol. 3, Senate Docs. 1849.

Report of Select Committee of Senate of 1849, (T. S. Williams, D. H. Little, John Fine,) giving history of work; Doc. 7, vol. 1, Senate Docs. 1849.

Communication from Comptroller (Millard Fillmore) concerning expenses occasioned by removal of obstructions therein, caused by the great fire of August, 1848; Doc. 18, vol. 1, Senate Docs. 1849.

BASIN, WEST TROY.

Report of Canal Commissioners in answer to a resolution of Senate in relation to feasibility of construction; Doc. 65, vol. 2, Senate Docs. 1849.

Mr. Glass' report; Doc. 171, vol. 3, Ass'y Docs. 1849.

LEWIS BASTEDO, N. B KINGSLAND.

Report of Canal Board; Doc. 129, vol. 4, Senate Docs. 1846. (Involving claim of Cayuga Bridge Company of exclusive jurisdiction for three miles.)

LORENZO BATES.

Mr. Pitt's report, claims; Doc. 39, vol. 2, Ass'y Docs. 1846.

Mr. J. E. Beers' report; claims; Doc. 115, vol. 4, Ass'y Docs. 1847.

Mr. N. Jones' report, claims; Doc. 78, vol. 2, Senate Docs. 1852.

Mr. Van Valkenburgh's report, claims; Doc. 48, vol. 2, Ass'y Docs. 1852.

ASA BAXTER.

Report of Commissioners of Land Office on claim for compensation for island in St. Lawrence river; Doc. 83, vol. 3, Ass'y Docs. 1846.

Mr. Miller's report; Doc. 179, vol. 5, Ass'y Docs. 1846.

Report of Commissioners of Land Office; Doc. 107, vol. 4, Senate Docs. 1847.

Mr. Thomas E. Clark's report.

Report of Commissioner of Land Office; Doc. 41, vol. 2, Ass'y Docs. 1848.

Mr. Schoonmaker's report, claims; Doc. 35, vol. 1, Senate Docs. 1850.

LEWIS BENTON.

Mr. Towers' report, claims; Doc. 73, vol. 3, Ass'y Docs. 1843.

HORACE A. BEACH.

Mr. McNamara's report; Doc. 246, vol. 8, Ass'y Docs. 1847.

EPHRAIM BEACH.

Mr. Miller's report, claims; Doc. 118, vol. 3, Ass'y Docs. 1854.

I. L. BEARDSLEY.

Report, as supreme court clerk, at Utica, of office expenses; Doc. 44, vol. 2, Senate Docs. 1846.

Report as to fees received for taxing costs; Doc. 22, vol. 1, Senate Docs. 1847.

LEVINIA BEARDSLEE.

Report of Canal Commissioners; Doc. 48, vol. 2, Ass'y Docs. 1846.

PETER BECKER.

Mr. N. Jones' report, claims; Doc. 71, vol. 2, Senate Docs. 1852.

Mr. W. A. Gilbert's report, claims; Ass'y Docs. 1852.

JAMES L. BEEBE AND JOHN W. BEEBE.

Mr. Lewis' report; Doc. 38, vol. 1, Ass'y Docs. 1854.

LEWIS W. BEECHER.

Mr. Fiske's report on claim for compensation as witness at the trial of Alexander McLeod, at Utica; Doc. 89, vol. 5, Ass'y Docs. 1850.

WILLIAM BENTLEY.

Report of Canal Board; Doc. 91, vol. 4, Ass'y Docs. 1843.

CLAIRE FELICITE, CAROLINE BERTHEMY.

George W. Strong's petition in relation to alien children; Doc. 72, vol. 2, Senate Docs. 1844.

JOHN L. BEVINS.

Report of Canal Board; Doc 25, vol 1, Ass'y Docs. 1844.

DARIUS BENTLEY, MATHEW STARLING, JOHN E. WESTLAKE AND ABEL SHUTE.

Mr. Barrows' report, claims; Doc. 113, vol. 3, Ass'y Docs. 1854.

N. S. BENTON, (Secretary of State.)

The entries will be found at length under the head of the different subjects.

SCHOOLS.

Doc. 30, vol. 2, Ass'y Docs. 1846. Doc. 10, vol. 1, Ass'y Docs. 1847. Doc. 5, vol. 1, Ass'y Docs. 1848.

NIAGARA COUNTY ASSEMBLY DISTRICTS.

Doc. 171, vol. 6, Ass'y Docs. 1847.

CENSUS MAPS.

Doc. 23, vol. 1, Ass'y Docs. 1846.

COUNTY CLERKS.

Doc. 76, vol. 2, Senate Docs. 1845. Doc. 58, vol. 5, Senate Docs. 1847.

CRIME.

Doc. 54, vol. 2, Ass'y. Docs. 1845; Doc. 98, vol. 3, Senate Docs 1846; Doc. 180, vol. 7, Ass'y. Docs. 1847.

DISTRICT SCHOOL JOURNAL.

Doc. 188, vol. 5, Ass'y. Docs. 1846.

INSPECTION RETURNS.

Doc. 53, vol. 2, Senate Docs. 1845; Docs. 82, vol. 3, Senate Docs. 1846.

LICENSE ELECTION RETURNS.

Doc. 40, vol. 1, Ass'y. Docs. 1847.

NATURAL HISTORY.

Doc. 43, vol. 1, Senate Docs. 1845.

POOR.

Doc. 97, vol. 5, Ass'y. Docs. 1845; Doc. 199, vol. 5, Ass'y. Docs. 1846; Doc. 100, vol. 3, Senate Docs. 1847.

RAILROADS.

Doc. 66, vol. 3, Ass'y. Docs. 1846; Doc. 102, vol. 4, Ass'y. Docs. 1847; Doc. 129, vol. 4, Ass'y. Docs. 1845; Doc. 80, vol. 3, Ass'y. Docs. 1846.

WILLIAM SMITH.

Doc. 212, vol. 6, Ass'y. Docs. 1845; Doc. 149, vol. 5, Ass'y. Docs. 1846.

BIBLE SOCIETY—AMERICAN AND FOREIGN.

Mr. Hervey's majority report; Doc. 38, vol. 3, Ass'y. Docs. 1845.

Mr. Garretson's minority report; Doc. 39, vol. 3, Ass'y. Docs. 1845.

JOSEPH BICKNELL.

Mr. H. W. Strong's report in relation to bill; Doc. 60, vol. 2, Senate Docs. 1844.

BIG CHAZY RIVER.

Mr. Leslie's report on allowing the Plattsburgh and Rouse's Point Railroad Company to erect a draw-bridge; Doc. 145, vol. 5, Ass'y Docs. 1851.

Mr. Austin Smith's report on appropriation for improvement; Doc. 57, vol. 2, Ass'y. Docs. 1852.

JOHN L. BIGELOW.

(Mary T. Bigelow, Elisha J. Davis, Aaron R. Wheeler, Administrators.)

Report of Mr. Markel; Doc. 157, vol. 3, Ass'y. Docs. 1849.

ANDREW BIGHAM.

Mr. W. A. Gilbert's report, claims, Doc. 83, vol. 2, Ass'y. Docs. 1852.

BENJAMIN BIRDSALL.

Report of Secretary of State, C. Morgan; Doc. 162, vol. 3, Ass'y. Docs. 1849.

BIRTHS, MARRIAGES AND DEATHS.

Mr. F. F. Backus' report, and legislation law; Doc. 81, vol. 3, Senate Docs. 1846.

Mr. F. F. Backus' further report; Doc. 8, vol. 1, Senate Docs 1847.

Report of Secretary of State Christopher Morgan for 1847; Doc. 73, vol. 3, Senate Docs. 1848.

Report of Secretary of State Christopher Morgan for 1848; Doc. 86, vol. 3, Senate Docs. 1849.

Report of Secretary of State Henry S. Randall, Doc. 59, vol. 1, Senate Docs. 1852.

Franklin Tuthill's treatise on the registration, made to State Medical Society; Doc. 67 (page 5), vol. 3, Ass. Docs. 1853.

Communication from T. K. Downing in relation to registration; Doc. 123, vol 3, Ass'y. Docs. 1854.

CHARLES BLACKMAN.

Mr. Woodruff's report, grievances; Doc. 84, vol. 3, Ass'y Docs. 1846.

Mr. Hitchcock's report; Doc. 220, vol. 7, Ass'y Docs. 1847.

BLACK RIVER.

Mr. Schoonmaker's report, claims; Doc. 78, vol. 3, Senate Docs. 1829. (This relates to a diversion of the waters of the river for the use of the Black River and Erie canals.)

BLACK RIVER CANAL.

Mr. Commissioner Enos' report as to estimate of completion; Doc. 49, vol. 1, Senate Docs. 1843.

Report of Canal Commissioners as to cost of completion; Doc. 131, vol. 4, Ass'y Docs. 1845.

Memorial of citizens in relation to the completion; Doc. 151 vol. 5, Ass'y Docs. 1845.

Memorial of George A. Simmons and other citizens for a survey of a railroad and steamboat route from Lake Champlain to the Black River canal at Boonsville; Doc. 73, vol. 3, Senate Docs. 1846.

Report of Surveyor-General H. Halsey in relation to the State lands owned on the route of the above proposed improvement; Doc. 88, vol. 3, Senate Docs. 1846.

Report of Canal Board in relation to supply of water; Doc. 98, vol. 3, Senate Docs. 1850.

Report of D. C. Jenne, resident engineer; Doc. 102, vol. 3, Senate Docs. 1850.

BLACK ROCK.

Report of Canal Commissioners upon the draining of land on Scajaquady creek; Doc. 27, vol. 1, Ass'y Docs. 1845.

Beport of select committee on above; Doc. 27, vol. 1, Ass'y Docs. 1847.

Report of Commissioners of Land Office, in relation to the stone quarry belonging to the State; Doc. 48, vol. 2, Senate Docs. 1847.

Report of State Engineer, Charles B. Stuart, in relation to improvement of harbor. Doc. 33, vol. 2, Senate Docs. 1849.

BLIND, NEW-YORK INSTITUTION.

Annual report; Doc. 77, vol. 4, Ass'y Docs. 1842.

Annual report; Doc. 88, vol. 4, Ass'y Docs. 1843.

Annual report; Doc. 57, vol. 3, Ass'y Docs. 1844.

Annual report; Doc. 18, vol. 1, Senate Docs. 1845. Doc. 45, vol. 3, Ass'y Docs. 1845.

Mr. A. G. Thompson's report on appropriation; Doc. 92, vol. 4, Ass'y Docs. 1845.

Annual report; Doc. 38, vol. 1, Senate Docs. 1846. Doc. 61, vol. 3, Ass'y Docs. 1846.

Annual report; Doc. 50, vol. 2, Ass'y Docs. 1847.

Annual report; Doc. 59, vol. 3, Ass'y Docs. 1848.

Annual report; Doc. 84, vol, 2, Ass'y Docs. 1849.

Secretary of State, (Morgan) report concerning appointment of three State Trustees; Doc. 109, vol. 3, Ass'y Docs. 1849.

Annual report; Doc. 76, vol. 4, Ass'y Docs. 1850.

Memorial of managers for aid; Doc. 34, vol. 2, Ass'y Docs. 1851.

Annual report; Doc. 48, vol. 3, Ass'y Docs. 1851.
do do 88, vol. 2, Senate Docs. 1852.
do do 54, vol. 2, Senate Docs. 1852.

BLOOMINGDALE ROAD.

Communication from Comptroller of New-York, T. J. Waters, in relation to opening; Doc. 216, vol. 5, Ass'y Docs. 1849.

BOLINGBROKE.

Mr. S. J. Wilkins' report on Lord Bolingbroke's land title; Doc. 53, vol. 2, Senate Docs. 1848.

BARNET BOND.

Report of Canal Board, in relation to loss of boat; Doc. 93, vol. 5, Ass'y Docs. 1842.

Mr. J. E. Beers' report, claims, Doc. 210, vol. 7, Ass'y Docs. 1847.

BOSTON CORNER.

Petition from inhabitants relative to annexation to New-York; Doc. 54, vol. 2, Ass'y Docs 1849.

Mr. Stevens's report; Doc. 194, vol. 3, Ass'y Docs. 1849.

GOVERNOR BOUCK.

Annual message; Doc. 1, vol. 1, Senate Docs. 1843. Doc. 2, vol. 1, Ass'y Docs. 1843.

Message, transmitting communication from Secretary of War, concerning cession of land to United States for military purposes; Doc. 107, vol. 4, Ass'y Docs. 1843.

Annual message; Doc. 2, vol. 1, Senate Docs. 1844. Doc. 2, vol. 1, Ass'y Docs. 1844.

Message conveying proceedings of Albany meeting, held at Capitol, Nov. 21, 1843, in relation to Constitutional reform; Doc. 32, vol. 1, Ass'y Docs. 1844.

SENECA BOUGHTON, GEORGE WRIGHT.

Mr. N. Jones' report, claims; Doc. 61, vol. 2, Senate Docs. 1852.

B. E. BOWEN.

Address delivered before Oswego county medical society; Doc. 85, (page 69) vol 2, Ass'y Docs. 1852.

JOHN H. BOYD.

Mr. Porter's report, claims ; Doc. 27, vol. 1, Senate Docs. 1845.

JAMES BRADY.

Mr. Martin's report on suit brought by Adsit and Co. ; Doc. 50, vol. 2, Ass'y Docs. 1849.

Mr. Fitzhugh's report ; Doc. 37, vol. 1, Ass'y Docs. 1849.

FRANCIS J. BRAYTON.

Mr. Hitchcock's report ; Doc. 82, vol. 2, Ass'y Docs. 1847.

HARVEY BRAYTON, MILTON BRAYTON, GEORGE BRAYTON.

Mr. Barrow's report, claims ; Doc. 12, vol. 1, Ass'y Docs. 1854.

BREAKS IN THE CANAL.

Report of Canal Commissioners giving a list of the interruptions to canal navigation on the Erie and Champlain canals, from 1843 to 1852, inclusive ; Doc. 128, vol. 6, Ass'y Docs. 1853.

BRIDGE AT ALBANY.

Memorial of city authorities of Troy, against the building of a bridge ; Doc. 72, vol. 3, Ass'y Docs. 1845.

Mr. Pardee's majority report, roads and bridges, adverse to the application for a bridge ; Doc. 196, vol. 6, Ass'y Docs. 1845. (With testimony.)

Mr. Moulton's minority report favorable to the application ; Doc. 199, vol. 6, Ass'y Docs. 1845.

Mr. Pray's adverse report ; Doc. 149, vol. 5, Ass'y Doc. 1848.

Mr. T. A. Ward's report in examination ; Doc. 115, vol. 5, Ass'y Docs. 1852.

BRIDGES OVER CANALS.

Over Erie canal, at Albany ; Doc. 128, vol. 4, Ass'y Docs. 1846.

Over the Chemung, at Elmira ; Doc. 152, vol. 6, Ass'y Docs. 1847.

Over the Genesee Valley, at Troup street, Rochester ; Doc. 221, vol. 7, Ass'y Docs. 1847.

BRIGHAM, STEWART & CO.

Mr. Orlando Allen's report; sec. 60, 14 Erie enlargement; Doc. 90, vol. 5, Ass'y Docs. 1850.

BRIGHT'S DISEASE.

John A. Swift's treatise; Doc. 67, (page 111,) vol. 3, Ass'y Docs. 1853.

SURRENUS BRITTON, WILLIAM BALDWIN.

Mr. Hale's report, claims; Doc. 163, vol. 3, Ass'y Docs. 1849.

J. ROMEYN BRODHEAD.

Report concerning the archieves and papers relative to American history at the courts of England and Holland; Doc. D, in Doc. 2, vol. 1, Senate Docs. 1842.

Same in vol. 1, Ass'y Docs. 1842.

Communication from same in relation to Colonial history; Doc. 88, vol. 4, Senate Docs. 1842.

Communication to Governor Seward at extra session, Doc. C, accommanying Governor Seward's extra session message; Doc. 106, vol. 4, Senate Doc. 1842, (with list of Documents;) Doc. C accommanying Doc. 195, vol. 7, Ass'y Docs. 1842.

Communication to Governor Bouck; Doc. A, accompanying Doc. 2, Senate Docs. 1843; Doc. A, Doc. 3, vol. 1, Ass'y Docs. 1843.

BROOKLYN.

Remonstrance of delegates of 8th and 9th wards of city of Brooklyn against proposed new charter; Doc. 28, vol. 1, Ass'y Docs. 1849.

Communication of John G. Bergen and others respecting new charter; Doc. 32, vol. 1, Ass'y Docs. 1849.

Mr. Baker's report in relation to cession of land to United States at navy yard.

Mr. E. W. Fiske's report on the reorganization of the common schools and the Board of Educations; Doc. 156, vol. 6, Ass'y Docs. 1850.

Mr. Cross' report on including with New-York city in one government; Doc. 74, vol. 3, Senate Docs. 1851.

Vital statistics, proposed by Chas. S. J. Goodrich; Doc. 85, (page 89) vol. 2, Ass'y Docs. 1852.

BROOKLYN GAS LIGHT COMPANY.

Mr. Crolius report; Doc. 22, vol. 1, Senate Docs. 1850.

BROOKLYN INSTITUTE.

Report of condition; Doc. 94, vol. 4, Ass'y Docs. 1845.

Report of condition; Doc. 199, vol. 6, Ass'y Docs. 1848.

Report of condition; Doc. 235, vol. 5, Ass'y Docs. 1849.

CORNELIUS M. BROSNAN, TREASURER ONONDAGA COUNTY.

Mr. J. Benedict's minority report on petition of Dennis McCarthy, Grove Lawrence, Asahal L. Smith, to be discharged from their liabilities as sureties; Doc. 50, vol. 3, Ass'y Docs. 1851.

Mr. John J. Townsend's majority report on same subject; Doc. 51, vol. 3, Ass'y Docs. 1851.

ELIAS BBOWN.

Report of Canal Commissioners; Doc. 22, vol. 1, Ass'y Docs. 1846.

LEVI BROWN.

Mr. N. Jones' report, claims; Doc. 37, vol. 1, Senate Docs. 1842.

MATHEW BROWN, (as surety for Cornelius Van Slyck.)

Mr. Ward's report; Doc. 140, vol 7, Ass'y Docs. 1842.

Mr. Haight's report; Doc. 23, vol. 2, Ass'y Docs. 1843.

Mr. Porter's report, claims; Doc. 87, vol. 2, Senate Docs. 1844.

MERRITT H. BROWN.

Mr. Hale's report, claims; Doc. 129, vol. 3, Ass'y Docs. 1849.

MARCUS BROWN, (CONRADT BROWN.)

Mr. Rugers' report, claims; Doc. 22, vol. 1, Senate Docs. 1843.

Mr. Gorham's report, claims; Doc. 122, vol. 5, Ass'y Docs. 1844.

Mr. Teft's report, claims; Doc. 130, vol. 4, Ass'y Docs. 1845.

Copy of papers on file in the office of Secretary of State; Doc. 132, vol. 4, Ass'y Docs. 1846.

Mr. J. E. Beers' report, claims; Doc. 19, vol. 1, Ass'y Docs. 1847.

Mr. McCarty's report, claims; Doc. 185, vol. 5, Ass'y Docs; 1848.

Mr. Boardman's report; Doc. 53, vol. 2, Ass'y Docs. 1849.

Affidavits relating to the claim of; Doc. 96, vol. 5, Ass'y Docs. 1852.

Mr. W. A. Gilbert's report, claims; Doc. 76, vol. 2, Ass'y Docs. 1852.

SOLOMON BROWN.

Mr. Jackson's report, claims; Doc. 20, vol. 2, Ass'y Docs. 1843.

Mr Nicolls' report, claims; Doc. 97, vol. 4, Ass'y Docs. 1843.

Report of Canal Board; Doc. 36, vol 3, Ass'y Docs. 1845.

THOMAS BROWN.

Report of Canal Commissioners; Doc. 101, vol. 3, Senate Docs. 1844.

PACKARD BRUCE.

Report of Canal Appraisers of allowance made in consequence of building Genesee Valley canal; Doc. 61, vol. 2, Ass'y Docs. 1847.

Mr. J. G. Floyd's report, claims; Doc. 38, vol 2, Senate Docs. 1849.

JANSEN BRUYN.

Mr. H. W. Strong's report as to the time for taking the oath as justice of the peace; Doc. 53, vol. 2, Senate Docs. 1844.

BUFFALO CITY.

Mr. Haight's report on the subject of the responsibility of the city for arms procured in 1836 by Samuel Wilkinson; Doc. 48, vol. 3, Ass'y. Docs. 1843.

Report of Canal Board upon enlargement of Canal and basin at city; Doc. 205, vol. 7, Ass'y. Docs. 1847.

Report upon bridges; Doc. 11, vol. 1, Senate Docs. 1848.

Report of Canal Board in relation to enlargement of canal and basin; Doc. 130, vol. 5, Ass'y. Docs. 1848.

Report of Canal Board in relation to harbor, Doc. 33, vol. 2, Senate Docs. 1849.

Report of Canal Board in relation to Erie and Ohio Canal basins, Doc. 26, vol. 1, Senate Docs. 1849.

Report of Canal Board in relation to obstructions in harbor, Doc. 90, vol. 3, Ass'y. Docs. 1851.

WILLIAM BUEL.

Report of Canal Commissioners; Doc. 119, vol. 4, Senate Docs. 1846.

Mr. Johnson's report, claims; Doc. 120, vol. 4, Senate Docs. 1846.

Mr. Dean's report, claims; Doc. 40, vol. 2, Ass'y Docs. 1846.

Memorial in relation to the report of select committee on canal frauds; Doc. 9, vol. 3, Senate Docs. 1847.

Mr. Cornwell's report on claim; Doc. 171, vol. 6, Ass'y Docs. 1847.

Memorial in relation to an agricultural college; Doc. 158, vol. 6, Ass'y Docs. 1850.

Memorial in relation to damages arising out of contracts for the Locport locks; Doc. 44, vol. 2, Ass'y Docs. 1851.

WILLIAM BUEL, 2.

Mr. Ward's report, claims; Doc. 17, vol. 1, Senate Docs. 1852.

Report of committee on claims; Doc. 74, vol. 3, Ass'y Docs. 1851.

THOMAS E. BUCHANAN, HENRY CARR.

Mr. Backhouse's report; Doc. 82, vol. 3, Ass'y Docs. 1851.

BULKHEADS AND WHARVES.

Mr. H. J. Allen's report; James B. Blatchford's petition in relation to Brooklyn water line; Doc. 141, vol. 6, Ass'y Docs. 1850.

Further report on same subject; Doc. 143, vol. 6, Ass'y Docs. 1850.

GEORGE W. BULL.

Report of select committee; Doc. 66, vol. 2, Senate Docs. 1851.

WILLIAM BULL.

Mr. Roger's report, claims; Doc. 31, vol. 1, Senate Docs. 1843.

JOHN BUMP.

Report of Canal Board; Doc. 141, vol. 4, Ass'y Docs. 1845.

JOHN BURCH.

Mr. Alvord's report, claims; Doc. 139, vol. 5, Ass'y Docs. 1844.

Report of Canal Board; Doc. 102, vol. 4, Ass'y Docs. 1845.

RUSSELL B. BURCH.

Mr. J. E. Beers' report, claims, in relation to school district, No. 16, New Berlin, Chenango county; Doc. 225, vol. 7, Ass'y Docs. 1847.

HUBBARD BURDICK.

Report of Canal Board; Doc. 217, vol. 6, Ass'y Docs. 1845.

Mr. Pitt's report, claims; Doc. 32, vol. 2, Ass'y Docs. 1846.

Mr. J. E. Beers' report, claims; Doc. 66, vol. 2, Ass'y Docs. 1847.

Mr. Beach's report; Doc. 37, vol. 2, Ass'y Docs. 1848.

Mr. McLean's report; Doc. 99, vol. 2, Ass'y Docs. 1849.

Mr. Orlando Allen's report; Doc. 79, vol. 5, Ass'y Docs. 1850.

THOMAS BURNS.

Mr. Gleason's report; Doc. 34, vol. 1, Ass'y Docs. 1854.

HARRIET R. BURT.

Report of Commissioners of Land Office, in relation to judgments against Daniel Burt and Erastus Sparrow; Doc. 102, vol. 3, Ass'y Docs. 1849.

BUTTERNUTTS, TOWN OF.

Mr. Morehouse's report as to bridges; Doc. 194, vol. 5, Ass'y Docs. 1846.

BUTTERNUTTS AND OXFORD TURNPIKE.

Mr. Noye's report in relation to the removal of a gate; Doc. 106, vol. 5, Ass'y Docs. 1844.

CABINET OF NATURAL HISTORY.

Report of Regents of University, on condition; Doc. 91, vol 8, Senate Docs. 1846.

Report of Regents of University, on condition; Doc. 72, vol 3, Senate Docs. 1848.

Report of Regents of University, on condition; Doc. 75, vol. 2, Senate Docs. 1850.

Report of Regents of University, on condition; Doc. 30. vol. 2, Senate Docs. 1851.

Report of Regents of University, on condition; Doc. 122, vol. 5, Ass'y Docs. 1852. (Illustrated with colored engravings.)

Report of Regents of University, on condition; Doc. 11, vol. 1, Senate Docs. 1853.

Report of Regents of University, on condition; Doc. 50, vol. 1, Senate Docs. 1854.

SHULER CADY.

Mr. A. Chamberlain's report; Doc. 73, vol. 2, Ass'y Docs. 1851. Doc. 75, vol. 3, Ass'y Docs. 1851.

GEORGE CALDWELL, JOSEPH W. CALDWELL.

Mr. N. Jones' report, claims; Doc. 38, vol. 2, Senate Docs. 1853.

Mr. Van Valkenburgh's report, claims; Doc. 71, vol. 2, Ass'y Docs. 1852.

Mr. Hopkins' report, claims; Doc. 69, vol. 2, Senate Docs. 1854.

GEORGE CALDWELL, JOSEPH WENTWORTH.

Mr. Rogers' report, claims; the loss was occasioned by the overflow of Bremen's creek, at Canajoharie; Doc. 57, vol. 3, Senate Docs. 1842.

JOHN CAMERDON.

Report of the Commissioners of the Land Office; Doc. 143, vol. 5, Ass'y Docs. 1848.

ALEXANDER CAMPBELL.

Report of Canal Board; Doc. 173, vol. 3, Ass'y Docs. 1849.

ARCHIBALD CAMPBELL, (and associates.)

Attorney General Van Buren's report as to title of land in Seneca county; Doc. 161, vol. 5, Ass'y Docs. 1846.

SQUIRE CAMPBELL.

Mr. E. F. Warren's report; Doc. 116, vol. 5, Ass'y Docs. 1842.

CAMPBELL AND MOODY.

Report of Commissioners of Land Office; Doc. 43, vol. 2, Senate Docs. 1851.

CANADA.

Communication from A. N. Morin, Speaker, in relation to books for Parliament library; Doc. 6, vol. 1, Senate Docs. 1850. Doc. 5, vol. 1, Ass'y Docs. 1850.

Mr. J. W. Beekman's report on above application; Doc. 9, vol. 1, Senate Docs. 1850.

Communication from Canadian Parliament, acknowledging receipt of donation of books; Doc. 69, vol. 3, Ass'y Docs. 1851.

CANADICE LAKE.

Report of Canal Board in relation to supply of water; Doc. 40, vol. 1, Senate Docs. 1850.

CAUGHNAWAGA BRIDGE COMPANY.

Mr. Averill's report; Doc. 73, vol. 2, Ass'y Docs. 1849.

CANAJOHARIE.

Mr. Converse's report on annexation of part of town to Minden; Doc. 96, vol. 3, Ass'y Docs. 1848.

Report in case of George Caldwell and Joseph Wentworth's case; Doc. 57, vol. 3, Senate Docs. 1842.

Report of John T. Clark, State Engineer, as to aqueduct over Boorman's creek; Doc. 61, vol. 2, Senate Docs. 1854.

CANAJOHARIE AND PALATINE BRIDGE COMPANY.

Report of condition; Doc. 51, vol. 2, Senate Docs. 1847.

Report of committee on roads and bridges as to reduction of tolls; Doc. 91, vol. 3, Senate Docs. 1847.

Report of Auditor Schoonmaker in relation to awards for the overflow of creek, March 9th and 10th, 1853; Doc. 114, vol. 3, Ass'y Docs. 4854.

CANAL BANK OF ALBANY.

Report of select committee (D. A. Bokee, W. J. Cornwell, J. G. Floyd), on the causes and circumstances of the failure; Doc. 63, vol. 2, Senate Docs. 1849.

Report of receiver, Andrew White; Doc. 185, vol. 3, Ass'y Docs. 1849.

Report of committee of investigation in relation to matters affecting the official integrity of the judiciary relating thereto; Doc. 221, vol. 5, Ass'y Docs. 1849.

Further report of receiver White; Doc. 222, vol. 5, Ass'y Docs. 1849.

CANALS—AND THE ENLARGEMENT.

Mr. John A. Dix's report on early opening; Doc. 110, vol. 5, Ass'y Docs. 1842.

Memorial of citizens of Niagara county, for the incorporation of a company to complete the enlargement of the Erie, the Genesee Valley, and the Black River canals; Doc. 160, vol. 7, Ass'y Docs. 1842.

Mr. John A. Dix's report on speedy enlargement; Doc. 190, vol. 7, Ass'y Docs. 1842.

Report of Canal Commissioners, as to contracts; Doc. 173, vol. 7, Ass'y Docs. 1842.

Comptroller Flagg's report, in relation to the contracts for the canal, between Albany and Troy; Doc. 15, vol. 1, Senate Docs. 1843.

Mr. Robert Flint's resolution; Doc. 70, vol. 3, Ass'y Docs. 1843.

Mr. Robert Denniston's report in relation to the necessity of the enlargement of that portion of the canal, near Root, Montgomery county; Doc. 102, vol. 3, Senate Docs. 1843.

Mr. Rhoades' minorty report on same subject; Doc. 103, vol. 3, Senate Docs. 1843.

Report of Comptroller Flagg relative to expenditures; Doc. 56, vol. 3, Ass'y Docs. 1843.

Report of Canal Board in relation to property shipped at Buffalo, Black Rock and Oswego; Doc. 142, vol. 5, Ass'y Docs. 1843.

Report of Comptroller Flagg as to the means necessary to be provided for canal purposes; Doc. 197, vol. 5, Ass'y Docs. 1843.

Mr. Flagler's minority report; Doc. 168, vol. 5, Ass'y Docs. 1843.

Mr. Murray's report; Doc. 170, vol. 5, Ass'y Docs. 1843.

Mr. Chamberlain's resolution, Genesee Valley; Doc. 45, vol. 1, Senate Docs. 1844.

Mr. Denniston's report; Doc. 98, vol. 3, Senate Docs. 1844.

Mr. H. Putnam's resolution; Doc. 108, vol. 3, Senate Docs. 1844.

Report of Attorney General Barker as to the appraisal of damages on the unfinished and suspended canals; Doc. 116, vol. 3, Senate Docs. 1844.

Report of the Canal Board as to the allowances to contractors on the suspended public works; Doc. 117, vol. 3, Senate Docs. 1844.

Comptroller Flagg's report as to extra allowances to canal contractors, from 1826 to 1844; Doc. 134, vol. 4, Senate Docs. 1844.

Report of Canal Board as to damages awarded for breaches of contract, occasioned by suspension law of 1842; Doc. 3. vol. 1, Ass'y Docs. 1844.

Report of Canal Appraisers as to rule of appraisement; Doc. 101, vol. 5, Ass'y Docs. 1844.

Comptroller Flagg's report relative to the expenditure on the canals; Doc. 105, vol. 5, Ass'y Docs. 1844.

Report of Commissioners of Canal Fund, communicating a table of receipts as payments up to 30 Sept. 1843; Doc. 120, vol. 5, Ass'y Docs. 1844.

Report of Canal Commissioners in relation to the land along the enlarged Erie canal; Doc. 132, vol. 5, Ass'y Docs. 1844.

Report of the Canal Commissioners in relation to the contracts for the enlargement; Doc. 146, vol. 6, Ass'y Docs. 1844.

Mr. Horatio Seymour's report; Doc. 177, vol. 7, Ass'y Docs. 1844.

Canal Commissioners report in relation to preservation or sale of perishable material for the enlargement; Doc. 72, vol. 2, Senate Docs. 1845.

Mr. R. Denniston's minority report on the Assembly bill entitled "an act in relation to the canals;" Doc. 110, vol. 3, Senate Docs. 1845.

Mr. Denniston's report on the subject of discriminating tolls on the Erie and Oswego canals; Doc. 113, vol. 3, Senate Docs. 1845.

Comptroller Flagg's report on the tolls paid on the Erie canal, on freight to or from the lateral canals; Doc. 116, vol. 3, Senate Docs. 1845.

Report of Canal Commissioners on the preservation of public work on the lateral canals; Doc. 150, vol. 5, Ass'y Docs. 1845.

Annual report of expenditures; Doc. 102, vol. 5, Ass'y Docs. 1845.

Comptroller Flagg's report as to issue and redemption of canal stocks; Doc. 175, vol. 5, Ass'y Docs. 1845.

Report of Canal Commissioners as to new work on enlarged Erie Canal, brought into use since 1842; Doc. 225, vol. 6, Ass'y Docs. 1845.

Mr. D. S. Howard's report on Governor Wright's message, and on the resumption of the work; Doc. 235, vol. 6, Ass'y Docs. 1845.

Governor Wright's message returning the canal bills, with his objections; Doc. 251, vol. 7, Ass'y Docs. 1845.

Canal Commissioners report as to policy of change in the mode of conducting repairs; Doc. 27, vol. 1, Senate Docs. 1846.

Mr. John Porter's report on the act giving bounty to the transportation of salt, coal and lead; Doc. 47, vol. 2, Senate Docs. 1846.

Report of Commissioners of Canal Fund in relation to a reduction in tolls; Doc. 89, vol. 3, Senate Doc. 1846.

Mr. Denniston's majority report on the bill to reduce the expense of canal superintendance and repairs; Doc. 104, vol. 3, Senate Docs. 1846.

Mr. Denniston's majority report in relation to the bill concerning the election of additional members to the Canal Board; Doc. 128, vol. 4, Senate Docs. 1846.

Report of Commissioners of Canal Fund as to tolls collected in October, November and December, 1845; Doc. 33, vol. 2, Ass'y Docs. 1846.

Comptroller Flagg's report as to expenditures; Doc. 90, vol. 4, Ass'y Docs. 1846.

Report of the Canal Commissioners in relation to doubling the locks on the Erie canal, west of Syracuse; Doc. 110, vol. 4, Ass'y Docs. 1846.

Comptroller Flagg's report as to tolls paid on the Erie canal as the products of the lateral canals; Doc. 113, vol. 4, Ass'y Docs. 1846.

Report of Canal Commissioners as to the expenditures of the canal; Doc. 119, vol. 4, Ass'y Docs. 1846.

Report of Canal Commissioners as to amount expended since 29th March, 1842, on Erie canal; Doc. 180, vol. 5, Ass'y Docs. 1846.

Report of Canal Commissioners as to the sums annually expended between Frankfort and Syracuse, and for the use of the Mohawk, and the quantity required; Doc. 171, vol. 5, Ass'y Docs. 1846.

Mr. Bishop Perkins' report on the bill to reduce the expense of canal repairs and against the contract system; Doc. 173, vol. 5, Ass'y Docs. 1846.

Report of select committee of investigation as to frauds; Doc. 100, vol. 3, Ass'y Docs. 1847.

Estimate for 1847, of sums paid by Commissioners of Canal Fund, on account of canal debt, superintendance and repairs; Doc. 43, vol. 2, Senate Docs. 1847.

Mr. Denniston's majority report and on the appropriations for canal purposes; Doc. 52, vol. 2, Senate Docs. 1847.

Mr. Beach's minority report on same subject; Doc. 81, vol. 3, Senate Docs. 1847.

Report of Canal Commissioners as to amount of material on hand for enlargement in 1842; Doc. 59, vol. 2, Senate Docs. 1847.

Mr. Denniston's majority report on Governor Young's message relative to canals, and especially in relation to the repair by contract system; Doc. 63, vol. 2, Senate Docs. 1847.

Mr. Beach's minority report on same subject; Doc. 79, vol. 2, Senate Docs. 1847. Also Doc. 25, vol. 2, Ass'y Docs. 1848.

Comptroller Flagg's report relative to available and unavailable canal funds; Doc. 66, vol. 2, Senate Docs. 1847.

Annual report of expenditures; Doc. 15, vol. 1, Ass'y Docs. 1847.

Report of Commissioners of Canal Fund as to the toll derived from the western trade in 1846; Doc. 42, vol. 1, Ass'y Docs. 1847.

Mr. Cornwell's report on Governor Young's message, in relation to canals, and the constitutional limit to appropriation; Doc. 128, vol. 4, Ass'y Docs. 1847.

Comptroller Flagg's report as to sums paid for superintendance and repair; Doc. 129, vol. 4, Ass'y Docs. 1847.

Mr. Cornwell's report as to the Comptrollers report on the expenditures on the canals; Doc. 147. vol. 4, Ass'y Docs. 1847.

Mr. Cornwell's report as to the bills for appropriation for the year; Doc. 167, vol. 6, Ass'y Docs. 1847.

Report of Commissioners of Canal Fund as to surplus of canal revenues unappropriated; Doc. 112, vol. 4, Senate Docs 1847.

Report in relation to the repairs on the eastern division; Doc. 125, vol. 4, Senate Docs. 1847.

Comptroller Flagg's report in relation to Canal Fund; Doc. 132, vol. 4, Senate Docs. 1847.

Mr. Joshua A. Spencer's report on rights and liabilities of common carriers on the canals; Doc. 142, vol. 4, Senate Docs. 1847.

Report of Commissioners of Canal Fund as to canal debt due 30 Sept. 1847; Doc. 151, vol. 4, Senate Docs. 1847.

Proceedings of a meeting at Rochester, in behalf of the speedy enlargement; Doc. 183, vol. 7, Ass'y Docs. 1847.

Report of Canal Commissioners in relation to amount of work done and under contract; Doc. 208, vol. 7, Ass'y Docs. 1847.

Comptroller Flagg's report in relation to expenditures; Doc. 60, vol. 3, Ass'y Docs. 1848.

Report of Canal Commissioners in relation to expense of bringing into use enlarged locks on Erie canal; Doc. 116, vol. 3, Ass'y Docs. 1848.

Report of Canal Board in relation to appropriations; Doc. 97, vol. 3, Ass'y Docs. 1848.

Comptroller Fillmore's report in relation to the expenditure of surplus revenues of the canals; Doc. 137, vol. 5, Ass'y Docs, 1848.

Mr. J. Fuller's report on general appropriation; Doc. 146, vol. 5, Ass'y Docs. 1848.

Communication from Auditor Ruggles respecting collection of tolls; Doc. 195, vol. 3, Ass'y Docs. 1849.

Mr. Fitzhugh's report on general appropriation; Doc. 178, vol. 3, Ass'y Docs. 1849.

Auditor Ruggles' report on canal expenditures; Doc. 30, vol. 1, Ass'y Docs. 1849.

Canal Commissioners report as to length and width of enlarged locks, size and form of boats, form and capacity of prism of canal; Doc. 50, vol. 2, Senate Docs. 1849.

Report of Canal Commissioners, as to the enlargement of the canals, except the Erie; Doc. 83, vol. 3, Senate Docs. 1850.

Mr. Follett's minority report; Doc. 88, vol. 3, Senate Docs, 1850.

Report of Auditor, F. H. Ruggle's, as to application of same; Doc. 81, vol. 5, Ass'y Docs. 1850.

Mr. F. S. Martin's report in relation to appropriations; Doc. 153, vol. 6, Ass'y Docs. 1850.

Report of Canal Commissioners in regard to improvement on canal; Doc. 17, vol. 3, Senate Docs. 1850.

Attorney General Chatfield's report as to the constitutionality of the canal law of 1851; Doc. 68, vol. 3, Senate Docs. 1851.

Mr. Upham's majority report on the same; Doc. 69, vol. 3, Senate Docs. 1851.

Mr. Alanson Skinner's minority report on the same; Doc. 70, vol. 3, Senate Docs. 1851.

Report of Canal Commissioners in relation to the plan of enlargement; Doc. 88, vol. 3, Senate Docs. 1851.

Report of Auditor, F. H. Ruggles, on expenditures; Doc. 97, vol. 3, Senate Docs. 1851.

Report of State Engineer, H. C. Seymour, on the condition of the canals, with maps and profiles; Doc. 45, vol. 3, Ass'y Docs. 1851.

Communication from Nelson J. Beach, on the subject of the enlargement; Doc. 63, vol. 3, Ass'y Docs. 1851.

Mr. Orlando Allen's report on so much of Governor Hunt's message as relates to the canals; Doc. 102, vol. 4, Ass'y Docs.

1851. (This contains the opinions of John C. Spencer, Samuel Stevens and Daniel Lord.)

Resolutions of Canal Board, asking for a complete investigation of the manner of letting contracts under the canal law of 1851; Doc. 8, vol. 1, Ass'y Docs. 1852.

Report of Auditor, G. W. Newell, as to extra allowances made on canal contracts; Doc. 23, vol. 1, Senate Docs. 1852.

Report of W. J. McAlpine, State Engineer, of the condition ot the canals, with profiles, and statement of bids made for work; Doc. 90, vol. 4, Ass'y Docs. 1852.

Mr. Vanderbilt's report, constitutional amendment; Doc. 42, vol. 2, Senate Docs. 1853.

Mr. G. T. Pierce and W. A. Davenport's minority report, constitutional amendment; Doc. 46, vol. 2, Senate Docs. 1853.

Mr. West's majority report on same; Doc. 98, vol. 4, Ass'y Docs. 1853.

Mr. Clapp's minority report on same; Doc. 99, vol. 4, Ass'y Docs. 1853.

Auditor Newell's report why certain claims against the treasu ry were not charged to Canal Debt Sinking Fund; Doc. 51, vol. 2, Senate Docs. 1853. (Letter from Judge Denio is appended.)

Report of State Engineer, W. J. McAlpine, as to cost of finishing the canals; Doc. 64, vol. 2, Senate Docs. 1853.

Message of Governor, Horatio Seymour, in relation to appropriations for the improvement of the Erie and Oswego canals; Doc. 67, vol. 2, Senate Docs. 1853. Doc. 91, vol. 4, Ass'y Docs. 1853.

Auditor Newell's report, concerning appropriations; Doc. 84, vol. 3, Senate Docs. 1853.

Report of Canal Commissioners in relation to old and new contracts; Doc. 18, vol. 2, Ass'y Docs. 1853.

Mr. West's report on so much of Governor Seymour's message as relates to canals; Doc. 64, vol. 3, Ass'y Docs. 1853.

Mr. West's majority report on the financial amendment; Doc. 98, vol. 4, Ass'y Docs. 1853.

Mr. Clapp's minority report on the same; Doc. 99, vol. 4, Ass'y Docs. 1853.

Report of Comptroller Wright in relation to the time when the State tax would be available for the improvement of the canals; Doc. 114, vol. 6, Ass'y Docs. 1853.

Report of the conference committees of Senate and Assembly, on the canal constitutional amendments; Doc. 116, vol. 6, Ass'y Docs. 1853.

Communication of Auditor, G. W. Newell, in relation to canal appropriation for 1853; Doc, 126, vol. 6, Ass'y Docs. 1853.

Mr. Germain's majority report on the general bill for the incorporation of companies to navigate the canals; Doc. 16, vol. 1, Ass'y Docs. 1854.

Mr. Hinkley's minority report; Doc. 32, vol. 1, Ass'y Docs. 1854.

Auditor Schoonmaker's report of money paid canal contractors for damages and extra compensation, from 1840 to 1853, inclusive; Doc. 148, vol. 5, Ass'y Docs. 1854.

Report of Auditor Schoonmaker as to costs paid in case of Phelps vs. Newell, to test constitutionality of canal law of 1851; Doc. 45, vol. 1, Senate Docs. 1854.

Report of State Engineer, W. J. McAlpine, on the condition of the canals, with profiles and statistics; Doc. 60, vol. 1, Senate Docs. 1854.

Official returns of election, in relation to the adoption of financial amendment; Doc. 85, vol. 3, Ass'y Docs. 1854.

Resolution of the Canal Board, relative to a reduction of tolls; Doc. 134, vol. 4, Ass'y Docs. 1854.

Mr. Field's report on enlargement; Doc. 119, vol. 3, Ass'y Docs. 1854.

CANAL BOATS.

Report of Canal Commissioners, as to length, size and form; Doc. 50, vol. 2, Senate Docs. 1849.

CANAL CLAIMS.

General Digest from 1842 to 1843, inclusive; Doc. 140, vol. 6, Ass'y Docs. 1844. (Reprinted. Doc, 252, vol. 7, Ass'y Docs. 1845.)

Mr. S. Cole's report, as to removal of causes from the Canal Board to the Supreme court by certiorari; Doc. 147, vol. 6, Ass'y Docs. 1844.

Mr. Bockee's report on the same subject; Doc. 103, vol. 3, Senate Doc. 1845.

Canal Committees report on same subject; Doc. 48, vol. 3, Ass'y Docs. 1845.

Mr. Coe's report on same subject; Doc. 195, vol. 5, Ass'y Docs. 1845.

Digest of 1845; Doc. 210, vol. 6, Ass'y Docs. 1846.

Mr. Schoonmaker's report on the preparation of papers by claimants before the Legislature; Doc. 27, vol. 1, Senate Docs. 1850.

Digest from 1844 to 1850 inclusive; Doc. 5, vol. 1, Senate Docs. 1851.

Digest 1851 and 1852; Doc. 6, vol. 1, Senate Docs. 1851.

Digest of claims presented to the Canal Board up to March 1, 1851; Doc. 50, vol. 2, Senate Docs. 1851.

Mr. Pettingill's report on general bill; Doc. 87, vol. 4, Ass'y Docs. 1853.

Digest of 1853; Doc. 51, vol. 1, Senate Docs. 1854.

Report of Commissioners of Canal Fund as to the application of surplus revenues to claims arrising prior to June 1, 1846; Doc. 125, vol. 6, Ass'y Docs. 1853.

CANAL COMMISSIONERS.

Annual report: Doc. 24, vol. 2, Ass'y Docs. 1842.

Report in relation to contracts on canals; Doc. 173, vol. 7, Ass'y Docs. 1842.

Mr. Flagg's report as to non-acting Canal Commissioners; Doc. 45, vol. 1, Senate Docs. 1843.

Further report; Doc. 80, vol. 3, Senate Docs. 1843.

Annual report; Doc. 25, vol. 2, Ass'y Docs. 1843.

Annual report; Doc. 16, vol. 1, Ass'y Docs. 1844. Doc. 16, vol. 1, Ass'y. Docs. 1844.

Report as to clerk hire; Doc. 19, vol. 1, Senate Docs. 1845.

Comptroller Flagg's report of payments to non-acting Canal Commissioners; Doc. 38, vol. 1, Senate Docs. 1845.

Annual report; Doc. 28, vol. 1, Ass'y Docs. 1845.

Annual report; Doc. 14, vol. 1, Ass'y Docs. 1846.

Report in relation to doubling the locks on Erie canal, west of Syracuse; Doc. 110, vol. 4, Ass'y Docs. 1846.

Comptroller Flagg's report as to office expenses; Doc. 118, vol. 4, Ass'y. Docs. 1846.

Report as to expenditures on canals; Doc. 119, vol. 4, Ass'y Docs. 1846.

Report as to amount expended since 29 March, 1842 on the Erie canal; Doc. 150, vol. 5, Ass'y Docs. 1846.

Report in case of Stephen V. R. Ableman; Doc. 191, vol 5, Ass'y Docs. 1846.

Report as to sums annually expended between Frankfort and Syracuse, and for the use of the Mohawk, and the quantity required; Doc. 171, vol. 5, Ass'y. Docs. 1846.

Report in relation to repairs on eastern division; Doc. 125, vol. 4, Senate Docs. 1847.

Annual report; Doc. 20, vol. 1, Ass'y Docs. 1847.

Report in relation to amount of work done and under contract; Doc. 208, vol. 7, Ass'y Docs. 1847.

Report as to materials on hand for the enlargement in 1842; Doc. 59, vol. 2, Senate Docs. 1847.

Report in relation to Horatio Averill, Lewis Averill, Joseph Bauder; Doc. 114, vol. 4, Senate Docs. 1847.

Report as to number of surveyors and agents in employ; Doc. 137, vol. 4, Ass'y Docs. 1847.

Annual report; Doc. 16, vol. 3, Ass'y Docs. 1848.

Report as to expense of bringing into use the enlarged docks on Erie canal; Doc. 116, vol. 3, Ass'y Docs. 1848.

Annual report; Doc. 40, vol. 2, Ass'y Docs. 1849.

Communication concerning tools and materials; Doc. 53, vol. 2, Ass'y Docs. 1849.

Report as to length and width of enlarged locks, size and form of boats, form and capacity of prism of enlarged canal; Doc. 50, vol. 2, Senate Docs. 1849.

Report as to supply of water between Tonawanda and Montezuma; Doc. 41, vol. 2, Senate Docs. 1850.

Report in relation to the enlargement of the canals, except the Erie; Doc. 83, vol. 3, Senate Docs. 1850.

Mr. Follett's minority report on same subject; Doc. 88, vol. 3, Senate Docs. 1850.

Annual report; Doc. 45, vol. 3, Ass'y Docs. 1850.

Report in relation to improvements on canal; Doc. 97, vol. 3, Senate Docs. 1850.

Annual report; Doc. 26, vol. 2, Ass'y Docs. 1851.

Report in relation to the plan of enlargement, Doc. 88, vol. 3, Senate Docs. 1851.

Annual report; Doc. 33, vol. 2, Ass'y Docs. 1852.

Annual report; Doc. 23, vol. 2, Ass'y Docs. 1853.

Report in relation to old and new contracts; Doc. 18, vol. 2, Ass'y Docs. 1853.

Report in relation to moneys loaned to banks and banking as sociations; Doc. 81, vol. 2, Senate Docs. 1852.

Financial report; Doc. 15, vol. 1, Ass'y Docs. 1852.

do do 15, vol. 2, Ass'y Docs. 1853.

Report of tolls, trade and tonnage, on the canals; Doc. 107, vol. 4, Ass'y Docs. 1853.

Financial report; Doc. 10, vol. 1, Ass'y Docs. 1844.

Report of tolls, trade and tonnage, on the canals; Doc. 145, vol. 5, Ass'y Docs. 1844.

Report in relation to improvements on canal; Doc. 97, vol. 3, Senate Docs. 1850.

Financial report; Doc. 69, vol. 4, Ass'y Docs. 1850.

Report of tolls, trade and tonnage of the canals; Doc. 140, vol. 6, Ass'y Docs. 1850.

Financial report; Doc. 27, vol. 2, Ass'y Docs. 1851.

Communicetion from Lieutenant Governor, S. E. Church, and Attorney General, L. S. Chatfield, impugning the validity of the annual report above, as not authorised by them; Doc. 30, vol. 2, Ass'y Docs. 1851.

Report of tolls, trade and tonnage of the canals; Doc. 56, vol. 3, Ass'y Docs. 1851.

Report of tolls, trade and tonnage of the canals; Doc. 94, vol. 3, Senate Docs. 1852.

CANTON PLANK ROAD.

Mr. Geddes' report; Doc. 62, vol. 2, Senate Docs. 1849.

Mr. E. D. Morgan' report; Doc. 13, vol. 1, Senate Docs. 1850

CAPITAL PUNISHMENT.

Memorial of citizens of Chenango county on abolition; Doc. 78, vol. 3, Senate Docs. 1842.

Memorial of citizens of Albany against abolition and in answer to Mr. O'Sullivan's report; Doc. 97, vol. 4, Senate Docs. 1842.

Memorial of citizens of Salina, against same; Doc. 133, vol. 7, Ass'y Docs. 1842.

Memorial of citizens of Greene co. for its repeal; Doc. 146, vol. 7, Ass'y Docs. 1842.

Memorial of citizens of Niagara co. for its repeal; Doc. 59, vol. 3, Ass'y Docs. 1843.

Mr. R. N. Morrison's report; Doc. 249, vol. 7, Ass'y Docs. 1845.

Mr. Titus's report; Doc. 213, vol. 6, Ass'y Docs. 1846.

Mr. Miller's report; Doc. 214, vol. 6, Ass'y Docs. 1846.

Mr. John Stanton Gould's majority report; Doc. 95, vol. 2, Ass'y Docs. 1847.

Mr. Underhill's minority report; Doc. 191, vol. 6, Ass'y Docs. 1848.

Mr. Brinkerhoff's report; Doc. 133, vol. 5. Ass'y Docs. 1848.

Memorial of Henry W. Taylor, protesting against the repeal of the law; Doc. 10, vol. 1, Senate Docs. 1849.

Mr. Baker's majority report favorable to the abolition; Doc. 110, vol. 4, Ass'y Docs. 1851.

CAPITOL.

Mr. A. G. Chatfield's majority report on removal; Doc. 153, vol. 5, Ass'y Docs. 1846.

Mr. Thomas Smith's minority report; Doc. 175, vol. 5, Ass'y Docs. 1846.

Mr. Charlock's report on removal; Doc. 148, vol. 5, Ass'y Docs. 1848.

Mr. Le Roy's report on removal; Doc. 106, vol. 4, Ass'y Docs. 1851.

CARPETING.

Attorney General Barker's report on the subject of the manufacture in State prisons; Doc. 75, vol. 3, Ass'y Docs. 1844.

CARTHAGE ROAD.

Report of Commissioners to lay out a road from Clinton to Carthage; Doc. 5, (page 116) vol. 1, Ass'y Docs. 1853.

SALLY CHAMBERLAIN CARR.

Mr. Barrow's report, claims; Doc. 83, vol. 3, Ass'y Docs. 1854.

JOHN CARVIS.

Mr. Buwell's report, claims; Doc. 73, vol. 3, Ass'y Docs. 1846. (This is in relation to service of a warrant to arrest a fugitive from justice.)

JOSEPH G. CASE.

Report of Canal Commissioners; Doc. 77, vol. 2, Senate Dcos. 1847.

LEVI CASLER.

Report of Canal Board; Doc. 84, vol. 5, Ass'y Docs. 1842.

ROBERT N. CASLER.

Report of Canal Board; Doc. 24, vol. 1, Ass'y Docs. 1844.
do do do 133, vol. 5, Ass'y Docs. 1844.

HOMER CASWELL.

Mr. Bevins' report, canals; Doc. 238, vol. 6, Ass'y Docs. 1845.

CATHOLIC CHILDREN.

Mr. Paterson's report in relation to education; Doc. 97, vol. 4, Ass'y Docs. 1853.

THEODORE CATLIN, FREDERICK GREEN.

Mr. H. W. Sage's report; Doc. 108, vol. 4, Ass'y Docs. 1847.
Mr. Martin's report; Doc. 114, vol. 3, Ass'y Docs. 1848.

CATTARAUGUS COUNTY.

Mr. Curry's report in relation to the sale of the poor house lot; Doc. 194, vol. 7, Ass'y Docs. 1847.

CAYUGA BRIDGE COMPANY.

Report of the Canal Board as to the right to exclusive jurisdiction for three miles; Doc. 129, vol. 4, Senate Docs. 1846. (Case of Lewis Basted, N. B. Kingsland.)

Attorney General Jordan's report as to whether the rights of the company have been affected by the construction of the Cayuga and Seneca canals; Doc. 140, vol. 5, Ass'y Docs. 1848.

CAYUGA INDIANS.

Mr. Wheeler's report on petition of Peter Wilson in relation to annuities; Doc. 55, vol. 2, Ass'y Docs. 1848.

Report of Secretary of State, Christopher Morgan, in relation to treaty made by the State of New-York; Doc. 61, vol. 3, Ass'y Docs. 1848.

Mr. William Samuel Johnson's report on Peter Wilson's memorial; Doc. 64, vol. 2, Senate Docs. 1849.

Report of Commissioners of Land Office; Doc. 165, vol. 3, Ass'y Docs. 1849.

Report of Commissioners of Land Office with speech of Dr. Peter Wilson, in behalf of the Cayugas, and with history of tribe.

Memorial for payment of annuities; Doc. 83, vol. 3, Ass'y Docs. 1851.

Memorial of Peter Wilson, (*Wa-o-wa-no-ouk*,) chief of the Cayugas, for an appropriation to the warriors of the nation; Doc. 56, vol. 2, Senate Docs. 1853.

Mr. Bristol's report on appropriation; Doc. 81, vol. 3, Senate Docs. 1853.

Mr. Malburn's report; Doc. 26, vol. 2, Ass'y Docs. 1853.

CAYUGA LAKE.

Report of select committee of Senate of 1847, on the embankment of Auburn and Rochester railroad across the Cayuga lake; Doc. 42, vol. 2, Senate Docs. 1848.

Report of commissioners H. Fitzhugh, J. B. Williams, W. H Adams on lowering in connection with the drainage of the Cayuga marshes; Doc. 66, vol. 2, Senate Docs. 1852. Winter of 1851–52, upon; Doc. 92, (page 400,) vol. 2, Senate Docs. 1852.

Mr. J. B. Williams' report; Doc. 35, vol. 2, Senate Docs. 1853.

CAYUGA MARSHES.

Report of commissioners W. H. Adams, Henry Fitzhugh, J. B. Williams, as to the drainage; Doc. 66, vol. 2, Senate Docs. 1852.

Mr. J. B. Williams' report on draining; Doc. 35, vol. 2, Senate Docs. 1853.

CAYUGA AND SENECA CANAL, (Outlet of Seneca Lake.

Report of Canal Commissioners; Doc. 102, vol. 4, Ass'y Docs. 1843.

Report of Canal Commissioners; Doc. 246, vol. 7, Ass'y Docs. 1845.

CENSUS OF THE STATE.

Mr. Folsom's report: Doc. 84, vol. 2, Senate Docs. 1845.

Census of 1845, as returned to the office of the Secretary of State; Doc. 5, vol. 1, Ass'y Docs. 1846.

Report of the Secretary of State, N. S. Benton, as to maps; Doc. 23, vol. 1, Ass'y Docs. 1846.

CENSUS OF THE UNITED STATES.

Communication from Alexander H. H. Stuart, Secretary of the Interior, in relation to the returns of population, under census of 1850; Doc. 33, vol. 2, Senate Docs. 1851.

Communication from Governor Hunt, with abstract of the seventh census; Doc. 157, vol. 6, Ass'y Docs. 1851.

CENTIGRADE THERMOMETER.

Report of Regents of the University on examination of the question of Fahrenheit or Centigrade; Doc. 94, vol. 4, Senate Docs. 1842.

CENTRE LOT. (Philadelphia and Ray, Jefferson Co.)

Report of Attorney General Barker as to the title; Doc. 115, vol. 3, Senate Doc. 1844.

CESSION OF LANDS TO UNITED STATES.

Letters of Secretary of War, (John C. Spencer) to Gov. Bouck, on cession at Black Rock; Doc. 107, vol. 4, Ass'y Docs. 1843.

Letters of Engineer J. G. Totten, accompanying the same; Doc. 107, vol. 4, Ass'y Docs. 1843.

Report of Commissioners of Land Office; Doc. 162, vol. 5, Ass'y Docs. 1843.

BUFFALO, SACKETTS HARBOR, MOUTH OF GENESEE ISLAND IN ST. LAWRENCE RIVER.

Governor Wright's message, with documents from the Secretary of War and Col. Totten; Doc. 164, vol. 5, Ass'y Docs. 1846.

Communication from Secretary of the Navy (J. Y. Mason) in relation to land at Sacketts Harbor; Doc. 96, vol. 2, Ass'y Docs. 1847. Doc. 156, vol. 6, Ass'y Docs. 1847.

Report of Commissioners of Land Office in relation to cession of land at Oswego; Doc. 37, vol. 2, Senate Docs. 1848.

Mr. Baker's report in relation to ceding lands in Brooklyn at Navy Yard; Doc. 183, vol. 8, Ass'y Docs. 1850.

Communication from Gov. Fish, transmitting a letter from William Ballard Preston, Secretary of the Navy, and a report to him (W. B. P.) of Joseph Smith from the Bureau of Yards and Docks in relation to the cession of lands at Navy Yard, Brooklyn; Doc. 171, vol. 6, Ass'y Docs. 1850.

Communication from the Secretary at War (C. M. Conrad) and Brevt. Col. G. Wright, through Gov. Hunt, in relation to lands at Oswego; Doc. 82, vol. 3, Senate Docs. 1851.

CHAMBER OF COMMERCE OF NEW-YORK.

Memorial in favor of the enlargement, and against tolls on railroads; Doc. 100, vol. 4, Ass'y Docs. 1854.

CALVIN T. CHAMBERLAIN.

Mr. Sear's report; Doc. 192, vol. 5, Ass'y Docs. 1845.

ENOCH CHAMBERLAIN—(Stephen M. Cook, for heirs of Silas Cook, Garry Loveridge, for Linus Loveridge, Abraham D. Hiles, John Hicks, Jacob Kendig, Hannah Peters, W. R. Cone, John H. Peters.)

Mr. Thompson's report; Doc. 197, vol. 3, Ass'y Docs. 1849.

JACOB CHAMBERLAIN.

Mr. Boardman's report; Doc. 114, vol. 3, Ass'y Docs. 1849.

ORRIN CHAMBERLAIN.

Mr. Ruger's report, claims; Doc. 85, vol. 3, Senate Docs. 1843.

CHAMPLAIN CANAL.

Mr. Orville Clark's report, as to the management and expenditures on the northern section, and the Glens Falls Feeder; Doc. 144, vol. 4, Senate Docs. 1846.

Mr. Martin's report on enlargement; Doc. 129, vol. 5, Ass'y Docs. 1850.

Mr. Martin's report in relation to the construction of an aqueduct over the Hudson river near the Saratoga dam; Doc. 144, vol. 6, Ass'y Docs. 1850.

Report of Canal Commissioners in relation to tolls received; Doc. 20, vol. 1, Senate Docs. 1853.

Auditor Newell's report; Doc. 29, vol. 1, Senate Docs. 1853.

Report of Canal Commissioner Mather; Doc. 80, vol. 3. Senate Docs. 1853.

Communication from Canal Commissioner Mather, as to towing bridge across the Mohawk at Cohoes; Doc. 110, vol. 4, Ass'y Docs. 1853.

ABEL CHANDLER.

Mr. Porter's report; claims; Doc. 68, vol. 2, Senate Docs. 1845.

Mr. Carpenter's report; grievances; Doc. 37, vol. 3, Ass'y Docs. 1845.

CHARITABLE, SCIENTIFIC AND BENEVOLENT SOCIETIES.

Mr. Fine's minority report on a general Law; Doc. 45, vol. 2, Senate Docs. 1848.

CHARTER OF NEW-YORK CITY.

Mr. Alden's report on amendments; Doc. 82, vol. 4, Ass'y Docs. 1853.

CHARITABLE INSTITUTIONS—(First Senate district)

Report of State Commissioners; Doc. 19, vol. 2, Ass'y Docs. 1842.

Report of, as above; Doc. 76, vol. 2, Senate Docs. 1844.

Report as above; Doc. 62, vol. 2, Senate Docs. 1845.

" " " Doc. 92, vol. 3, Senate Docs. 1847.

" " " Doc. 139, vol. 5, Ass'y Docs. 1848.

CHARLOTTE, WILLIAM, DANIEL AND MARY ANN ROWLAND.

Mr. Davis' report; aliens; Doc. 33, vol. 1, Ass'y Docs. 1844.

ISAAC ROWLAND.

Report of Comptroller Flagg; Doc. 110, vol. 5, Ass'y Docs.

JOHN ROWLAND.

Mr. J A. Lott's report, on title of land; Doc. 85, vol. 2, Senate Docs. 1844.

MICHAEL RUSH.

Mr. Barrow's report; claims; Doc. 37, vol. 1, Ass'y Docs. 1854.

RUSSELL AND AU SABLE TURNPIKE COMPANY.

Mr. J. G. Hubbell's report; Doc. 84, vol. 4, Ass'y Docs. 1843.

L. S. CHATFIELD, ATTORNEY GENERAL.

Mr. J. J. Townsend's report from a select committee of investigation on an alleged attempt to bribe; Doc. 158, vol. 6, Ass'y Docs. 1851.

Report of H. S. Randall as to books purchased for the Library of the Attorney General; Doc. 120, vol. 5, Ass'y Docs. 1852.

Report as to clerical force in his office; Doc. 61, vol. 2, Senate Docs. 1853.

Report on the subject of the Indian title to the Manors; Doc. 59, vol. 3, Ass'y Docs. 1853.

Report of E. G. Spalding, Treasurer, as to fees received; Doc. 10, vol. 1, Senate Docs. 1854.

CHAUTAUQUE COUNTY MUTUAL INSURANCE COMPANY.

Mr. Danforth's report on renewal and extension of charter; Doc. 20, vol. 1, Senate Docs. 1854.

SAMUEL CHEEVER.

Report of Canal Commissioners; Doc. 130, vol. 5, Ass'y Docs. 1844.

CHEMICAL MANUFACTURING COMPANY.

Report; Doc. 135, vol. 7, Ass'y Docs. 1842.

CHEMUNG CANAL.

Report of Commissioners of Canal Fund respecting loan; Doc. 69, vol. 3, Senate Docs. 1842.

Report of Comptroller Collier, of amount of premium received in stocks; Doc. 87, vol. 4, Senate Docs. 1842.

Mr. Dix's report, canals, an extension of feeder; Doc. 188, vol. 7, Ass'y Docs. 1842.

Report of Canal Commissioners as to amount expended in removing obstructions; Doc. 55, vol. 2, Senate Docs. 1845.

Mr. Bishop Perkin's report as to a canal to connect the Chemung canal with the Pennsylvania works; Doc. 112, vol. 4, Ass'y Docs. 1846.

Report of Canal Board in relation to the dam at the head of the feeder; Doc. 195, vol. 7, Ass'y Docs. 1847.

CHENANGO BRIDGE.

Mr. T. R. Lee's report as to the conflict of the bill with vested rights; Doc. 229, vol. 3, Ass'y Docs. 1845.

CHENANGO CANAL.

Report of committee on canals—Mr. Dix—on subject of payment by citizens of Oriskany Falls, for location of canal; Doc. 69, vol. 4, Ass'y Docs. 1842.

Report of Comptroller Collier, as to premium received on stock; Doc. 87, vol. 4, Senate Docs. 1842.

Mr. Niles' report, canals, on the repayment to citizens of Oriskany Falls, of moneys paid by them in consideration of location; Doc. 105, vol. 4, Ass'y Docs. 1843.

Mr. Gorham's report, claims, on same; Doc. 77, vol. 3, Ass'y Docs. 1844.

Mr. Alvord's minority report; Doc. 82, vol. 3, Ass'y Docs. 1844.

Report of Canal Board in relation to surplus waters; Doc. 195, vol. 5, Ass'y Docs. 1846.

CHLOROFORM.

George N. Burwell's treatise; Doc. 67, (page 77) vol. 3, Ass'y Docs. 1853.

SARAH CHURCH, (an infant.)

Mr. Boyle's report; Doc. 127, vol. 3, Ass'y Docs. 1849.

CHANCERY.

Report of Comptroller in relation to fees of registers and clerks; Doc. 30, vol. 2, Senate Docs. 1842.

Report of judiciary committee, Mr. Loomis, on the court and its relief; Doc. 94, vol. 5, Ass'y Docs. 1842.

Report of Chancellor Walworth, in relation to chancery fund and chancery library fund; Doc. 57, vol. 3, Ass'y Docs. 1843.

Report of Chancellor in relation to the dispatch of business in his court; Doc. 86, vol. 4, Ass'y Docs. 1843.

Report of chancellor, with catalogue of chancery library; Doc. 166, vol. 5, Ass'y Docs. 1843.

Comptroller Flagg's report as to fees of the register, assistant register, and clerks; Doc. 48, vol. 2, Senate Docs. 1845.

Further report; Doc. 49, vol. 2, Senate Docs. 1845.
do do 50, vol. 2, Senate Docs. 1845.

Report of register, J. M. Davison, as to clerical force and expenses; Doc. 39, vol. 1, Senate Docs. 1846.

Ex-chancellor Walworth's report as to the funds in chancery; Doc. 113, vol. 4, Senate Docs. 1847.

Further and detailed report, by same officer of the chancery fund; Doc. 120, vol. 4, Senate Docs. 1847.

Mr. S. G. Wilson's report on situation of funds; Doc. 73, vol. 3, Senate Docs. 1849.

Report of investigating committee—James Maurice, Daniel Clark Briggs, Hamilton Harris, on the funds of the court of chancery, with statements and tables; Doc. 56, vol. 2, Ass'y Docs. 1852.

CIRCUIT COURTS.

Comptroller Flagg's report as to expenses of holding courts in sixth circuit, since the resignation of Judge Monell; Doc. 35, vol. 1, Senate Docs. 1846.

Comptroller Flagg's report of moneys paid to circuit judges for expenses of trials out of the districts in which they reside; Doc. 47, vol. 2, Ass'y Docs. 1847.

CITIZENSHIP.

Mr. John Young's report, judiciary, on the petition of James R. Brice, to be restored to rights of citizenship; Doc. 70, vol 3, Ass'y Docs. 1846.

Governor Wright's message concerning the restoration of Marcus Aylesworth; Doc. 208, vol. 6, Ass'y Docs. 1846.

CITY STOCKS.

Governor Seymour's veto message on the bill to admit such stocks as a basis for banking; Doc. 113, vol. 6, Ass'y Docs. 1853.

A. CLARK.

Address, as president to the State Medical Society; Doc. 67, (page 271) vol. 3, Ass'y Docs. 1853.

CHESTER CLARK.

Mr. Alvord's report, claims; Doc. 78, vol. 3, Ass'y Docs. 1844.

GUSTAVUS CLARK.

Mr. Hopkins's report, claims; Doc. 59, vol. 1, Senate Docs. 1854.

JAMES R. CLARK.

Mr. McLean's report; Doc. 80, vol. 2, Ass'y Docs. 1849.

JASON CLARK.

Report of committee on internal affairs of towns and counties; Doc. 43, vol. 1, Senate Docs. 1852.

MINT CLARK, REED CLARK, AMBROSE CLARK, GEORGE P. WHEELER.

Mr. Nicoll's report, claims; Doc. 173, vol. 5, Ass'y Docs. 1843.

Mr. Gorham's report; Doc. 90, vol. 3, Ass'y Docs. 1844.

Mr. T. J. Wheeler's report, claims; Doc. 124, vol. 4, Senate Docs. 1846.

Mr. Foster's report, claims; Doc. 71, vol. 3, Ass'y Docs. 1846.

Auditor Schoonmaker's report; Doc. 62, vol. 2, Senate Docs. 1854.

SYLVESTER CLARK.

Mr. Tupper's report; Doc. 21, vol. 2, Ass'y Docs. 1842.

CLERKS IN PUBLIC OFFICES.

Report of Secretary of State, N. S. Benton, as to number of clerks and compensation; Doc. 33, vol. 1, Senate Docs. 1845.

Report of Comptroller A. C. Flagg, on same subject; Doc. 45, vol. 1, Senate Docs. 1845.

Report of State Engineer, W. J. McAlpine, as to clerks in his department; Doc. 18, vol. 1, Senate Docs. 1853.

CLINTON STATE PRISON.

Mr. Pentz's report; Doc. 72, vol. 3, Ass'y Docs. 1843.

Mr. Suydam's report; Doc. 41, vol. 3, Ass'y Docs. 1844.

Ransom Cook's report as agent; Doc. 16, vol. 1, Senate Docs. 1845.

Ransom Cook's report as agent; Doc. 14, vol. 1, Senate Docs. 1846.

Communication from Surveyor General H. Halsey, as to road from the prison to Lake Champlain; Doc. 55, vol. 2, Ass'y Docs. 1846.

Ransom Cook's report concerning punishments; Doc. 138, vol. 4, Ass'y Docs. 1846.

Ransom Cook's annual report; Doc. 10, vol. 1, Senate Docs. 1847.

Visit to, by Governor Wright and Comptroller Flagg; Doc. 18, vol. 1, Senate Docs. 1847.

Ransom Cook's communication informing Governor that the funds are exhausted; Doc. 105, vol. 4, Ass'y Docs. 1847.

Mr. Johnson's report of investigation; Doc. 122, vol. 4, Senate Docs. 1847.

Communication from Ebenezer Emmons, on mineral character of locality; Doc. 211, vol. 7, Ass'y Docs. 1847.

Report of visit of joint committee; Doc. 228, vol. 8, Ass'y Docs. 1847.

Report of Mr. Butrick, one of the committee of investigation; Doc. 236, vol. 8, Ass'y Docs. 1847.

Mr. Rowe's report on the manufacture of iron; Doc. 62, vol. 2, Ass'y Docs. 1852.

Inspector Darius Clark's report as to indebtedness; Doc. 66, vol. 2, Senate Docs. 1854.

JOHN BAPTISTE CLUTE.

Mr. Gorham's report, claims; Doc. 18, vol. 1, Ass'y Docs. 1844.

CLAUDIUS E. COAN.

Mr. Haight's report, grievances; Doc. 68, vol. 3., Ass'y Docs. 1843.

Mr. Johnson's report, claims; Doc. 35, vol. 5, Senate Docs. 1845.

EDWARD COBURN.

Mr. H. G. Root's report, claims; Doc. 113, vol. 5, Ass'y Docs. 1850.

Mr. James Maurice's report; Doc. 62, vol. 3, Ass'y Docs. 1851,

CLAVERACK AND GREENPORT SCHOOL DISTRICT.

Mr. Burchard's majority report; Doc. 201, vol. 7, Ass'y Docs. 1847.

Mr. Watson's minority report; Doc. 214, vol. 7, Ass'y Docs. 1847.

CLINTON, TOWN.

Mr. J. A. Lott's report, judiciary, on the election of town officers; Doc. 75, vol. 2, Senate Docs. 1846.

Mr. Burnet's report in relation to tax of Clinton county; Doc. 122, vol. 3, Ass'y Docs. 1854.

CODIFICATION OF THE LAWS.

Communication of R. H. Walworth, declining office of commissioner to codify; Doc. 102, vol. 3, Senate Docs. 1847. (This gives a general view of codes and their practicability.)

Communication of John A. Collier in relation to progress in work; Doc. 146, vol. 4, Senate Docs. 1847.

Communication of Anthony L. Robertson, on the same—same document.

Communication of Alvah Worden, on the same—same document.

Mr. Wilkins' report, with communications from Messrs. Worden, Robertson, and Hawley; Doc. 69, vol. 2, Senate Docs. 1848.

Communication from John A. Collier, resigning his office; Doc. 28, vol. 2, Ass'y Docs. 1848.

Communication of Messrs. Robertson and Worden, in relation to progress; Doc. 31, vol. 2 Ass'y Docs. 1848.

Report of Commissioners Alvah Worden, Seth C. Hawley, with chapter relative to highways, and bridges, and ferries; Doc. 5, vol. 1, Senate Docs. 1849. Doc. 12, vol. 1, Ass'y Docs. 1849.

Report of Comptroller W. Hunt, of sums paid to commissioners; Doc. 44, vol. 3, Ass'y Docs. 1850.

Communication of Seth C. Hawley, commissioner in relation to the prosecution of the work; Doc. 137, vol. 5, Ass'y Docs. 1850.

AMOS COLE.

Mr. P. Dieffendorf's report; Doc. 71, vol. 4, Ass'y Docs. 1842.

COLE, CALKINS, & CO.

Mr. McCarty's report, claims; Doc. 44, vol. 2, Ass'y Docs. 1848.

GEORGE COLE.

Report of Auditor George W. Newell, as to mileage as engineer on canals; Doc. 122, vol. 62, Ass'y Docs. 1853.

Mr. R. D. Livingston's report; Doc. 132, vol. 6, Ass'y Docs. 1853.

COLLECTION OF DEBTS.

Mr. O'Sullivan's report, judiciary; Doc. 178, vol. 7, Ass'y Docs. 1842.

CICERO COLLINS, CHARLES W. WOOLSTON, ERASTUS HUGHES.

Mr. McCarty's report, claims; Doc. 174, vol. 5, Ass'y Docs. 1848.

Mr. Schoonmaker's report. claims; Doc. 22, vol. 2, Senate Docs. 1851.

COLLINS AND HITCHCOCK.

Mr. Upham's report; Doc. 21, vol. 2, Senate Docs 1851.

Report of Canal Board; Doc. 18, vol. 1, Senate Docs. 1851.

JOHN A. COLLIER, COMPTROLLER. (Finances, Taxes and Stocks.)

Doc. 16, vol. 1, Senate Docs. 1842. Doc. 87, vol. 4, Senate Docs. 1842. Doc. 64, vol. 4, Ass'y Docs. 1842. Doc. 98, vol. 4, Senate Docs. 1842.

ANNUAL REPORT.

1841, (reprint); Doc. 63, vol. 3, Ass'y Docs. 1843.

1842; Doc. 15, vol. 1, Ass'y Docs. 1842.

COLONIAL HISTORY.

Message of Governor Seward, recommending appropriation; Doc. 85, vol. 4, Senate Docs. 1842.

Communication from J. Romeyn Brodhead concerning; Doc. 88, vol. 4, Senate Docs. 1842.

Mr. Lawrence's report, select committee; Doc. 42, vol. 1, Senate Docs. 1844.

Report to Governor Wright, of J. R. Brodhead, with catalogue of Holland, London and Paris documents; Doc. 47, vol. 1, Senate Docs. 1845.

Mr. Folsom's report; Doc. 111, vol. 3, Senate Docs 1845.

Communication from Secretary of State, C. Morgan; Doc. 188, vol. 3, Ass'y Docs. 1849.

Communication from Governor Fish, and Secretary of State, C. Morgan, in relation to progress of work; Doc. 66, vol. 3, Ass'y Docs. 1851.

E. B. O'Callaghan's statement; Doc. 24, vol. 1, Senate Docs. 1853.

Report of Secretary of State, H. S. Randall, relative to publication; Doc. 43, vol. 2, Senate Docs. 1853.

Contracts for printing and editing; Doc. 5, (page 108,) vol. 1, Ass'y Docs. 1853.

COLONIZATION SOCIETY—AMERICAN.

Communication from, to Governor Bouck, Doc. E. accompanying Doc. 2, vol. 1, Senate Docs. 1843. Doc. E. Doc. 3, vol. 1, Ass'y Docs. 1843.

Mr. Ward's report upon appropriation; Doc. 71, vol. 3, Ass'y Docs. 1851.

Mr. Strong's report in relation to an appropriation; Doc. 44, vol. 2, Ass'y. Docs. 1852.

COLORED HOME.

Mr. Orville Clark's report in relation to an appropriation; Doc. 112, vol. 3, Senate Docs. 1845.

COLORED ORPHANS, NEW-YORK,

Mr. Ward's report on appropriation; Doc. 43, vol. 2, Ass'y Docs. 1851.

COLORED PEOPLE—SUFFRAGE.

Mr. John Cramer's report; Doc. 155, vol. 7, Ass'y Docs. 1842.

COLUMBIA COUNTY.

Comptroller Flagg's report in relation to the expenditures incurred in maintenance of law in those counties; Doc. 99, vol. 2, Ass'y Docs. 1847.

SARAH COURTS.

Mr. S. A. Brown's report, aliens; Doc. 47, vol. 3, Ass'y Docs. 1845.

COMMERCE.

Proceedings of meeting held in the city of New-York, March 18, 1842, in relation to the deranged condition; Doc. 82, vol 3, Senate Docs. 1842.

COLUMBIA COLLEGE.

Mr. Hubbard's report, in relation to application for appropriation; Doc. 30, vol. 2, Ass'y Docs. 1843.

Report of condition made to Regents of the University; Doc. 77, (page 24) vol. 2, Senate Docs. 1854.

COMMISSARY GENERAL.

Annual report, Adoniram Chandler; Doc. 80, vol. 5, Ass'y Docs. 1842.

Annual report, Henry Storms; Doc. 40, vol. 2, Ass'y Docs. 1843.

Annual report, Henry Storms; Doc. 50, vol. 1, Ass'y Docs. 1844.

Gov. Wright's message respecting annual report of 1845, Doc. 51, vol. 3, Ass'y Docs. 1845. Doc. 99, vol. 4, Ass'y Docs. 1845.

Annual report, Henry Storms; Doc. 99, vol. 4, Ass'y Docs. 1845.

Annual report, Henry Storms; Doc. 75, vol. 3, Ass'y Docs. 1848.

Annual report, Henry Storms; Doc. 59, vol. 2, Ass'y Docs. 1846.

Annual report, Henry Storms; Doc. 110, vol. 4, Ass'y Docs. 1847.

Annual report, John Stewart, including communication from Ordnance department, Washington ; Doc. 120, vol. 3, Ass'y Docs. 1849.

Report, John Stewart, as to condition of arsenals in this State; Doc. 238, vol. 5, Ass'y Docs. 1849.

Annual report, John Stewart; Doc. 105, vol. 8, Ass'y Docs. 1850.

Annual report, Daniel Lee; Doc. 20, vol. 1, Ass'y Docs. 1851.
do do do 26, vol. 1, Ass'y Docs. 1852.
do do do 147, vol. 5, Ass'y Docs. 1854.

COMMISSIONERS OF CANAL FUND.

Financial report; Doc. 60, vol. 2, Ass'y Docs. 1847.

Report as to tolls derived from the western trade in 1846; Doc. 42, vol. 1, Ass'y Docs. 1847.

Report in relation to the surplus of canal revenues unappropriated; Doc. 112, vol. 4, Senate Docs. 1847.

Report as to canal debt due 30th September, 1847; Doc. 151, vol. 4, Senate Docs. 1847.

Report of tolls, trade and tonnage of the canals; Doc. 40, vol. 2, Senate Docs. 1848.

Financial report; Doc. 11, vol. 1, Ass'y Docs. 1848.

Report of payments for fiscal year ending 20th September, 1848; Doc. 15, vol. 1, Ass'y Docs. 1848.

Report of tolls, trade and tonnage of canal; Doc. 170, vol. 3, Ass'y Docs. 1849.

Report of tolls, trade and tonnage of canal; Doc. 60, vol. 2, Senate Docs. 1849.

Report in relation to stocks, city of Albany, Bank Fund, Lewis county bank.

Financial report, 1848, Doc. 100, vol. 2, Ass'y Docs. 1849.

Report in relation to tolls at Buffalo, Black Rock and Oswego; Doc. 35, vol. 1, Senate Docs. 1844.

Report of tolls, trade and tonnage of the canals; Doc. 118, vol. 4, Senate Docs. 1844.

Financial report; Doc. 40, vol. 3, Ass'y Docs. 1844.

Report of the tolls, tonnage and trade of the canals; Doc. 115, vol. 3, Senate Docs. 1845.

Financial report; Doc. 165, vol. 5, Ass'y Docs. 1845.

Report of tolls, trade and tonnage of the canals; Doc. 59, vol. 2, Senate Docs 1846.

Report in relation to the reduction in tolls; Doc. 89, vol. 3, Senate Docs. 1846.

Financial report; Doc. 4, vol. 1, Ass'y Docs. 1846.

Report as to tolls collected in October, November, December, 1845; Doc. 33, vol. 2, Ass'y Docs. 1846.

Report of tolls, trade and tonnage; Doc. 90, vol. 3, Senate Docs. 1847.

Report of tolls, trade and tonnage; Doc. 33, vol. 2, Senate Docs. 1842.

Report in relation to moneys paid for repairs, loans to banks, stock paid off; Doc. 70, vol. 2, Senate Docs. 1843.

Report in relation to loans of Canal Fund to banks; Doc. 92, vol. 3, Senate Docs. 1843.

Report of tolls, trade and tonnage; Doc. 100, vol. 3, Senate Docs. 1843.

Report of finances; Doc. 36, vol. 2, Ass'y Docs. 1843.

Report, communicating a table of receipts and payments, up to 30th September, 1843; Doc. 120, vol. 5, Ass'y Docs. 1844.

Report of Commissioners of Canal Fund, as to the application of surplus revenues to claims arising prior to June 1, 1846; Doc. 125, vol. 6, Ass'y Docs. 1853.

COMMITTEES OF THE LEGISLATURE.

Attorney General Chatfield's report on their powers; Doc. 110, vol. 5, Ass'y Docs. 1850.

COMMON CARRIERS.

Mr. Joshua A. Spencer's report on rights and liabilities of common carriers on the canals; Doc. 142, vol. 4, Senate Docs. 1847.

COMMON SCHOOLS.

Mr. Maclay's report on Gov. Seward's message in relation to schools in New-York city; Doc. 60, vol. 4, Ass'y Docs. 1846.

Memorial of citizens of Rochester, for uniform class books; Doc. 101, vol. 4, Ass'y Docs. 1846.

Mr. Benedict's report; Doc. 146, vol. 4, Ass'y Docs. 1846.

Mr. Burchard's report; Doc. 254, vol. 8, Ass'y Docs. 1847.

Secretary Morgan's report relative to digest of laws; Doc. 115, vol. 3, Ass'y Docs. 1848.

Mr. Beekman's report relative to certain academies, instructing common school teachers; Doc. 28, vol. 2, Senate Docs. 1851.

COMMON SCHOOLS.

Mr. Lysander H. Brown's report; Doc. 206, vol. 6, Ass'y Docs. 1845.

Mr. Ludlow's report; Doc. 133, vol. 4, Ass'y Docs. 1846.

COMMON SCHOOL FUND.

Mr. Harden's report in relation to an increase of the capital; Doc. 177, vol. 5, Ass'y Docs. 1845.

List of lands belonging to the fund; vol. 1, Senate Docs. 1854.

RUSSELL COMSTOCK.

Draft bill and testimonials in relation to discovery in agricultural science; Doc. 23, vol. 3, Ass'y Docs. 1850.

CONESUS LAKE.

Report of Canal Board in relation to supply of water; Doc. 40, vol. 1, Senate Docs. 1850.

CONGRESSIONAL DOCUMENTS.

Mr. Morris Brown's report (colleges, academies and common schools), on distribution of certain congressional documents; Doc. 31, vol. 2, Ass'y Docs. 1843.

Communication from Secretary of State, N. S. Benton; Doc. 71, vol. 2, Senate Docs. 1845.

CONNECTICUT.

Resolutions of Legislature on subject of tariff; Doc. 26, vol. 2, Ass'y Docs. 1842.

Resolutions of Legislature in relation to limitation of office of President of United States, to one term; Doc. 28, vol. 2, Ass'y Docs. 1842.

Resolutions of Legislature in relation to the public lands—pre-emptive rights—tariff—West Point academy—the bankrupt law; Doc. 11, vol. 1, Ass'y Docs. 1843.

Resolutions of Legislature in relation to French spoliations, West Point academy, tariff, Doc. 7, vol. 1, Ass'y Docs. 1844. Franking privilege; Doc. 14, vol. 1, Ass'y Docs. 1844.

CONSOLIDATION—(New-York, Brooklyn and Williamsburgh.)

Mr. John A. Cross's report, on the expediency of uniting the cities of New-York, Brooklyn and Williamsburgh, into one city; Doc. 74, vol. 3, Senate Docs. 1851.

CONSTABLES.

Mr. McMurray's report in relation to their compensation for attending the terms of the supreme court; Doc. 14, vol. 1, Senate Docs. 1853.

CONSTITUTION OF 1846.

Index; Doc. 16, vol. 1, Senate Docs. 1847.

Copy of, with marginal notes, prepared by Clerk Ellwood; Doc. 4, vol. 1, Ass'y Docs. 1847.

Comptroller Flagg's report containing list of papers publishing, and their terms; Doc. 126, vol. 4, Ass'y Docs. 1847.

Further report on same subject; Doc. 157, vol. 6, Ass'y Docs. 1847.

Copy with marginal notes; Doc. 6, vol. 1, Senate Docs. 1848.

Duplicate copy; Doc. 7, vol. 1, Ass'y Docs. 1848.

Copy with index and marginal notes; Doc. 7, vol. 2, Ass'y Docs. 1849.

Mr. Vanderbilt's majority report and proposed financial amendment; Doc. 42, vol. 2, Senate Docs. 1853.

Mr. G. T. Pierce's majority report on the same; Doc. 46, vol. 2, Senate Docs. 1853.

CONSTITUTIONAL AMENDMENTS.

Mr. Foster's propositions in relation to a loan of the State credit to corporations, the debt of the State, the election of State officers; Doc. 11, vol. 1, Senate Docs. 1844.

Mr. Foster's further propositions in relation to justices of the supreme court and chancery, and the court of errors; Doc. 13, vol. 1, Senate Docs. 1844.

Mr. Hand's propositions in relation to the supreme court, circuit courts, assistant chancellors, right of suffrage; Doc. 13, vol. 1, Senate Docs. 1844.

Mr. Porter's propositions in relation to usury laws, banks, masters and examiners in chancery; Doc. 15, vol. 1, Senate Docs 1844.

Mr. Johnson's proposition in relation to State debt, mill tax; Doc. 16, vol. 1, Senate Docs. 1844.

Mr. Platt's proposition in relation to appointments by Governor and Senate; Doc. 16, vol. 1, Senate Docs. 1844.

Mr. Porter's proposition in relation to the court of errors; Doc. 17, vol. 1, Senate Docs. 1844.

Mr. Clark's propositions in relation to the supreme court and court of chancery; Doc. 22, vol. 1, Senate Docs. 1844.

Mr. Scott's proposition in relation to the court of errors, chancery, supreme court, superior court, removal of judges; Doc. 29, vol. 1, Senate Docs. 1844.

Mr. Le Grand Marvin's petition, with propositions in relation to the judiciary; Doc. 36, vol. 1, Senate Docs. 1844.

Report of committee on judiciary, propositions concerning judiciary; Doc. 90, vol. 2, Senate Docs. 1844.

Mr. Lester's proposition in relation to chancery and supreme court; Doc. 104, vol. 3, Senate Docs. 1844.

Report of committee of conference; Dec. 123, vol. 4, Senate Docs. 1844.

Proceedings of Albany meeting, held at Capitol 21 Nov. 1843, in relation to constitutional reform; Doc. 32, vol. 1, Ass'y Docs. 1844.

Mr. B. F. Hall's proposition relative to single districts; Doc. 61, vol. 3. Ass'y Docs. 1844.

Report of select committee; Doc. 150, vol. 6, Ass'y Docs. 1844. (On the difference between Senate and Assembly in their propositions.)

Report of committee of conference; Doc. 166, vol. 7, Ass'y Docs. 1844.

Further report of committee of conference; Doc. 178, vol. 7, Ass'y Docs. 1844.

Report of Secretary of State, S. Young, relative to publication of proposed amendments; Doc. 7, vol. 1, Ass'y Docs. 1845.

Mr. Worden's propositions in relation to the eligibility to the Legislature of officers under the federal government, and of persons excluded from being Senator of the United States; Doc. 24, vol. 1, Ass'y Docs. 1845.

Mr. Comstock's report, select committee; Doc. 43, vol. 3, Ass'y Docs. 1845.

Mr. West's majority report on proposed financial amendment; Doc. 98, vol. 4, Ass'y Docs. 1853.

Mr. Clapp's minority report on same; Doc. 99, vol. 4, Ass'y Docs. 1853.

Returns of election held on the adoption of the financial amendment, February, 1854, Doc. 65, vol. 2, Senate Docs. 1854.

CONTESTED ELECTIONS.—(George J. J. Barber, and Abraham Aker, Cortland.)

Mr. Niven's unanimous report, favorable to Mr. Barber, the occupant; Doc. 21, vol. 1, Ass'y Docs. 1845.

EPENETUS CROSBY, AND GEORGE T. PIERCE, (Dutchess.)

Mr. Bishop Perkins' majority report, favorable to Mr. Crosby, the contestant; Doc. 45, vol. 2, Ass'y Docs. 1846.

Mr. Seacord's minority report, favorable to Mr. Pierce, the occupant; Doc. 46, vol. 2, Ass'y Docs. 1846.

DE LA MONTANYE, AND HASBROUCK, (Ulster.)

Mr. Thomas Smith's majority report, favorable to Mr. De La Montanye; Doc. 16, vol. 1, Ass'y Docs. 1847.

Mr. Robert D. Watson's minority report, favorable to Mr. Hasbrouck; Doc. 17, vol. 1, Ass'y Docs. 1847.

JAMES E. BEERS. AND JOHN R, HAYWARD, (case, Westchester.)

Mr. Thomas Smith's report, unanimous, in favor of Mr. Beers, the occupant; Doc. 29, vol. 1, Ass'y Docs. 1847.

SOLOMON MOSS, AND MORGAN JOHNSON, (case, Niagara.)

Attorney General Jordan's report as to the propriety of taking testimony after commencement of session; Doc. 30, vol. 6, Ass'y Docs. 1848.

Mr. S. G. Raymond's majority report, favorable to Mr. Johnson; Doc. 147, vol. 5, Ass'y Docs. 1848.

Mr. C. G. Myers' report, against Mr. Johnson; Doc. 147, vol. 5, Ass'y Docs. 1848.

DANIEL T. DURLAND, AND DANIEL FULLERTON, (case, Orange.)

Mr. Dinninny's report, with testimony favorable to Mr. Durland; Doc. 67, vol. 4, Ass'y Docs. 1850.

SAMUEL JAYNE, Jr., JOHN UNDERWOOD, (Yates County.)

Mr. Bishop's majority report; Doc. 55, vol. 3, Ass'y Docs. 1851.

Mr. Maurice's minority report; Doc. 55, vol. 3, Ass'y Docs. 1851. (Both these reports are preliminary to further investigation.)

Mr. Bishop's majority report, with evidence adverse to Mr. Underwood; Doc. 128, vol. 4, Ass'y Docs. 1851.

EPHRAIM L. SNOW, RUSSELL SMITH.

Mr. Sheldon's majority report, favorable to Mr. Snow, with testimony; Doc. 46, vol. 2, Ass'y Docs. 1852.

Mr. Keese's minority report, favorable to Mr. Smith, with testimony; Doc. 46, (page 28,) vol. 2, Ass'y Docs. 1852.

WILLIAM J. GILBERT, AND GEORGE B. GUINNIP, (26th Senatorial District.)

Mr. J. A. Cross' majority report, favorable to Mr. Gilbert; Doc. 84, vol. 3, Senate Docs. 1851.

Mr. T. Cook's minority report, in dissent; Doc. 84, vol. 3, Senate Docs. 1851. (Testimony is annexed.)

Communication from Charles G. Higby; Doc. 92, vol. 3, Senate Docs. 1851.

HENRY B. STANTON, AND JOSIAH B. WILLIAMS, (25th Senatorial District.)

Mr. J. A. Cross' report of examination, with testimony; Doc. 85, vol. 3, Senate Docs. 1851.

JOB G. ELMORE, contestant, JACOB WESTBROOK, Jr., sitting member (Ulster.)

Mr. Sheldon's report, adverse to Mr. Westbrook; Doc. 28, vol. 2, Ass'y Docs. 1852.

Mr. Sayles' report in relation to payment to contestant; Doc. 65, vol. 2, Ass'y Docs. 1852.

EBENEZER BLAKELEY, AND ADAM STORING.

emorial of Adam Storing; Doc. 9, vol. 1, Senate Docs. 1854.

Statement of Ebenezer Blakeley; same document.

Mr. Crosby's majority report, favorable to Mr. Blakeley; Doc. 57, vol. 1, Senate Docs. 1854.

Mr. Zenas Clark's minority report, favorable to Mr. Storing; Doc. 57, vol. 1, Senate Docs. 1854.

CONTINGENT FUND AND EXPENSES.

Report of Comptroller J. C. Wright; Doc. 124, vol. 5, Ass'y Docs. 1852.

Mr. Davenport's report; Doc. 26, vol. 1, Senate Docs. 1853.

CONTRACTS OF 1851.

The majority report from a committee of investigation of the facts connected with the canal lettings of 1851; Doc. 89, vol. 3, Ass'y Docs. 1852. (This report is signed by A. H. Moss, H. B. Bull, A. S. Upham.)

Mr. Cushing's report on same subject; Doc. 89, (page 23,) vol. 3, Ass'y Docs. 1852.

Mr. Conger's report on same subject; Doc. 89, (page 29,) vol. 3, Ass'y Docs. 1852.

The appendix contains statistics of contracts and minutes of Canal Board.

CONVENTION OF THE PEOPLE.

Mr. Bockee's majority report on the bill from the Assembly recommending a convention; Doc. 107, vol. 3, Senate Docs. 1845.

Mr. Lott's minority report; Doc. 108, vol. 3, Senate Docs. 1845.

Mr. W. C. Crain's report; Doc. 211, vol. 6, Ass'y Docs. 1845.

Messrs. Comstock, Sager, McKey and Pierce's report on Mr. Crain's bill; Doc. 231, vol. 6, Ass'y Docs. 1845.

Attorney General Van Buren's report as to the number of delegates to which each county will be entitled; Doc. 111, vol. 4, Ass'y Docs. 1846.

Report as to the justices of the supreme court, as to the apportionment of delegates; Doc. 181, vol. 5, Ass'y Docs. 1846.

CALVIN CONVERSE.

Mr. Dimmick's report; Doc. 12, vol. 1, Senate Docs. 1850.

PATRICK CORNEY.

Mr. Johnson's report, claims; Doc. 45, vol. 2, Senate Docs. 1846.

CHARLES A. COOK.

Mr. Schoonmaker's majority report of investigation on charges preferred against him as Canal Commissioner, by Senator Guinnip; Doc. 105, vol. 3, Senate Docs. 1850.

JOHN J. COOK, JOSEPH T. COOK.

Report of Canal Commissioners; Doc. 99, vol. 3, Ass'y Docs. 1844.

JAMES M. COOK, (Comptroller.)

The entries will be found at length under the heads of the subjects.

FIRE INSURANCE.

Doc. 95, vol. 3, Ass'y Docs. 1854.

NON-RESIDENT TAXES.

Doc. 101, vol. 3, Ass'y Docs. 1853.

STATIONERY.

Doc. 55, vol. 1, Senate Docs. 1854.

CHARLES COOK.

Mr. S. Baldwin's report, claims; Doc. 115, vol. 3, Ass'y Docs. 1854.

JOHN COPELAND.

Report committee on claims, on his petition for damages concerning raising Mud lock, section 8, Erie canal; Doc. 105, vol. 3, Ass'y Docs. 1849.

DANIEL CORNELL, RANSOM CLARKE.

Mr. McLean's report, claims; Doc. 158, vol. 3, Ass'y Docs. 1849.

Mr. Hale's report, claims; Doc. 87, vol. 2, Ass'y Docs. 1849.

Mr. Cushman's report; Doc. 26, vol. 3, Ass'y Docs. 1850.

Mr. Colt's report; Doc. 100, vol. 3, Senate Docs. 1850.

Mr. Vanderbilt's report; Doc. 14, vol. 1, Senate Docs. 1852.

AUGUSTUS CORNWALL.

Report of committee on public lands, in relation to an escheat; Doc. 113, vol. 5, Ass'y Docs. 1852.

CORONERS OF NEW-YORK CITY.

Report of fees; Doc. 36, vol. 3, Ass'y Docs. 1848.

CORPORATIONS.

Attorney General Van Buren's report on the subject of the constitutional power of the Legislature, to restrict the rights of any class of corporations by a general bill; Doc. 159, vol. 5, Ass'y Docs. 1845.

CORPORATION COUNSEL OF NEW-YORK.

Memorial of citizens of New-York on the subject of fees and costs; Doc. 18, vol. 1, Senate Docs. 1854.

CORTLAND.

Comptroller Fillmore's report on taxes on lands; Doc. 136, vol. 5, Ass'y Docs. 1848.

CHARLES CONGELL, WILLIAM CONGELL.

Mr. Spencer's report relative to their medical license; Doc. 83, vol. 5, Ass'y Docs. 1842.

ELIAS COST.

Report of Commissioners of Land Office in relation to compensation for notice of an escheat; Doc. 57, vol. 2, Senate Docs. 1847.

COSTS AND FEES IN COURTS.

Mr. McCarthy's report, with propriety of reducing costs; Doc. 227, vol. 6, Ass'y Docs. 1845.

Mr. Ansel Bascom's resolutions concerning; Doc. 37, vol. 1, Ass'y Docs. 1847.

Memorial of bar of New-York, in relation to the taxation of bills of costs by county clerk; Doc. 192, vol. 7, Ass'y Docs. 1847.

THOMAS COUNTRYMAN.

Mr. Curtis's report; Doc. 46, vol. 2, Senate Docs. 1851.

Mr. J. B. Williams's report; Doc. 12, vol. 1, Senate Docs. 1852. Doc. 34, vol. 1, Senate Docs. 1853.

COUNTY CLERKS.

Report of Secretary of State, N. S. Benton, as to their returns to his office of their statements of fees; Doc. 70, vol. 2, Senate Docs. 1845.

Report of judiciary committee in relation to fees of clerk of New-York; Doc. 126, vol. 3, Senate Docs. 1845.

Report of Secretary of State, N. S. Benton, as to those who did not report their fees in 1846; Doc. 141, vol. 4, Senate Docs. 1846.

Report of Secretary of State, N. S. Benton, as to fees for 1845, 1846; Doc. 58, vol. 2, Senate Docs. 1847.

Report of Secretary of State, Christopher Morgan, on fees received by clerk of New-York; Doc. 78, vol. 3, Senate Docs. 1849.

Report of Secretary of State. C. Morgan, as to reports; Doc. 152, vol. 6, Ass'y Docs. 1850.

Report of Secretary of State, H. S. Randall, in relation to fees; Doc. 118, vol. 5, Ass'y Docs. 1852.

COUNTY CLERKS OF NEW-YORK CITY.

Report of James Conner; Doc. 86, vol. 2, Ass'y Docs. 1849.

COUNTY COURTS.

Petition of E. T. Bullard and others, in relation to jurisdiction of, with opinion of Mr. Justice Willard; Doc. 142, vol. 3, Ass'y Docs. 1849.

COUNTY EXPENSES.

Mr. Barlow's report on the abuses; Doc. 76, vol. 3, Senate Docs. 1846.

Reports of clerks of boards of supervisors, as to expenses of board; Doc. 65, vol. 2, Senate Docs. 1847.

COUNTY SUPERINTENDENTS OF SCHOOLS.

Mr. Maclay's report; Doc. 168, vol. 7, Ass'y Docs. 1842.

Mr. Hubbard's report; Doc. 100, vol. 4, Ass'y Docs. 1843.

Mr. Burchard's report as to their compensation; Doc. 242, vol. 8, Ass'y Docs. 1847.

Comptroller Flagg's report in relation to the same; Doc. 245, vol. 8, Ass'y Docs. 1847.

Memorial of citizens of Pompey, against the office; Doc. 166, vol. 6, Ass'y Docs. 1850.

COURTS OF CONCILIATION.

Communication of Steen Bille, charge 'des affaires of Sweden to the United States, in relation to the arrangement and operation of such tribunals in Sweden; Doc. 98, vol. 3, Senate Docs. 1847.

COURT OF ERRORS.

Mr. Joshua A. Spencer's report on the provision of the new constitution respecting duration; Doc. 4, vol. 1, Senate Docs. 1847.

Mr. A. C. Hand's report on same; Doc. 9, vol. 1, Senate Docs. 1847.

Lieutenant Governor, Addison Gardner's opinion on same; Doc. 20, vol. 1, Senate Docs. 1847.

COURTS—MARTIAL.

Mr. Root's report—militia—concerning abolition or reduction of expenses; Doc. 74, vol. 3, Senate Docs. 1843.

ESEK COWEN.

Arrangements for his funeral, as justice of the Supreme court; Doc. 54, vol. 2, Senate Docs. 1844.

JAMES COX, ISAAC COX.

Mr. Tupper's report, claims; Doc. 128, vol. 5, Ass'y Docs. 1842.

CLARK CRANDALL.

Mr. Corey's report in relation to injuries received in the militia service of the State; Doc. 149, vol. 6, Ass'y Docs. 1850.

Mr. Simmons's report; Doc. 106, vol. 5, Ass'y Docs. 1852.

HENRY CRANDALL.

Mr. Boardman's report; Doc. 150, vol. 3, Ass'y Docs. 1849.

CREDIT AND FAITH OF THE STATE.

Mr. Erastus Root's resolutions; Doc. 23, vol. 2, Senate Docs. 1842.

CRIME IN STATE OF NEW-YORK.

Annual report, Secretary of State, Samuel Young; Doc. 51, vol. 3, Senate Docs. 1842.

Annual report of Secretary, S. Young; Doc. 110, vol. 4, Ass'y Docs. 1843.

Annual report of Secretary, S. Young; Doc. 92, vol. 2, Senate Docs. 1844.

Annual report of Secretary, N. S. Benton; Doc. 54, vol. 2, Senate Docs. 1845.

Annual report of Secretary, N. S. Benton; Doc. 98, vol. 3, Senate Docs. 1846.

Reports of clerks of counties as to criminal statistics; Doc. 80, vol. 2, Senate Docs. 1847.

Report of Secretary of State, N. S. Benton, with abstracts of convictions; Doc. 180, vol. 7, Ass'y Docs. 1847.

Report of Secretary of State, C. Morgan, with abstracts of convictions: Doc. 193, vol. 6, Ass'y Docs. 1848.

Report of Secretary of State, C. Morgan; Doc. 242, vol. 85, Ass'y Docs. 1849.

Report of Secretary of State, C. Morgan; Doc. 195, vol. 8, Ass'y Docs. 1850.

Report of Gov. Fish in relation to commissions for vagrancy; Doc. 43, vol. 2, Senate Docs. 1850.

Report of Secretary of State, Christopher Morgan; Doc. 140, vol. 5, Ass'y Docs. 1851.

Report of Secretary of State, H. S. Randall, with abstracts of convictions; Doc. 97, vol. 3, Senate Docs. 1852.

Report of Secretary of State, Henry S. Randall, with abstract of returns in counties; Doc. 77, vol. 3, Senate Docs. 1853.

Report of Secretary of State, E. W. Leavenworth, with statistics; Doc. 54, vol. 1, Senate Docs. 1854.

CRIMINAL COURTS IN NEW-YORK CITY.

Report of committee on Judiciary, Mr. O'Sullivan, on repeal of the law of 1840, relative to the criminal courts of New-York city; Doc. 30, vol. 2, Ass'y Docs. 1842.

Message of Gov. Seward, vetoing the bill repealing the New-York Criminal Court act. Doc. 90, vol. 6, Senate Docs. 1842.

JOSEPH R. CROSS.

Mr. Mark's report, claims, in relation to the arrest of fugitives from justice ; Doc. 224, vol. 7, Ass'y Docs. 1847.

CROTON AQUEDUCT.

Scientific description of Croton Aqueduct, by Mr. Jervis, document B, accompanying Gov. Seward's extra session message; Doc. 106, vol. 4, Senate Docs. 1842. Doc. B, accompanying Doc. 195, vol. 7, Ass'y Docs. 1842.

CROUP.

Morgan Snyder's treatise; Doc. 67, (page 126,) vol. 3, Ass'y Docs. 1843.

HENRY CROUSE.

Mr. Severance's report, claims; Doc. 38, vol. 2, Ass'y Docs. 1851.

CRYSTAL PALACE IN LONDON.

Communication from Gov. Fish and the British Consul, Anthony Barclay, with English documents having relation thereto; Doc. 177, vol. 8, Ass'y Docs. 1850.

JAMES CUNNINGHAM.

Mr. Wood's report, claims; Doc. 45, vol. 2, Ass'y Docs. 1853.

JOHN W. CURRAN.

Mr. Schoonmaker's report, claims; Doc. 31, vol. 2, Senate Docs. 1851.

CYPRESS HILL CEMETERY.

Mr. G. R. Babcock's report; Doc. 31, vol. 1, Senate Docs. 1850.

JAMES DANA, WILLIAM YOUNGS, DAVID A. RICHTMYER.

Mr. Carpenter's report, grievances; Doc. 77, vol. 3, Ass'y Docs. 1845.

DANSVILLE, BANK OF.

Mr. Sherman's report, judiciaty; Doc. 17, vol. 1, Senate Docs. 1845.

M. Lawrence's majority report; Doc. 224, vol. 6, Ass'y Docs. 1846. (Discusses the question of the power of the Legislature over Banks formed under the General Law.)

Mr. H. Z. Hayner's minority report; Doc. 225, vol. 6, Ass'y Docs. 1846.

Petition of Richard W. Porter and others for investigation; Doc. 73, vol 2, Ass'y Docs. 1847.

Remonstrance of Cashier Woodruff against charges, and petition for investigation; Doc. 93, vol. 2, Ass'y Docs. 1847.

Mr. Hadley's report as to a lost paper; Doc. 125, vol. 4, Ass'y Docs. 1847.

Mr. Hadley's report on investigation, and on power of Legislature over General Banking Law Banks; Doc. 145, vol. 4, Ass'y Docs. 1847.

Further report of Mr. Hadley; Doc. 155, vol. 6, Ass'y Docs. 1847.

DANSVILLE BRANCH OF GENESEE VALLEY CANAL.

Mr. Horatio Seymour's report; Doc. 164, vol. 7, Ass'y Docs. 1844.

Mr. H. R. Riddle's report, same document.

Affidavits in relation thereto; Doc. 182, vol. 7, Ass'y Docs. 1844.

Further affidavits; Doc. 187, vol. 7, Ass'y Docs. 1844.

Report as to Steel Creek; Doc. 75, vol. 2, Senate Docs. 1845.

Mr. Denniston's report; Doc. 82, vol. 2, Senate Docs. 1845.

Mr. Denniston's further report; Doc. 96, vol. 3, Senate Docs. 1845.

Mr. Coe's report, canals; Doc. 117, vol. 3, Ass'y Docs. 1845.

Report of Canal Commissioners; Doc. 135, vol. 4, Ass'y Docs. 1845.

JONATHAN W. DAVIS.

Mr. Folger's report; Doc. 41, vol. 2, Ass'y Docs. 1849.

Comptroller Fillmore's report; Doc. 98, vol. 2, Ass'y Docs. 1849.

DAY, TOWN.

Report of Attorney General Jordan; Doc. 181, vol. 3, Ass'y Docs. 1849.

JOHN H. DAYTON.

Mr. Nivins' report as to the eligibility of Mr. Dayton, a member elect, he having accepted the office of Collector of the Customs for Sag Harbor district, an office conferred by the Federal Government; Doc. 12, vol. 1, Ass'y Docs. 1845. This report is that the seat is vacant.

Mr. T. R. Lee's majority report, judiciary; Doc. 19, vol. 1, Ass'y Docs. 1845. This report is that the seat is *not* vacant.

Mr. Wheeler's minority report, judiciary; Doc. 20, vol. 1, Ass'y Docs. 1845. This report is that the seat is vacant.

DEAF AND DUMB INSTITUTION, NEW-YORK.

Annual report; Doc. 57, vol. 4, Ass'y Docs. 1842.
" " Doc. 74, vol. 3, Ass'y Docs. 1843.
" " Doc. 26, vol. 1, Ass'y Docs. 1844.

Report of Comptroller Flagg, as to sums paid from State Treasury; Doc. 52, vol. 2, Senate Docs. 1845.

Mr. A. G. Thompson's report; Doc. 60, vol. 3, Ass'y Docs. 1845.

Annual report; Doc. 70, vol. 3, Ass'y Docs. 1845.
" " Doc. 140, vol. 5, Ass'y Docs. 1846.
" " Doc. 51, vol. 2, Ass'y Docs. 1847.
" " Doc. 47, vol. 2, Ass'y Docs. 1848.

Petition for appropriation to extinguish their debt of $15,000; Doc. 38, vol. 1, Ass'y Docs. 1849.

Annual Report; Doc. 89, vol. 2, Ass'y Docs. 1849.
" " Doc. 70, vol. 4, Ass'y Docs. 1850.
" " Doc. 22, vol. 2, Ass'y Docs. 1851. (Proceedings of the first Convention of American Instructors of the Deaf and Dumb, New-York, August 28, 29, 30, 1850, are annexed.)

Annual report; Doc. 112, vol. 5, Ass'y Docs. 1852. This contains tribute to the memory of J. H. Gallaudet; Mr. H. P. Peet's record of foreign institutions.

Peter Van Buren's treatise on Deaf and Dumb Institutions; Doc. 85, (page 75) vol. 2, Ass'y Docs. 1852.

Hervey P. Peet's treatise on the statistics. Doc. 67, (page 44) vol. 3, Ass'y Docs. 1853.

P. Van Buren's reply to H. P. Peet; Doc. 67, (page 173) vol. 3, Ass'y Docs. 1853.

Annual report; Doc. 93, vol. 4, Ass'y Docs. 1853.

Report of Superintendent of Public Instruction, Victor M. Rice, as to deaf mutes; Doc. 29, vol. 1, Senate Docs. 1854.

Communication of directors in relation to sale of real estate, and purchase of new location for buildings; Doc. 127, vol. 4, Ass'y Docs. 1854.

Annual report; Doc. 125, vol. 3, Ass'y Docs. 1854.

DEBTORS, ABSCONDING—(concealed and non-resident)

Mr. H. W. Strong's report; Doc. 42, vol. 2, Senate Docs. 1842.

NICHOLAS H. DECKER, JOHN WARNER JOSEPH H. DECKER.

Report of Canal Commissioners on details of contract for sections 51, 52, 53, 54, 55, 56, 57, Erie canal; Doc. 101, vol. 4, Ass'y Docs. 1845.

DECLARATION OF INDEPENDENCE.

Resolutions of the authorities of Philadelphia, relative to the erection of a monument in Independence Hall; Doc. 6, vol. 1, Senate Docs. 1852.

Proceedings of a convention held at Philadelphia, in 1852; Doc. 89, vol. 4, Ass'y Docs. 1853.

Mr. Session's report, in favor of co-operation by New-York; Doc. 102, vol. 4, Ass'y Docs. 1853.

Message from Gov. Seymour, in relation to the proposed monument; Doc. 89, vol. 4, Ass'y Docs. 1853.

DAVID DEFENDORF, CHARLES DEVENDORF.

Mr. A. Chamberlain's report; Doc. 68, vol. 2, Ass'y Docs. 1852.

DELAWARE—(County.)

Gov. Wright's proclamation concerning disturbances; appendix to Doc. 2, vol. 1, Senate Docs. 1846.

Further proclamation, declaring its insurrection quelled; appended to same document.

Comptroller Flagg's report as to expenses incurred in preserving order and maintaining the laws in said county; Doc. 37, vol. 1, Senate Docs. 1846. Doc. 99, vol. 2, Ass'y Docs. 1847.

DELAWARE—(State.)

Resolutions of Legislature in relation to slavery; Doc. 27, vol. 2, Ass'y Docs. 1842.

DELAWARE AND HUDSON CANAL.

Report of Comptroller Flagg in relation to the difference between this company and the Erie railroad company; Doc. 162, vol. 7, Ass'y Docs. 1842. Doc. 155, vol. 5, Ass'y Docs. 1845.

Mr. John L. Lawrence's report on restitution of premium received; Doc. 43, vol. 2, Senate Docs. 1848.

Report of Comptroller Fillmore as to stocks issued on account of this company; Doc. 41, vol. 2, Senate Docs. 1849.

Mr. Van Valkenburgh's majority report in relation to alleged violation of charter; Doc. 60, vol. 2, Ass'y Docs. 1852.

Mr. Alvah Hurlburt's minority report on same subject; Doc. 70, vol. 2, Ass'y Docs. 1852.

DEMILT DISPENSARY.

Annual report; Doc. 60, vol. 2, Senate Docs. 1853.

JOSEPH DEMONT, ORRIN TYLER, EDWARD MYNDERSE.

Report of Canal Appraisers; Doc. 46, vol. 3, Ass'y Docs. 1845.

HIRAM DENIO.

Report of fees, as Supreme court clerk; Doc. 48, vol. 1, Senate Docs. 1843.

Report; Doc. 92, vol. 4, Ass'y Docs. 1843.

Letter to George W. Newell, Auditor, concerning State debt, Canal Debt and Sinking Fund; Doc. 51, (page 10) vol. 2, Senate Docs. 1853.

ISAAC DENNISTON.

Comptroller Flagg's report on claim as Indian agent; Doc. 110, vol. 3, Senate Docs. 1847.

DENTAL SURGERY COLLEGE.

Mr. D. P. Wood's report; Doc. 139, vol. 4, Ass'y Docs. 1854.

DEPOSITE FUND—(United States.)

Comptroller Flagg's report; Doc. 83, vol. 4, Ass'y Docs. 1843.

Gov. Bouck's message concerning; Doc. 138, vol. 5, Ass'y Docs. 1843.

Proceedings of meeting of people of Bainbridge, concerning; Doc. 138, vol. 5, Ass'y Docs. 1843.

Mr. Allen's report, ways and means, on the subject of receiving the money by the State; Doc. 144, vol. 5, Ass'y Docs. 1843.

Comptroller Flagg's report as to the condition of amount received; Doc. 75, vol. 3, Ass'y Docs. 1845.

Gov. Wright's message respecting the last instalment of $10,-000; Doc. 88, vol. 4, Ass'y Docs. 1845.

Comptroller Fillmore's report in relation to the balance of $1,373.33, due treasury, Sept. 30th 1847; Doc. 111, vol. 3, Ass'y Docs. 1849.

DE RUYTER INSTITUTE.

Memorial of Benjamin Enos and others, for an agricultural department; Doc. 78, vol. 2, Ass'y Docs. 1849.

CHARLES DEWEY.

Mr. Johnson's report; Doc. 52, vol. 2, Senate Docs. 1846.

WILLIAM S. DE ZENG.

Mr. Ruger's report, claims; Doc. 50, vol. 1, Senate Docs. 1853.

DIRECT RAILWAY—(Syracuse and Rochester.)

Mr. Mowry's majority report, adverse to incorporation; Doc. 81, vol. 2, Ass'y Docs. 1849.

Mr. Boyce's minority report on same; Doc. 82, vol. 2, Ass'y Docs. 1849.

Proceedings of meeting of citizens of Palmyra; Doc. 122, vol. 3, Ass'y Docs. 1849.

Memorial of Auburn and Rochester railway company against same; Doc. 13, vol. 1, Ass'y Docs. 1850.

Memorial of Auburn and Syracuse Railway Company, against same; Doc. 13, vol. 1, Ass'y Docs. 1850.

Memorial of "Direct Railway Company" for the same; Doc. 14, vol. 1, Ass'y Docs. 1850.

Mr. Story's report; Doc. 37, vol. 3, Ass'y Docs. 1850.

JOHN Q. A. DISBROW.

Report of committee on judiciary, Mr. Loomis, on claims; Doc. 38, vol. 2, Ass'y Docs. 1842.

DISLOCATION.

Wm. W. Reid's treatise, before State Medical Society; Doc. 85, (page 25) vol. 2, Ass'y Docs. 1852.

DISPENSARY AT BUFFALO.

Report; Doc. 16, vol. 1, Senate Docs. 1854.

DISPENSARIES IN THE CITY OF NEW-YORK.

Mr. Whitney's report in favor of an appropriation; Doc. 140, vol. 4, Ass'y Docs. 1845.

DISPENSARY—(Eastern New-York.)

Report; Doc. 80, vol 3, Senate Docs. 1842.
do do 47, vol. 1, Senate Docs. 1843.
do do 174, vol. 7, Ass'y Docs. 1844.
do do 113, vol. 4, Ass'y Docs. 1847.
do do 197, vol. 6, Ass'y Docs. 1848.
do do 234, vol. 5, Ass'y Docs. 1849.
do do 119, vol. 4, Ass'y Docs. 1851.

DISPENSARY, NEW-YORK

Annual report; Doc. 99, vol. 5, Ass'y Docs. 1842. Doc. 64, vol. 3, Senate Docs. 1842.

Annual report; Doc. 169, vol. 7, Ass'y Docs. 1844.
do do 207, vol. 6, Ass'y Docs. 1846.

Report; Doc. 76, vol. 3, Senate Docs. 1848.
do do 103, vol. 3, Senate Docs. 1850.
do do 52, vol. 2, Senate Docs. 1851.

DISPENSARY, NORTHERN NEW-YORK.

Annual report; Doc. 61, vol. 3, Senate Docs. 1842.

Annual report, Doc. 33, vol. 1, Senate Docs. 1843. Doc. 61, vol. 3, Ass'y Docs. 1843.

Annual report; Doc. 88, vol 2, Senate Docs. 1844. Doc. 163, vol. 7, Ass'y Docs. 1844.

Annual report; Doc. 37, vol. 1, Senate Docs. 1845. Doc. 160, vol. 5, Ass'y Docs. 1845.

Annual report; Doc. 145, vol. 4, Senate Docs. 1846.
do do 29, vol. 1, Senate Docs. 1847.
do do 82, vol. 3, Senate Docs. 1849.

NEW-YORK DISPENSARY—NORTHERN 2D.

Annual report; Doc. 107, vol. 3, Senate Docs. 1850.
do do 21, vol. 2, Senate Docs. 1851.
do do 11, vol. 1, Senate Docs. 1852.
do do 40, vol. 1, Senate Docs. 1854.

DISSECTION.

Mr. O'Sullivan's report on means necessary to protect the sanctity; Doc. 186, vol. 7, Ass'y Docs. 1842.

Mr. Sprague's report; Doc. 21, vol. 2, Ass'y Docs. 1853.

Remonstrance of Irish Emigrant Society against the bill in relation to dissection; Doc. 31, vol. 1, Ass'y Docs. 1854.

DISTRICT OF COLUMBIA.

Mr. Worden's resolutions respecting slavery; Doc. 162, vol. 5, Ass'y Docs. 1846.

DISTRICT ATTORNEYS.

Report of Secretary of State, Samuel Young, relative to fees; Doc. 89, vol. 5, Ass'y Docs. 1842.

DISTRICT SCHOOL JOURNAL.

Report of Secretary of State, N. S. Benton, as to moneys paid for publication; Doc. 188, vol. 5, Ass'y Docs. 1846.

DIVORCE.

Mr. Palmer's report, judiciary, on the question of intemperance, as a cause for divorce; Doc. 156, vol. 6, Ass'y Docs. 1844.

Mr. Allen's report, judiciary, on the petition of Jacob Scrumling, for a divorce; Doc. 199, vol. 7, Ass'y Docs. 1844.

Mr. T. R. Lee's report, judiciary, on petition of Jacob Scrumling; Doc. 139, vol. 4, Ass'y Docs. 1845.

Mr. Wheeler's report, judiciary, on the petition of Mary Ann Van Riper, for a divorce; Doc. 237, vol. 6, Ass'y Docs. 1845.

Mr. Lott's report, judiciary, on the bill for the relief of Cornelia L. Lilie, and Eben A. Hall; Doc. 125, vol. 4, Senate Docs. 1846.

Mr. Lott's report, judiciary, on the Livingston Schuyler case; Doc. 130, vol. 4, Senate Docs. 1846.

Mr. B. F. Cooper's majority report, judiciary; Doc. 219, vol. 6, Ass'y Docs. 1846.

Mr. George J. Cornell's report in cases of John Black and William H. Pillow; Doc. 66, vol. 2, Ass'y Docs. 1849.

Mr. Burrough's report; Doc. 72, vol. 4, Ass'y Docs. 1850.

Report of committee on judiciary in the case of Edwin H. Cobb; Doc. 16, vol. 1, Ass'y Docs. 1852.

Mr. Van Santvoord's report; Doc. 73, vol. 2, Ass'y Docs. 1852.

MISS DIX.

Report on the condition of the insane in the various poor houses of the State, communication subjoined to Doc. 21, vol. 1, Ass'y Docs. 1844.

THOMAS W. DIXON.

Report of judiciary committee; Doc. 91, vol. 4, Ass'y Docs. 1851.

JAMES DOBBIN.

Copy of his last will; Doc. 80, vol. 3, Senate Docs. 1846.

DOCUMENTS OF LEGISLATURE.

Report of select committee in relation to fraud and negligence in distribution; Doc. 105, vol. 6, Ass'y Docs. 1847.

DOCUMENTARY HISTORY.

Report of Secretary of State, E. W. Leavenworth; Doc. 136, vol. 4, Ass'y Docs. 1854.

HORACE DODGE, JAMES ROGERS, JOHN MONROE, GILBERT RILEY.

Mr. Bishop Perkins' report, claims; Doc. 123, vol. 4, Ass'y Docs. 1846.

Mr. Lewis' report; Doc. 108, vol. 5, Ass'y Docs. 1850.

ORIN DODGE.

Report of Mr. Fitzhugh; Doc. 147, vol. 3, Ass'y Docs. 1849.

NICHOLAS B. DOE.

Report of Commissioners of Land Office; Doc. 158, vol. 5, Ass'y Docs. 1843.

Report of Commissioners of Land Office; Doc. 32, vol. 2, Senate Docs. 1848.

DOGS.

Report upon, from committee on internal affairs; Doc. 4, vol. 1, Ass'y Docs. 1851.

JOHN DONELLY.

Mr. McCarty's report, claims; Doc. 89, vol. 3, Ass'y Docs. 1848.

Report of Canal Commissioners; Doc. 99, vol. 3, Ass'y Docs. 1845.

THOMAS W. DORR, of Rhode Island.

Mr. McKey's report; Doc. 248, vol. 7, Ass'y Docs. 1845.

TIMOTHY DOUGHTY.

Mr. H. Putnam's report, claims; Doc. 54, vol. 2, Senate Docs. 1843.

DOWER.

Mr. A. C. Hand's report on conveyances by *femes covert;* Doc. 37, vol. 1, Senate Docs. 1847.

ERASTUS DRESSER.

Mr. J. E. Beers' report, claims; for loss of canal boat; Doc. 142, vol. 4, Ass'y Docs. 1847.

PHILANDER DUNHAM.

Comptroller Flagg's report in relation to claim for services in executing a requisition; Doc. 82, vol. 3, Ass'y Docs. 1846.

DUNDEE SALT SPRINGS.

Mr. Austin Smith's report in relation to aid by the State in testing the availability of the Salt Springs, at that place; Doc. 91, vol. 5, Ass'y Docs. 1852.

CYRUS P. DURHAM.

Mr. N. Jones' report, claims; Doc. 55, vol. 2, Senate Docs. 1853.

DUTCHESS COUNTY.

Mr. James Munroe's report on the expenses incurred in quelling a riot on the Hudson River Railroad, in January, 1849; Doc. 170, vol. 6, Ass'y Docs. 1850.

JOHN E. DUTTON, GEORGE SALMON, GEORGE F. FALLEY, CHARLES G. CASE.

Mr. J. E. Beers' report, claims; Doc. 72, vol. 2, Ass'y Docs. 1847.

DYEING AND PRINTING ESTABLISHMENT, NEW-YORK,

Mr. Falkner's report; Doc. 62, vol. 2, Senate Docs. 1843.

A. DYGERT.

Mr. Mitchell's report; Doc. 26, vol. 1, Ass'y Docs. 1854.

ELIJAH EATON.

Report of Commissioners of Land Office on resale of lands in Locke; Doc. 54, vol. 2, Senate Docs. 1847.

ECLECTIC MEDICAL COLLEGE OF CENTRAL NEW-YORK, Rochester.

Mr. Bradford's report on special incorporation; Doc. 108, vol. 5, Ass'y Docs. 1852.

OTIS EDDY, HARRIET EDDY.

Mr. H. Putnam's report, claims; Doc. 58, vol. 2, Senate Docs. 1843.

Mr. Nicoll's report, claims; Doc. 43, vol. 3, Ass'y Docs. 1843.

Report of Canal Board; Doc. 43, vol. 1, Senate Docs. 1844.

Mr. W. Platt's minority report; Doc. 109, vol. 3, Senate Docs. 1844.

TIMOTHY EDDY.

Report of Canal Commissioners; Doc. 48, vol. 1, Senate Docs. 1844.

Mr. Lawrence's report, claims; Doc. 56, vol. 2, Senate Docs. 1844.

Report of Canal Board; Doc. 34, vol. 1, Senate Docs. 1845. (The testimony is subjoined.)

Mr. Hand's report, finance; Doc. 41, vol. 1, Senate Docs. 1845.

MARY E. EDWARDS.

Report of State Engineer Charles B. Stuart; Doc. 176, vol. 5, Ass'y Docs. 1849.

Report of Commissioners of Land Office; Doc. 64, vol. 2, Ass'y Docs. 1849.

Mr. Bownes' report; Doc. 46, vol. 3, Ass'y Docs. 1850.

Appendix to above report, containing extracts from record of Commissioners of Land Office, since 1790; Doc. 61, vol. 4, Ass'y Docs. 1850.

SILAS EGGLESTON.

Report of Canal Board; Doc. 147, vol. 5, Ass'y Docs. 1846.

CHARLES EHLE.

Report of committee on claims; Doc. 73, vol. 2, Senate Docs. 1847.

Report of Canal Commissioners; Doc. 76, vol. 2, Senate Docs. 1847.

Report of committee on canals; Doc. 161, vol. 2, Ass'y Docs. 1849.

Mr. E. D. Morgan's report; Doc. 42, vol. 2, Senate Docs. 1850.

Mr. Schoonmaker's report, claims; Doc. 94, vol. 3, Senate Docs. 1851.

Mr. Chamberlain's report; Doc. 48, vol. 3, Ass'y Docs. 1851.

Mr. Ward's report, claims; Doc. 44, vol. 1, Senate Docs. 1852.

ELIZABETH EINSTEIN.

Report of Commissioners of Land Office, upon bill to convey lands; Doc. 22, vol. 2, Senate Docs. 1842.

ELECTIONS.

Mr. Cramer's report on the changes necessary in the general election law; Doc. 36, vol. 2, Ass'y Docs. 1842.

Mr. G. C. Sherman's report as to the residence qualification; Doc. 132, vol. 4, Senate Docs. 1844.

Mr. A. C. Hand's report on revision of the law to conform to the Constitution of 1846; Doc. 55, vol. 2, Senate Docs. 1847.

Mr. Week's report in relation to the constitutional amendment concerning the elective iranchise; Doc. 60, vol. 3, Ass'y Docs. 1853.

ELLICOTT AND TONAWANDA CREEKS.

Report of Canal Board, on subject of draining adjacent lands; Doc. 198, vol. 7, Ass'y Docs. 1847.

JOHN ELLIS.

Report of Canal Board; Doc. 81, vol. 3, Ass'y Docs. 1846.

Mr. Cornwell's report; Doc. 53, vol. 2, Ass'y Docs. 1847.

SAMUEL S. ELLSWORTH, JAMES ROBINSON, HIRAM CHAPMAN.

Mr. B. Swartwout's report, claims; Doc. 147, vol. 7, Ass'y Docs. 1842.

LUCAS ELMENDORF.

Mr. Ruger's report, claims; Doc. 61, vol. 2, Senate Docs. 1843.

HERVEY ELY.

Report of Canal Board; Doc. 65, vol. 2, Senate Docs. 1844.

ELLENBURGH.

Mr. J. A. Lott's report as to legality of election of town officers; Doc. 72, vol. 2, Senate Docs. 1842.

EMIGRATION.

Report of minority of committee on internal affairs, on foreign poor; Doc. 129, vol. 5, Ass'y Docs. 1842.

Memorial of city authorities, New-York, for act for relief; Doc. 139, vol. 5, Ass'y Docs. 1843.

Mr. D. E. Wheler's report; Doc. 216, vol. 6, Ass'y Docs. 1845.

Report of Commissioners of Emigration; Doc. 119, vol. 4, Senate Docs. 1847.

Mr. Thomas Smith's report, select committee, of frauds upon emigrants; Doc. 250, vol. 8, Ass'y Docs. 1847.

Report of Commissioners of Emigration; Doc. 47, vol. 2, Senate Docs. 1848.

Memorial of Commissioners of Emigration, soliciting appropriation for Marine hospital; Doc. 46, vol. 2, Senate Docs. 1848.

Report of printing committee in relation to printing report of frauds upon emigrants; Doc. 46, vol. 2, Ass'y Docs. 1848.

Memorial of German society; Doc. 165, vol. 5, Ass'y Docs. 1848.

Mr. Disosway's report on the emigration laws; Doc. 219, vol. 5, Ass'y Docs. 1849.

Letter from Gulian C. Verplanck to Comptroller Fillmore; Doc. 39, vol. 2, Senate Docs. 1849.

Annual report of Commissioners; Doc. 50, vol. 2, Ass'y Docs. 1849.

Communication from Commissioners respecting necessities of quarantine establishment; Doc. 58, vol. 2, Ass'y Docs. 1849.

Comptroller Fillmore's report concerning funds; Doc. 140, vol. 3, Ass'y Docs. 1849.

Report of agents and employees of Commissioners; Doc. 214, vol. 5, Ass'y Docs. 1849.

Report of commutation money received at port of Sackett's Harbor; Doc. 240, vol. 5, Ass'y Docs. 1849.

Annual report of Commissioners; Doc. 48, vol. 2, Senate Docs. 1850. Doc. 52, vol. 4, Ass'y Docs. 1850.

Communication from Commissioners respecting amendments to the law respecting alien passengers; Doc. 99, vol. 5, Ass'y Docs. 1850.

Communication from Commissioners in relation to certain amendments of the laws respecting alien passengers; Doc. 71, vol. 2, Senate Docs. 1850.

Mr. R. S. Williams's report on communication from St. George's society requesting that the president of that society be made one of the Commissioners; Doc. 24, vol. 2, Senate Docs. 1851.

Annual report of the Commissioners; Doc. 37, vol. 2, Ass'y Docs. 1851.

Mr. Orlando Allen's report; Doc. 92, vol. 4, Ass'y Docs. 1851.

Annual report of the Commissioners; Doc. 59, vol. 2, Senate Docs. 1852.

Mr. Dewey and Mr. Cady's report from committee of investigation into the affairs of the Commissioners; Doc. 34, vol. 3, Ass'y Docs. 1852.

Annual report of Commissioners Doc. 37, vol. 2, Senate Docs. 1853.

Memorial of Commissioners asking for an appropriation; Doc. 79, vol. 3, Senate Docs. 1853.

Annual report of Commissioners; Doc. 97, vol. 3, Ass'y Docs. 1854.

ROBERT EMMET.

Report of, as assistant register in chancery, of office expenses; Doc. 54, vol. 2, Senate Docs. 1846.

RICHARD EMPEY.

Report of the committee on claims; Doc. 84, vol. 3, Ass'y Docs. 1851.

ENACTING CLAUSE.

Report of Secretary of State, C. Morgan, as to change in bill on file; Doc. 59, vol. 4, Ass'y Docs. 1850.

ISAAC L. ENDRESS.

Mr. Bockee's report; Doc. 55, vol. 2, Senate Docs. 1843.

FRANCIS ENGLISHBEE.

Memorial of M. S. Myers; Doc. 25, vol. 1, Senate Docs. 1848.

EPIDEMIC—(Diarrhœa.)

Wm. Woodward's treatise before the State medical society; Doc. 85, (page 43) vol. 2, Ass'y Docs. 1852.

EPISCOPAL PUBLIC SOCIETY, NEW-YORK.

Mr. Orville Clark's report, in relation to change of corporate name; Doc. 46, vol. 1, Senate Docs. 1845.

ERIE CANAL FEEDER.

Commissioner Enos' report as to estimate of completion; Doc. 49, vol. 1, Senate Docs. 1843.

ERIE COUNTY.

Mr. J. L. Dox's report in relation to expenses incurred in quelling riot on the Erie canal enlargement; Doc. 93, vol. 5, Ass'y Docs. 1850.

Mr. Irish's report in relation to the erection of the town of Red Jacket; Doc. 167, vol. 6, Ass'y Docs. 1850.

ERRONEOUS PAYMENT OF TAXES.

Report of Comptroller Washington Hunt, giving a list of the erroneous and double payments for taxes, made since 1799; Doc. 120, vol. 5, Ass'y Docs. 1850.

ESCHEATS.

Report of Commissioners of Land Office, giving statistics; Doc. 12, vol. 1, Senate Docs. 1844.

EXCISE IN BUFFALO.

Report of select committee, W. Case, on application of supervisors of Erie; Doc. 46, vol. 2, Ass'y Docs. 1842.

Exemption of property from sale under execution.

Mr. H. W. Strong's report; Doc. 76, vol. 3, Senate Docs. 1842. Doc. 43, vol. 1, Senate Docs 1843.

Mr. O'Sullivan's report; Doc. 145, vol. 7, Ass'y Docs. 1842.

EXTRA SESSIONS.

Comptroller Flagg's report as to the probable expense had an extra session of the Senate, been called by Governor Wright in June 1845, for the purpose of making appointments; Doc. 53, vol. 2, Senate Docs. 1846.

SAMUEL EVERETT.

Mr. Ruger's report, claims; Doc. 40, vol. 1, Senate Docs. 1843.

EYE INFIRMARY—NEW-YORK.

Report of committee on medical societies and colleges—Mr. Spencer; Doc. 98, vol. 5, Ass'y Docs. 1842.

Report of surgeons; Doc. 180, vol. 5, Ass'y Docs. 1846.

Report of condition; Doc. 236, vol, 5, Ass'y Docs. 1849.

EYE AND EAR INFIRMARY.

Mr. Garretson's report in favor of an appropriation; Doc. 146, vol. 4, Ass'y Docs. 1845.

FAIRFIELD ACADEMY.

Mr. W. Taylor's report; Doc. 63, vol. 2, Ass'y Docs. 1852.

FAIRFIELD MEDICAL COLLEGE.

Mr. C. Drake's report on appropriation; Doc. 217, vol. 6, Ass'y Docs. 1846.

FARE ON RAILWAYS.

Remonstrance of railway companies from Albany to Buffalo; Doc. 194, vol. 5, Ass'y Docs. 1845.

Mr. R. K. Morrison's report; Doc. 224, vol. 6, Ass'y Docs. 1846.

Mr. Tefft's report against reduction; Doc. 51, vol. 2, Ass'y Docs. 1846.

Mr. Blodgett's report, relative to the Tonawanda road; Doc. 58, vol. 2, Ass'y Docs. 1846.

Memorial of Utica and Syracuse railroad company against reduction of fare; Doc. 69, vol. 3, Ass'y Docs. 1848.

Report of committee on railroads; Doc. 163, vol. 3, Ass'y Docs. 1849.

Mr. J. B. Varnum, jr., report on reduction; Doc. 88, vol. 3, Ass'y Docs. 1851.

JAMES G. FERGUSON, PATRICK NORTON.

Mr. Benedict's report, claims, on petition; Doc. 137, vol. 7, Ass'y Docs. 1842.

ROBERT FEN.

Report of Canal Board; Doc. 153, vol. 6, Ass'y Docs. 1844. (With testimony.)

JOHN FERRIS.

Mr. Hale's report; Doc. 57, vol. 2, Ass'y Docs. 1849.

FERRIES.

Report of Commissioners of Codification, A. Worden, S. C. Hawley, with proposed general law; Doc. 5, vol. 1, Senate Docs. 1849. Doc. 12, vol. 1, Ass'y Docs. 1849.

Opinion of Attorney General O. Hoffman, relative to regulation of ferries by the Legislature; Doc. 131, vol. 4, Ass'y Docs. 1854.

MILLARD FILLMORE.

Report on bill for relief of Elizabeth Gilchrist; Doc. 40, vol. 2, Senate Docs. 1848.

Report on returns of insurance companies in the city of New-York; Doc. 41, vol. 2, Senate Docs. 1848.

Report on Bank Fund Stock; Doc. 44, vol. 2, Senate Docs. 1848.

Report on allowance to be made to Safety Fund Banks, on payment in advance; Doc. 56, vol. 2, Senate Docs. 1848.

Report on expenses of governments for 1848-9; Doc. 14, vol. 1, Ass'y Docs. 1848.

Report of sale of land for taxes, in counties where situated; Doc. 63, vol. 3, Ass'y Docs. 1848.

Report in relation to registration and issue of bank notes; Doc. 91, vol. 3, Ass'y Docs. 1848.

Report on land taxes in Cortland Co.; Doc. 136, vol. 5, Ass'y Docs. 1848.

Report on expenditure of surplus revenues of canals; Doc. 137, vol. 5, Ass'y Docs. 1848.

Report concerning funds of Emigration Commissioners; Doc. 140, vol. 3, Ass'y Docs. 1849.

Report on deposit of money in certain banks; Doc. 182, vol. 5, Ass'y Docs. 1848.

Report as to expenses of commissioners of practice and pleadings; Doc. 69, vol. 2, Ass'y Docs. 1849.

Report as to sales of land for taxes in counties where situated; Doc. 8, vol. 1, Ass'y Docs. 1849.

Communication in respect to Albany basin; Doc. 18, vol. 1, Senate Docs. 1849.

Annual report; Doc. 5, vol. 1, Ass'y Docs. 1849.

Report in the case of Jonathan W. Davis; Doc. 98, vol. 2 Ass'y Docs. 1849.

Report on finances of State; Doc. 13, vol. 2, Ass'y Docs. 1849.

Further report on same subject; Doc. 33, vol. 1, Ass'y Docs. 1849.

Report in relation to Chauncey Smith; Doc. 99, vol. 2, Ass'y Docs. 1849.

Report in relation to foreign insurance companies; Doc. 36, vol. 1, Senate Docs. 1849.

Report as to State stocks, and where held; Doc. 29, vol. 1, Senate Docs. 1849.

Further report on same subject; Doc. 41, vol. 2, Senate Docs 1849.

Report in relation to William Radford; Doc. 92, vol. 2, Ass'y Docs. 1849.

FINANCES OF STATE.

Report of Comptroller Collier and the Commissioners of Canal Fund and Canal Commissioners in answer to Mr. Michael Hoffman's resolutions of enquiry; Doc. 64, vol. 4, Ass'y Docs. 1842.

Report of Comptroller Flagg; Doc. 62, vol. 3, Senate Docs. 1842.

Mr. M. Hoffman's majority report; Doc. 88, vol. 5, Ass'y Docs. 1842.

Mr. Albert Smith's minority report; Doc. 166, vol. 7, Ass'y Docs. 1842.

Communication from Comptroller Flagg; Doc. 61, vol. 4, Ass'y Docs. 1842.

Report of Comptroller Flagg; Doc. 18, vol. 1, Senate Docs. 1843.

Mr. Bokee's report; Doc. 69, vol. 2, Senate Docs. 1843.

Comptroller Flagg's report respecting amount of appropriation for internal improvements, and amount of stock issued; Doc. 65, vol. 3, Ass'y Docs. 1843.

Comptroller Flagg's report concerning proceeds of the mill tax; Doc. 66, vol. 3, Ass'y Docs. 1843.

Mr. Bokee's report, finance; Doc. 126, vol. 4, Senate Docs. 1844.

Republication of the act to pay the debt and preserve the credit of the State, of March 29, 1842; Doc. 103, vol. 5, Ass'y Docs. 1842.

Mr. Hoffman's report, majority, ways and means; Doc. 185, vol. 7, Ass'y Docs. 1844.

Mr. N. W. Davis' minority report; Doc. 186, vol. 7, Ass'y Docs. 1844.

Mr. Bosworth's report, ways and means; Doc. 188, vol. 7, Ass'y Docs. 1844.

Comptroller Flagg's report as to the General Fund, and the means necessary to replenish it; Doc. 178, vol. 5, Ass'y Docs. 1846.

Mr. Bailey's report, ways and means; Doc. 187, vol. 5, Ass'y Docs. 1846.

Mr. G. O. Chase's majority report, ways and means; Doc. 189, vol. 5, Ass'y Docs., 1846.

Mr. Worden's minority report; Doc. 190, vol. 5, Ass'y Docs. 1846.

Comptroller Flagg'sreport as to moneys due from the General Fund; Doc. 193, vol. 5, Ass'y Docs. 1846.

Mr. Worden's minority report, ways and means, on the expediency of resuming the public works; Doc. 212, vol. 6, Ass'y Docs. 1846.

Comptroller Flagg's report as to General Fund debt and Sinking Fund; Doc. 130, vol. 4, Senate Docs. 1847.

Comptroller Fillmore's report; Doc. 13, vol. 2, Ass'y Docs· 1849.

Another report on same subject; Doc. 33, vol. 1, Ass'y Docs. 1849.

Mr. Elijah Ford's majority report; Doc. 189, vol. 8, Ass'y Docs. 1850.

Mr. Pruyn's minority report; Doc. 196, vol. 8, Ass'y Docs. 1850.

Report of Comptroller W. Hunt, in answer to a resolution of the Assembly relative to a plan for raising the money to meet appropriations; Doc. 132, vol. 5, Ass'y Docs. 1850.

Mr. Elijah Ford's report on so much of Governor Fish's message as relates to premiums on the loan of 1849; Doc. 133, vol. 5, Ass'y Docs. 1850.

Mr. E. D. Morgan's report on so much of Gov. Fish's message as relates to premiums and loans; Doc. 68, vol. 2, Senate Docs. 1850.

Mr. E. D. Morgan's report on so much of Gov. Fish's message as relates to school revenues; Doc. 70, vol. 2, Senate Docs. 1850.

Comptroller Fuller's report; Doc. 48, vol. 2, Senate Docs. 1851.

Mr. E. D. Morgan's report; Doc. 49, vol. 2, Senate Docs. 1851.

Mr. Morgan's report on unclaimed interest on stocks issued by State; Doc. 24, vol. 2, Senate Docs. 1851.

Comptroller Fuller's report on unclaimed interest on State stocks; Doc. 83, vol. 3, Senate Docs. 1851.

Comptroller Fuller's report on condition of treasury; Doc. 91, vol. 3, Senate Docs. 1851.

Treasurer Alvah Hunt's report on same; Doc. 93, vol. 3, Senate Docs. 1851.

Comptroller Fuller's report in relation to additional appropriations; Doc. 17, vol. 1, Ass'y Docs. 1851.

Comptroller Wright's report in relation to General Fund debt; Doc. 68, vol. 2, Senate Docs. 1852.

Mr. McMurray's majority report on the State debt; Doc. 69, vol. 2. Senate Docs. 1852.

Mr. E. D. Morgan's minority report on same subject; Doc. 77, vol. 2, Senate Docs. 1852.

Mr. McMurray's report on the reduction of the half mill tax; Doc. 83, vol. 2, Senate Docs. 1852.

Comptroller Wright's report as to the amount of State debt on 1st June, 1846; Doc. 87, vol. 2, Senate Docs. 1852.

Comptroller Wright's estimate of General Fund receipts; Doc. 103, vol. 5, Ass'y Docs. 1852.

Mr. McMurray's report in relation to certain expenses chargeable upon the Canal Fund; Doc. 10, vol. 1, Senate Docs. 1853.

Auditor Newell's report concerning charges on canal debt sinking fund; Doc. 51, vol. 2, Senate Docs. 1853.

Auditor Newell's report concerning appropriations for canals; Doc. 84, vol. 3, Senate Docs. 1853.

Comptroller Wright's report of State debt from 1835 to 1853; Doc. 24, vol. 2, Ass'y Docs. 1853.

Communication of Auditor G. W. Newell in relation to canal appropriation for 1853; Doc. 126, vol. 6, Ass'y Docs. 1853.

Mr. Loomis' report; Doc. 48, vol. 2, Ass'y Docs. 1853.

Mr. Ellsworth's report; Doc. 54, vol. 2, Ass'y Docs. 1853.

Report of Commissioners of Canal Fund, as to the application of surplus revenues, to claims arising prior to June 1, 1846; Doc. 125, vol. 6, Ass'y Docs. 1853.

Report of Comptroller Wright in relation to the time when the State tax would be available for the improvement of the canals; Doc. 114, vol. 6, Ass'y Docs. 1853.

WILLIAM FINN.

Report of Canal Board; Doc. 100, vol. 5, Ass'y Docs. 1842.

HAMILTON FISH.

Annual message; Doc. 2, vol. 1, Senate Docs. 1849. Doc. 2, vol. 1, Ass'y Docs. 1849.

Annual message; Doc. 3, vol. 1, Senate Docs. 1849. Doc. 1, Ass'y Docs. 1850.

ALFRED FISHER.

Report of committee on claims, Mr. J. G. Hopkins, on claim; Doc. 73, vol. 3, Senate Docs. 1842.

Mr. Lawrenee's report, claims; Doc. 41, vol. 1, Senate Docs.

FISH CREEK.

Report of Canal Board in relation to towing path; Doc. 193, vol. 5, Ass'y Docs. 1845.

FISHKILL.

Mr. Lott's report on the appropriation of certain moneys by the town; Doc. 33, vol. 1, Senate Docs. 1846.

FIRST SENATE DISTRICT—CHARITABLE INSTITUTIONS.

Report of commissioners to investigate; Doc. 42, vol. 1, Senate Docs. 1843.

Report of commissioners to investigate; Doc. 121, vol. 4, Ass'y Docs. 1851.

Report of commissioners to investigate; Doc. 89, vol. 2, Senate Docs. 1852.

Report of commissioners to investigate; Doc. 92, vol. 4, Ass'y Docs. 1853.

ABIJAH FITCH, THOMAS M. HUNT, HENRY H. COOLY.

Mr. Underwood's report; Doc. 76, vol. 3, Ass'y Docs. 1851.

Mr. W. Clark's report; Doc. 75, vol. 2, Senate Docs. 1854.

HENRY FITZHUGH.

Communication in relation to charges preferred against him by Mr. Gale; Doc. 27, vol. 2, Ass'y Docs. 1853.

Mr. Gale's report from a committee of investigation; Doc. 90, vol. 4, Ass'y Docs. 1853.

PATRICK FITZSIMMONS, JAMES BRADY.

Report of Canal Board on petition for allowance; Doc. 86, vol. 4, Senate Docs. 1842.

Further report; Doc. 93, vol. 4, Senate Docs. 1842.

Report of committee on claims; Doc. 16, vol. 1, Senate Docs. 1843.

Mr. Boughton's report, grievances; Doc. 56, vol. 3, Ass'y Docs. 1845.

Mr. Dean's report, claims; Doc. 29, vol. 1, Ass'y Docs. 1846.

Mr. J. E. Beers' report, claims; Doc. 23, vol. 1, Ass'y Docs. 1847.

Mr. Schoonmaker's report, claims; Doc. 77, vol. 3, Senate Docs. 1851.

Mr. Robinson's report; Doc. 47, vol. 2, Senate Docs. 1851.

AZARIAH C. FLAGG.

(The entries will be found at length under the head of the subjects treated.)

NEW STATE HALL.

Doc. 139, vol. 7, Ass'y Docs. 1842.

STOCKS, AND FINANCES, AND TAXES.

Doc. 62, vol. 3, Senate Docs. 1842. Doc. 61, vol. 4, Ass'y Docs. 1842. Doc. 18, vol. 1, Senate Docs. 1843. Doc. 65, vol. 4, Ass'y Docs. 1843. Doc. 66, vol. 3, Ass'y Docs. 1843. Doc. 167, vol. 3, Ass'y Docs. 1843. Doc. 105, vol. 5, Ass'y Docs. 1844. Doc. 64, vol. 3, Ass'y Docs. 1845. Doc. 175, vol. 5, Ass'y Docs. 1845. Doc. 66, vol. 2, Senate Docs. 1847. Doc. 132, vol. 4, Senate Docs. 1847.

CANAL CONTRACTS AND CONTRACTORS.

Doc. 15, vol. 1, Senate Docs. 1843. Doc. 134, vol. 4, Senate Docs. 1844.

CANAL EXPENDITURES AND REPAIRS.

Doc. 56, vol. 3, Ass'y Docs. 1843. Doc. 90, vol. 4, Ass'y Docs. 1846. Doc. 129, vol. 4, Ass'y Docs. 1847. Doc. 50, vol. 3, Ass'y Docs. 1848.

NON-ACTING CANAL COMMISSIONERS.

Doc. 45, vol. 1, Senate Docs. 1843. Doc. 80, vol. 3, Senate Docs. 1843. Doc. 38, vol. 1, Senate Docs. 1845.

DEPOSITE FUND.

Doc. 83, vol. 4, Ass'y Docs. 1842. Doc. 75, vol. 3, Ass'y Docs. 1845.

NON-RESIDENT TAXES.

Doc. 13, vol. Senate Docs. 1843.

CANAL PASSENGER TOLLS.

Doc. 21, vol. 1, Senate Docs. 1843.

PUBLIC PRINTING.

Doc. 3, vol. 1, Senate Docs. 1843. Doc. 12, vol. 1, Senate Docs. 1843. Doc. 94, vol. 5, Senate Docs. 1844. Doc. 56, vol. 2, Senate Docs. 1846. Doc. 75, vol. 3, Ass'y Docs. 1846. Doc. 91, vol. 4, Ass'y Docs. 1846. Doc. 134, vol. 4, Ass'y Docs. 1847.

GENESEE WESLEYAN SEMINARY.

Doc. 38, vol. 3, Ass'y Docs. 1844.

TAXES—INCORPORATED COMPANIES.

Doc. 98, vol. 3, Ass'y Docs. 1844.

GEOLOGICAL SURVEY.

Doc. 153, vol, 5, Ass'y Docs. 1845.

MARINERS' FUND.

Doc. 29, vol. 1, Senate Docs. 1845.

NATURAL HISTORY.

Doc. 153, vol. 5, Ass'y Docs. 1845.

QUIT RENTS.

Doc. 228, vol. 6, Ass'y Docs. 1845.

SUPREME COURT CLERKS.

Doc. 48, 49, 50, vol. 2, Senate Docs. 1845. Doc. 10, vol. 1, Senate Docs. 1846.

EXTRA COMPENSATION.

Doc. 102, vol. 3, Senate Docs. 1846. Doc. 28, vol. Senate Docs. 1846. Doc. 47, vol. 2, Ass'y Docs. 1847.

BANKS AND BANKING.

Doc. 100, vol. 3, Senate Docs. 1845. Doc. 161, vol. 5, Ass'y Docs. 1845. Doc. 31, vol. 2, Ass'y Docs. 1846. Doc. 186, vol. 5, Ass'y Docs. 1846. Doc. 202, vol. 6, Ass'y Docs. 1846. Doc. 135, vol. 4, Ass'y Docs. 1847. Doc. 123, vol. 4, Senate Docs. 1847. Doc. 145, vol. 4, Senate Docs. 1847.

LATERAL CANALS.

Doc. 116, vol. 3, Senate Docs. 1845. Doc. 113, vol. 4, Ass'y Docs. 1846.

CHANCERY OFFICERS.

Doc. 48, vol. 2, Senate Docs. 1845. Doc. 49, vol. 2, Senate Docs. 1845. Doc. 50, vol. 2, Senate Docs. 1845.

DEAF AND DUMB.

Doc. 52, vol. 2, Senate Docs. 1845.

DELAWARE AND HUDSON CANAL COMPANY.

Doc. 162, vol. 7, Ass'y Docs. 1842.

ANNUAL REPORTS.

1843—Doc. 10, vol. 1, Ass'y Docs.
1844—Doc. 4, vol. 1, Ass'y Docs.
1845—Doc. 25, vol. 1, Ass'y Docs.
1846—Doc. 25, vol. 1, Ass'y Docs.
1847—Doc. vol. Docs.

CANAL APPRAISERS.

Doc. 74, vol. Senate Docs. 1845.

AUCTION DUTIES.

Doc. 208, vol. 6, Ass'y Docs. 1845.

OFFICE EXPENSES—(Canal Commissioners.)

Doc. 118, vol. 4, Ass'y Docs. 1846.

CITY BANK, BUFFALO.

Doc. 120, vol. 4, Ass'y Docs. 1846.

SIXTH CIRCUIT COURTS.

Doc. 35, vol. 1, Senate Docs. 1846. Doc. 47, vol. 2, Ass'y Docs. 1847.

CLINTON STATE PRISON.

Doc. 18, vol. 1, Senate Docs. 1847.

COLUMBIA AND DELAWARE.

Doc. 99, vol. 2, Ass'y Docs. 1847. Doc. 37, vol. 1, Senate Docs. 1846.

COUNTY SUPERINTENDENTS.

Doc. 245, vol. 8, Ass'y Docs. 1847.

ISAAC DENNISTON.

Doc. 110, vol. 3, Senate Docs. 1847.

PHILANDER DUNHAM.

Doc. 82, vol. 3, Ass'y Docs. 1846.

EXTRA SESSIONS.

Doc. 53, vol. 2, Senate Docs. 1846.

FRAUDS ON GENESEE VALLEY CANAL.

Doc. 90, vol. 4, Ass'y Docs. 1846.

GRAND ISLAND.

Doc. 155, vol. 5, Senate Docs. 1846.

LEGAL NOTICES.

Doc. 13, vol. 1, Senate Docs. 1847.

LOAN COMMISSIONERS.

Doc. 32, vol. 1, Senate Docs. 1847.

FLAG ON THE CAPITOL.

Mr. Fonda's report; Doc. 230, vol. 6, Ass'y Docs. 1845.

FLOATING DRY DOCK COMPANY, (Buffalo.)

Mr. Shumway's report in favor of a special act of incorporation; Doc. 63, vol. 2, Ass'y Docs. 1847.

FLORIDA BRIDGE COMPANY.

Report of Canal Board; Doc. 127, vol. 4, Ass'y Docs. 1846.

Mr. J. C. Curtis' report; Doc. 34, vol. 1, Senate Docs. 1850.

FLORIDA.

Resolutions of Legislature in relation to the establishment of a board of Agriculture at Washington; Doc. 126, vol. 4, Ass'y Docs. 1851.

JOHN FLYNN.

Mr. Hopkins' report, claims; Doc. 74, vol. 2, Senate Docs. 1854.

JAMES FOLTZ.

Report of Canal Board as to bridge at Frankfort; Doc. 200, vol. 7, Ass'y Docs. 1847.

Mr. Fitzhugh's report; Doc. 119, vol. 3, Ass'y Docs. 1849.

Mr. Schoonmaker's report, claims; Doc. 51, vol. 2, Senate Docs. 1850.

GEORGE FOLTS.

Mr. Benedict's report, claims; Doc. 37, vol. 2, Ass'y Docs. 1852.

STAATS O. S. FONDA.

Report of committee on claims; Doc. 65, vol. 4, Ass'y Docs. 1850.

FOREST TREES.

Catalogue of varieties in southern tier of counties; Doc. 92, (page 392) vol. 2, Senate Docs. 1852.

WINFIELD S. FOREMAN.

Mr. Benedict's report, claims, in relation to the loss of canal boat; Doc. 80, vol. 2, Ass'y Docs. 1842.

FORT HUNTER SUSPENSION BRIDGE.

Mr. Bennett's report on the subject of a special incorporation; Doc. 86, vol. 2, Senate Docs. 1852.

FORT BREWERTON BRIDGE COMPANY

Report of condition; Doc. 68, vol. 2, Ass'y Docs. 1847.

Mr. Orlando Allen's report; Doc. 29, vol. 2, Ass'y Docs. 1851.

FORT MILLER DAM.

Report of Canal Board, in relation to removal; Doc. 114, vol. 5, Ass'y Docs. 1842.

Report of Canal Board; Doc. 125, vol. 3, Ass'y Docs. 1849.

Report of Canal Board, John Harris' petition; Doc. 66, vol. 2, Senate Docs. 1850.

MICHAEL FRANCISCO.

Report of committee on militia—Mr. Griffin—on his claim for land for revolutionary services; Doc. 16, vol. 2, Ass'y Docs. 1842.

Mr. Straton's report, claims; Doc. 124. vol. 5, Ass'y Docs. 1843.

Mr. Fonda's report, militia; Doc. 40, vol. 3, Ass'y Docs. 1845.

FRAUDS ON THE CANALS.

Report of select committee of investigation, Sidney Lawrence, L. S. Viele, George T. Pierce, A. G. Chatfield, John T. Bush, with testimony; Doc. 100, vol. 3, Ass'y Docs. 1847.

Memorial of John D. Fay, in relation thereto; Doc. 93, vol. 3, Senate Docs. 1847.

Memorial of Holmes Hutchinson, in relation thereto; Doc. 218, vol. 7, Ass'y Docs. 1847.

Memorial of Wm. Buell in relation thereto; Doc. 94, vol. 3, Senate Docs 1847.

Memorial of Daniel P. Bissell, Canal Commissioner, in relation thereto; Doc. 109, vol. 3, Senate Docs. 1847.

Mr. Cornwell's report; Doc. 78, vol. 2, Ass'y Docs. 1847.

Report of printing committee concerning; Doc. 84, vol. 2, Ass'y Docs. 1847.

Further report of printing committee; Doc. 85, vol. 2, Ass'y Docs. 1847.

Mr. Wakeman's report; Doc. 158, vol. 8, Ass'y Docs. 1851.

Testimony and exhibit taken by committee of whom Mr. L. D. Smith was chairman of the Assembly of 1850; Doc. 158, vol. 6, Ass'y Docs. 1851.

FRAZEE AND FOSTER.

Mr. Porter's report, claims; Doc. 77, vol. 2, Senate Docs. 1845.

Henry A. Foster's memorial relative to above; Doc. 90, vol. 3, Senate Docs. 1845.

Mr. Sawyer's report, claims; Doc. 20, vol. 1, Ass'y Docs. 1846

Report of Canal Commissioners; Doc. 74, vol. 2, Senate Docs 1847.

BENJAMIN FRAZEE.

Mr. Wood's report, claims; Doc. 72, vol. 3, Ass'y Docs. 1853.

FREE ACADEMY.

Mr. E. D. Morgan's report; Doc. 90, vol. 3, Senate Docs. 1850.

Mr. J. W. Beekman's report on subject of appropriation for a library; Doc. 21, vol. 2, Senate Docs. 1851.

FREE SCHOOL.

Mr. Ludlow's report; Doc. 222, vol. 6, Ass'y Docs. 1846.

Memorial of Onondaga county institute; Doc. 115, vol. 3, Ass'y Docs. 1849.

Report of Secretary of State, C. Morgan; Doc. 50, vol. 4, Ass'y Docs. 1850.

Mr. James W. Beekman's report; Doc. 38, vol. 1, Senate Docs. 1850.

Attorney General Chatfield's report on the constitutionality of the law; Doc. 107, vol. 5, Ass'y Docs. 1850.

Mr. Kingsley's report; Doc. 180, vol. 6, Ass'y Docs. 1850.

Memorial of citizens of Pompey, for the repeal of the free school act; Doc. 166, vol. 6, Ass'y Docs. 1850.

Mr. J. W. Beekman's majority report; Doc. 111, vol. 3, Senate Docs. 1850.

Mr. T. H. Benedict's majority report in relation to the repeal or amendment of the free school law; Doc. 41, vol. 2, Ass'y Doc's. 1851.

M. S. M. Burrough's minority report on same subject; Doc. 42, vol. 2, Ass'y Docs. 1851.

FREE TRADE.

Memorial of free trade association of New-York city; Doc. 22, vol. 2, Ass'y Docs. 1843.

FREEHOLDER QUALIFICATION FOR GOVERNOR.

Resolution to amend the Constitution; Doc. 5, vol. 1, Ass'y Docs. 1842.

FREIGHT ON RAILWAYS.

Report of W. J. McAlpine, State Engineer, of the freight carried on the railways of the State; Doc. 59, vol. 2, Senate Docs. 1853.

LEMUEL FRENCH.

Mr. N. Jones' report, claims; Doc. 25, vol. 1, Senate Docs. 1852.

FRENCH SPOLIATIONS.

Mr. Jeremiah's report on petition of George Griswold, Theodore Sedgwick, and others, for legislative resolution of recommendation for Congressional relief; Doc. 67, vol. 3, Ass'y Docs. 1844.

FRESH KILLS.

Mr. Lesley's report on the application of the Port Richmond Plank Road Company, to construct a draw bridge; Doc. 99, vol. 4, Ass'y Docs. 1851.

FRIENDS, SOCIETY OF

Mr. Thomas Smith's majority report in relation to exemption from taxation; Doc. 190, vol. 7, Ass'y Docs. 1847.

Mr. E. Pratt's report in relation to taxation; Doc. 117, vol. 5, Ass'y Docs. 1850.

PHILO C. FULLER, Comptroller.

Report in regard to Union college; Doc. 27, vol. 2, Senate Docs. 1851.

Report of sums paid for cost, fees, counsel fees, and other expenses in the prosecutions for the recovery of manorich lands; Doc. 33, vol. 2, Senate Docs. 1851.

Report upon revenue; Doc. 48, vol. 2, Senate Docs. 1851.

Report upon sums paid for printing, binding and engraving; Doc. 56, vol. 2, Senate Docs. 1851.

Report in relation to unclaimed interest; Doc. 83, vol. 3, Senate Docs. 1851.

Annual report; Doc. 9, vol. 1, Ass'y Docs. 1851.

Report in relation to taxation; Doc. 87, vol. 3, Ass'y Docs. 1851.

Report in relation to additional appropriations; Doc. 17, vol. 1, Ass'y Docs. 1851.

FUGITIVE SLAVES.

Remonstrance of citizens of Salina against repeal of the law of 1840, granting right of trial by jury; Doc. 60, vol. 3, Ass'y Docs. 1843.

Mr. Jones' majority report, judiciary, on bills introduced; Doc. 128, vol. 5, Ass'y Docs. 1843.

Mr. E. F. Warner's minority report; Doc. 141, vol. 5, Ass'y Docs. 1843.

Mr. Bloss' report; Doc. 168, vol. 6, Ass'y Docs. 1847.

FULTON COUNTY.

Mr. H. W. Strong's report, overseers of the poor; Doc. 44, vol. 2, Senate Docs. 1842.

SAMUEL G. GAGE.

Attorney General Jordan's report in relation to the confirmation of his official acts; Doc. 118, vol. 3, Ass'y Docs. 1848.

WILLIAM GALL, HEIRS OF

Mr. E. C. Church's report on the petition of Maria Johnson for bounty land; Doc. 66, vol. 4, Ass'y Docs. 1842.

Mr. S. Moore's report; Doc. 146, vol. 4, Ass'y Docs. 1847.

Mr. McLean's report; Doc. 25, vol. 1, Ass'y Docs. 1849.

THOMAS H. GALLAUDET.

Tribute to the memory of, by directors of the New-York institution for the instruction of the deaf and dumb; Doc. 112, (page 71,) vol. 5, Ass'y Docs. 1852.

ADDISON GARDNER.

Opinion as Lieutenant Governor on the duration of the powers of the court of errors; Doc. 20, vol. 1, Senate Docs. 1847.

GEORGE GARDNER.

Mr. Burhans' minority report, claims; Doc. 62, vol. 3, Ass'y Docs. 1844.

Mr. T. J. Wheeler's report, claims; Doc. 53, vol. Senate Docs. 1847.

TITUS FELIX GAZYNSKI.

Mr. James Monroe's report; Doc. 94, vol. 5, Ass'y Docs. 1850.

GEDDES.

Report of Canal Board in relation to the route of the Erie canal; Doc. 103, vol. 5, Ass'y Docs. 1850.

D. S. AND S. P. GEER.

Report of Canal Commissioners; Doc. 96, vol. 3, Senate Docs. 1847.

Mr. J. E. Beers' report, claims; Doc. 32, vol. 1, Ass'y Docs. 1847.

ROBERT GEER, PHILO C. WEAVER.

Mr. Alvord's report, claims; Doc. 118, vol. 5, Ass'y Docs. 1844.

Mr. Teft's report, claims; Doc. 32, vol. 3, Ass'y Docs. 1845.

R. NELSON GEER, CHARLES W. STEVES.

Report of committee on claims; Doc. 49, vol. 1, Senate Docs. 1852.

GENESEE COLLEGE.

Report of condition made to Regents of the University; Doc. 77, (page 129,) vol. 2, Senate Docs. 1854.

GENESEE RIVER.

Mr. Bishop Perkins' report as to water drawn for the Erie canal; Doc. 204, vol. 6, Ass'y Docs. 1846.

Mr. Carpenter's report as to the removal of the dam across the river, erected for State purposes; Doc. 182, vol. 7, Ass'y Docs. 1857.

GENESEE SUSPENSION BRIDGE.

Mr. D. Wilson's report on special incorporation; Doc. 45, vol. 2, Ass'y Docs. 1852.

GENESEE WESLEYAN SEMINARY.

Report of Comptroller Flagg in relation to a proposed loan; Doc. 38, vol. 3, Ass'y Docs. 1844.

Mr. Hubbard's report; Doc. 92, vol. 3, Ass'y Docs. 1844.

GENESEE VALLEY CANAL.

Report of Canal Commissioners; Doc. 77, vol. 3, Senate Docs. 1843.

Report of Canal Commissioner Bissell; Doc. 111, vol. 3, Senate Docs. 1844.

Report of Canal Commissioners Bissell, Little, Earll, Enos, as to probable cost; Doc. 112, vol. 3, Senate Docs. 1844.

Report of Canal Commissioners as to expense of preserving the unfinished work; Doc. 154, vol. 5, Ass'y Docs. 1845.

Report of Canal Board in relation to change of plan of constructing locks; Doc. 202, vol. 6, Ass'y Docs. 1845.

Comptroller Flagg's report as to frauds: Doc. 90, vol. 4, Ass'y Docs. 1846.

Canal Commissioners' report in regard to probable cost; Doc. 58, vol. 2, Senate Docs. 1848.

GEOGRAPHICAL AND STATISTICAL SOCIETY, (American.)

Memorial of Henry Grinnell and others in relation to the objects of the society; Doc. 98, vol. 3, Ass'y Docs. 1854.

GENEVA COLLEGE.

Mr. T. H. Bond's report on appropriation; Doc. 23, vol. 1, Senate Docs. 1848.

GEOGRAPHICAL SURVEY OF STATE.

Memorial of American Association; Doc. 41, vol. 1, Senate Docs. 1852.

GEOLOGICAL SURVEY.

Communication from Governor Seward; Doc. 68, vol. 3, Senate Docs. 1842.

Communication from James Hall; Doc. 59, vol. 2, Senate Docs. 1843.

Communication from James Hall and Ebenezer Emmons; Doc. 60, vol. 2, Senate Docs. 1843.

Communication from Secretary of State, S. Young, as to distribution of books; Doc. 67, vol. 2, Senate Docs. 1842.

Further communication from Secretary; Doc. 72, vol. 3, Senate Docs. 1843.

Report of Comptroller Flagg as to expenditure; Doc. 153, vol. 5, Ass'y Docs. 1845.

Mr. Bowen's report; Doc. 186, vol. 8, Ass'y Docs. 1850.

Report of James Hall; Doc. 32, vol. 2, Senate Docs. 1851.

Report of Christopher Morgan, Secretary of State, and T. Romeyn Beck, Secretary of the Regents of the University, as commissioners of investigation into financial affairs; Doc. 124, vol. 4, Ass'y Docs. 1851.

Further report of same commissioners; Doc. 23, vol. 1, Ass'y Docs. 1852.

GEORGIA.

Resolutions of Legislature concerning constitution United States, Presidential Veto, Bank United States, Public Land, Loan Bill, Bankrupt Bill, Revenue Bill, Sub Treasury, Widow Harrison Bill, Edward Everett, General Post Office, Rules of House of Representatives; Doc. 58, vol. 4, Ass'y Docs. 1842.

Resolutions of Legislature in relation to citizenship of persons of color; Doc. 51, vol. 3, Ass'y Docs. 1843.

Resolutions of Legislature in relation to assumption of State debts by the General Government; Doc. 52, vol. 3, Ass'y Docs. 1843.

Resolution of same in relation to the repudiation of State debts; Doc. 195, vol. 7, Ass'y Docs. 1844.

Resolutions of State relative to slavery; Doc. 176, vol. 8, Ass'y Docs. 1850.

GERE, KASSON AND BREED.

Report of Canal Board; Doc. 133, vol. 4, Senate Docs. 1844.

Report of Canal Board Doc. 23, vol. 1, Ass'y Docs. 1844.

Report of Canal Board; Doc. 58, vol. 3, Ass'y Docs. 1844.

Mr. Alvord's report, claims; Doc. 116, vol. 5, Ass'y Docs. 1844.

WILLIAM H. GIBSON, JOHN MATTEMORE.

Report of Canal Board on petition; Doc. 102, vol. 5, Ass'y Docs. 1842.

JASPER W. GILBERT.

Attorney General Barker's report in relation to sale of land under Deposite Fund mortgage; Doc. 40, vol. 1, Senate Docs. 1844.

Mr. Bokee's report, finance; Doc. 71, vol. 2, Senate Docs. 1844.

THOMAS J. GILBERT.

Mr. Johnson's report, claims; Doc. 64, vol. 2, Senate Docs. 1845.

GILBOA.

Mr. J. T. Raymond's minority report against the bill to erect this town; Doc. 234, vol. 6, Ass'y Docs. 1845.

Mr. J. Brook's majority report in favor; Doc. 241, vol. 7, Ass'y Docs. 1845.

ELIZABETH GILCHRIST, THERON ROBLEE.

Report of committee on public lands, Mr. Kelly, as to lands in Johnsburgh, Warren Co.; Doc. 68, vol. 4, Ass'y Docs. 1842.

Report of Commissioners of Land Office; Doc. 161, vol. 5, Ass'y Docs. 1843.

Surveyor General Jones' report; Doc. 77, vol. 2, Senate Docs. 1844.

Comptroller Fillmore's report for relief; Doc. 40, vol. 2, Senate Docs. 1848.

Mr. S. J. Wilkin's report, Doc. 58, vol. 2, Senate Docs. 1849.

ARCHIBALD GILCHRIST.

Mr. Hubbard's report, claims; Doc. 120, vol. 4, Ass'y Docs. 1843.

ZACHARIAH P. GILLETT.

Mr. Foster's report; Doc. 124, vol. 4, Ass'y Docs. 1846.

Report of Commissioners of Land Office; Doc. 22, vol. 1, Ass'y Docs. 1847.

Mr. Boardman's report; Doc. 91, vol. 2, Ass'y Docs. 1849.

JOHM GILES, SAMUEL GILES.

Report of Commissioners of Land Office; Doc. 7, vol. 1, Ass'y Docs. 1843.

WILLIAM GILLILAND.

Mr. Alvord's report, claims; Doc. 117, vol. 5, Ass'y Docs. 1844.

ELIAS P. GILMAN.

Mr. S. Baldwin's report, claims; Doc. 87, Ass'y Docs. 1854.

CALEB GOODRICH.

Mr. Schoonmaker's report, claims; Doc. 66, vol. 3, Senate Docs. 1851.

THOMAS GOODSELL.

Mr. Severance's report, claims; Doc. 122, vol. 4, Ass'y Docs. 1851.

Mr. Van Valkenburgh's report, claims; Doc. 51, vol. 2, Ass'y Docs. 1852.

Report of committee on claims; Doc. 19, vol. 1, Ass'y Docs. 1854.

S. A. GOODWIN.

Report as to moneys and salary as clerk of 7th chancery circuit; Doc. 51, vol. 2, Senate Docs. 1843.

FREDERICK GOSSKOFF.

Mr. Hopkins' report, claims; Doc. 21, vol. 1, Senate Docs. 1854.

IRA GOULD.

Report of Canal Commissioners; Doc. 84, vol. 4, Senate Docs. 1842.

GOVERNOR'S APPROVAL OF BILLS.

Resolution of Mr. Root in relation to Governor Seward's approval of bill respecting repeal of bill in relation to appointment of receivers of moneyed institutions, and of Mr. Foster in relation to same; Doc. 21, vol. 2, Senate Docs. 1842.

GRAND ISLAND.

Comptroller Flagg's report respecting sale of lands therein, Niagara river; Doc. 155, vol. 5, Senate Docs. 1846.

ELIZABETH S. GRANGER, WARREN L. GRANGER, JAMES N. GRANGER.

Mr. Thompson's report; Doc. 196, vol. 3, Ass'y Docs. 1849.

Mr. Upham's report; Doc. 44, vol. 2, Senate Docs. 1850.

Report of Canal Board; Doc. 101, vol. 3, Senate Docs. 1850.

OSCAR GRANGER, WALTER S. TODD.

Mr. Noble's report; Doc. 93, vol. 2, Ass'y Docs. 1849.

Mr. Guinnip's report; Doc. 73, vol. 2, Senate Docs. 1850.

ABRAHAM P. GRANT.

Report of Commissioners of Land Office on memorial in relation to sale of land in East Oswego; Doc. 53, vol. 4, Ass'y Docs. 1850.

GRANT. TURNER AND RYAN.

Mr. H. Putnam's report, claims; Doc. 37, vol. 1, Senate Docs. 1843.

Report of Canal Commissioner, Nathaniel Jones; Doc. 212, vol. 7, Ass'y Docs. 1847.

Mr. McCarty's report, claims; Doc. 42, vol. 2, Ass'y Docs. 1848.

Mr. O. Allen's report; Doc. 78, vol. 3, Ass'y Docs. 1851.

Mr. N. Jones' report, claims; Doc. 90, vol. 2, Senate Docs. 1852.

GRAVESEND AND CONEY ISLAND.

Bridge and road company, report of condition; Doc. 180, vol. 5, Ass'y Docs. 1848.

GREENBORO'.

Mr. Rutherford's report on repeal of town incorporation; Doc. 262, vol. 8, Ass'y Docs. 1847.

Mr. Glass' report; Doc. 94, vol. 3, Ass'y Docs. 1848.

CALEB GREEN.

Address before the Cortland county medical society; Doc. 67, (page 159) vol. 3, Ass'y Docs. 1853.

JOHN R. GREEN.

Report of Commissioners of Land Office; Doc. 87, vol. 3, Senate Docs. 1847.

LESTER GREEN.

Biographical sketch—Transactions of State Medical society, Albany; Doc. 125, (page 199) vol. 4, Ass'y Docs. 1851.

LEVY B. GREEN, and wife—SARAH McKINSTER.

Mr. McLean's report, claims; Doc. 135, vol. 3, Ass'y Docs. 1849.

THOMAS GREENLY.

Proceedings of Canal Board, and testimony on investigation; Doc. 71, vol. 3, Senate Docs. 1853.

STORM HAIGHT, JOHN BLOOD, AND ASA W. CADY.

Mr. Sawyer's report, claims; Doc. 107, vol. 4, Ass'y Docs. 1846.

Mr. J. E. Beers' report, claims; Doc. 28, vol. 1, Ass'y Docs. 1847.

DEBORAH ANN HALLETT.

Report of Commissioners of Land Office; Doc. 21, vol. 1, Senate Docs. 1845.

W. P. HALLETT—(Clerk Supreme Court.)

Report; Doc. 121, vol. 5, Ass'y Docs. 1843.

Report in relation to fees for searches; Doc. 149, vol. 5, Ass'y Docs. 1843.

Report as to office expenses; Doc. 42, vol. 2, Senate Docs. 1846.

Report as to fees received for taxing costs; Doc. 23, vol. 1, Senate Docs. 1847.

HAMILTON COLLEGE.

Mr. T. H. Bond's report on appropriation; Doc. 23, vol. 1, 1848.

Report of condition made to Regents of the University; Doc. 77, (page 86) vol. 2, Senate Docs. 1854.

HAMILTON COUNTY.

State Engineer, Hezekiah C. Seymour's report, as to quantity of State land in county; Doc. 19, vol. 1, Senate Docs. 1851.

ELI HAMILTON, PETER D. HAMILTON.

Mr. Cornwell's report; Doc. 36, vol. 1, Ass'y Docs. 1847.

ORRIN HAMILTON.

Report of Attorney General Barker; Doc. 14, vol. 1, Senate Docs. 1844.

HELENA HAND.

Mr. Pierce's report, aliens; Doc. 105, vol. 5, Ass'y Docs. 1842.

HARBORS.

Mr. Fine's resolution in relation to improvement of harbors; Doc. 4, vol. 1, Senate Docs. 1848.

Mr. Bowen's majority report; Doc. 71, vol. 3, Ass'y Docs. 1848.

Mr. Myers' minority report; Doc. 72, vol. 3, Ass'y Docs. 1848.

HARBOR AT NEW-YORK.

Report of Commissioners of Land Office, on petition of Samuel I. Hunt, and Cornelius Du Bois, relative to land under water at Williamsburgh; Doc. 103, vol. 3, Senate Docs. 1844.

Meeting of merchants' at Exchange in New-York city in relation to the harbor improvement; Doc. 8, vol. 1, Senate Docs. 1854.

Report of John T. Clark, State Engineer, as to lands under water in harbor; Doc. 12, vol. 1, Senate Docs. 1854. Doc. 34, vol. 1, Senate Docs. 1854.

Remonstrance of citizens of Brooklyn against the appointment of commissioners in relation to the piers and bulkheads; Doc. 42, vol. 1, Senate Docs. 1854.

Report of Attorney General, Ogden Hoffman, in relation to grant at the harbor of New-York; Doc. 105, vol. 3, Ass'y Docs. 1854.

HARBOR MASTER, (Albany.)

Annual report;	Doc.	186,	vol. 5,	Ass'y Docs.	1843.
do	do	173,	do 7,	do	1844.
do	do	49,	do 3,	do	1845.
do	do	220,	do 6,	do	1846.
do	do	38,	do 1,	do	1847.
do	do	184,	do 5,	do	1848.

LYDIA HARDIN—(an Indian.)

Report of Commissioners of Land Office; Doc. 189, vol. 7, Ass'y Docs. 1847.

Mr. Wm. Samuel Johnson's report; Doc. 66, vol. 2, Senate Docs. 1849.

SAMUEL W. HARNED.

Mr. Pruyn's report; Doc. 21, vol. 2, Ass'y Docs. 1848.

SAMUEL HART, WM. CANDEE.

Mr. B. Swartwout's report, claims; Doc. 104, vol. 5, Ass'y Docs. 1842.

CAMPBELL HARRIS.

Mr. J. G. Floyd's report; Doc. 68, vol. 2, Senate Docs. 1849.

JAMES HARRINGTON, JAMES SLEEPER.

Mr. J. W. Jermain's report; Doc. 95, vol. 5, Ass'y Docs. 1850.

SAMUEL HART—WM. CANDEE.

Report of Canal Board; Doc. 55, vol. 8, Ass'y Docs. 1845.

JOHN HARTMAN.

Mr. A. Chamberlain's report; Doc. 94, vol. 5, Ass'y Docs. 1852.

E. B. HARWOOD.

Mr. Martin's report; Doc. 82, vol. 3, Ass'y Docs. 1848.

PETER HASBROUCK.

Report of Commissioners of the Land Office; Doc. 79, vol. 3, Senate Docs. 1843.

HASTINGS.

Mr. A. C. Hand's report on the memorial of citizens to authorise the overflow of land; Doc. 49, vol. 2, Senate Docs. 1847.

JARVIS M. HATCH.

Mr. Johnson's report, claims; Doc. 11, vol. 1, Senate Docs. 1846.

MALCOM N. HAWKINS.

Report of Commissioners of Land Office; Doc. 183, vol. 5, Ass'y Docs. 1846.

Report of Commissioners of Land Office; Doc. 89, vol. 2, Ass'y Docs. 1847.

GEORGE HAWKINS.

Report of committee on claims; Doc. 117, vol. 4, Ass'y Docs. 1851.

Mr. N. Jones' report, claims; Doc. 52, vol. 2, Senate Docs 1852.

J. W. HAUN.

Mr. Fitzhugh's report; Doc. 79, vol. 2, Ass'y Docs. 1849.

JAMES HAY.

(See John G. Leake.)

WILLIAM HAYDEN.

Mr. Reamer's report; Doc. 159, vol. 5, Ass'y Docs. 1848.

PERKINS G. HAYES.

Mr. Ward's report; Doc. 77, vol. 2, Ass'y Docs. 1849.

R. B. HEACOCK.

Report of Canal Commissioners; Doc. 207, vol. 6, Ass'y Docs. 1845.

HEALTH OFFICE.

Mr. Glazier's report on reduction of fees; Doc. 104, vol. 4, Ass'y Docs. 1843.

Report; Doc. 11, vol. 1, Senate Docs. 1850.

HEALTH OF STATE.

Mr. McNeil's report on the act to preserve the public health; Doc. 19, vol. 1, Ass'y Docs. 1846.

Communication from Gov. Fish; Doc. 36, vol. 1, Senate Docs. 1850.

Attorney General Chatfield's report as to the reviving, by proclamation of the Governor, of the act of June 22, 1832; Doc. 126, vol. 5, Ass'y Docs. 1850.

Mr. Robinson's report (with communications from physicians); Doc. 92, vol. 3, Senate Docs. 1850.

GEORGE HEATH.

Report of Canal Board, as to valve gate claim; Doc. 91, vol. 3, Ass'y Docs. 1844.

Report of Canal Board; Doc. 201, vol. 6, Ass'y Docs. 1846.

Mr. Bishop Perkins' report; Doc. 216, vol. 6, Ass'y Docs. 1846.

HENRY HEATH.

Report of Canal Board; Doc. 150, vol. 7, Ass'y Docs. 1842.

Mr. Pitt's report, claims; Doc. 62, vol. 3, Ass'y Docs. 1846.

HEMLOCK LAKE.

Report of Canal Board, in relation to a supply of water; Doc. 40, vol. 1, Senate Docs. 1850.

SUSAN HENDRICK (an Indian).

Report of the Commissioners of the Land Office; Doc. 127, vol. 4, Senate Docs. 1846.

HERKIMER COUNTY.

State Engineer, H. C. Seymour's report of quantity of State land in county; Doc. 19, vol. 1, Senate Docs. 1851.

HERKIMER DEMOCRATIC DELEGATES.

Memorial of a convention, in relation to State debt; Doc. 90, vol. 4, Ass'y Docs. 1843.

Mr. McMurray's majority report on such memorial; Doc. 152, vol. 5, Ass'y Docs. 1843.

Mr. Wells Brooks' minority report; Doc. 152, vol. 5, Ass'y Docs. 1843.

MARIAH M. HESS.

Mr. Russell's report, aliens; Doc. 174, vol. 7, Ass'y Docs. 1842.

HENRY I. HEWETT, WILLIAM BEACH.

Mr. Joshua A. Spencer's report on loss of canal boat; Doc. 150, vol. 4, Senate Docs. 1847.

Mr. J. E. Beer's report, claims; Doc. 230, vol. 8, Ass'y Docs. 1847.

Mr. J. M. Cook's report, claims; Doc. 12, vol. 1, Senate Docs. 1848.

JOSEPH P. HEWETT, JOHN M. BUTTERY.

Report of Canal Board; Doc. 134, vol. 5, Ass'y Docs. 1844.

HIGHWAYS.

Report of commissioners of codification, S. C. Hawley, Alvah Worden, with proposed general law; Doc. 5, vol. 1, Senate Docs. 1849. Doc. 12, vol. 1, Ass'y Docs. 1849.

Mr. S. Willett's report; Doc. 34, vol. 2, Senate Docs. 1851.

GEORGE W. HILDRETH.

Report of Canal Board as to valve gate claim with testimony; Doc. 201, vol. 6, Ass'y Docs. 1846.

Mr. Bishop Perkins' report; Doc. 216, vol. 6, Ass'y Docs. 1846.

ANTHONY JOHN HILL.

Mr. McMurray's report; Doc. 73, vol. 4, Ass'y Docs. 1842.

CHARLES J. HILL.

Report of Canal Commissioners; Doc. 209, vol. 6, Ass'y Docs. 1845.

JACOB HINDS.

Memorial of Jonas Ingraham presenting charges; Doc. 81, vol. 5, Ass'y Docs. 1850.

Mr. Hinds' memorial in reply, and asking for a committee of investigation; Doc. 102, vol. 5, Ass'y Docs. 1850.

Further communication from Mr. Hinds', on the same subject; Doc. 106, vol. 5, Ass'y Docs. 1850.

ELI HINMAN.

Mr. Folger's report in relation to lands leased of Stockbridge Indians; Doc. 23, vol. 1, Ass'y Docs. 1849.

HISTORICAL SOCIETY—(New-York.)

Memorial of Henry R. Schoolcraft, John. W. Edmonds, J. Romeyn Brodhead, a committee of the society, calling attention to the Aboriginal History of the State; Doc. 55, vol. 2, Senate Docs. 1846.

Memorial for appropriation for fire proof building; Doc. 15, vol. 1, Senate Docs. 1850.

Mr. J. W. Beekman's report on above memorial; Doc. 95, vol. 2, Ass'y Docs. 1849.

FRANCIS HITCHIN, JOHN HITCHIN, STEPHEN HITCHIN.

Mr. Carpenter's report; Doc. 143, vol. 4, Ass'y Docs. 1847.

HOBART FREE COLLEGE.

Report of condition made to Regents of the University; Doc. 77, (page 93,) vol. 2, Senate Docs. 1854.

Report of condition of medical department, is page 99 of same document.

OGDEN HOFFMAN—(Attorney General.)

Report in relation to militia acts, Oct., 21, 1814, and April 21, 1818.

Opinion in relation to legislative regulation of ferries; Doc. 131, vol. 4, Ass'y Docs. 1854.

Report in relation to grants in the harbor of New-York; Doc. 105, vol. 3, Ass'y Docs. 1854.

Opinion in relation to responsibility of State prison agents; Doc. 121, vol. 3, Ass'y Docs. 1854.

MICHAEL HOFFMAN.

Resolutions in relation to State debt; Doc. 23, vol. 2, Ass'y Docs. 1842.

Report of State officers in answer; Doc. 64, vol. 4, Ass'y Docs. 1842.

Report on the finances of the State; Doc. 88, vol. 5, Ass'y Docs. 1842.

HOLLAND LAND COMPANY.

Mr. H. Putnam's report on the perpetuation of evidence as to former owners; Doc. 18, vol. 1, Senate Docs. 1846.

NATHAN S. HOLLISTER.

Mr. Strowbridge's report, claims; Doc. 178, vol. 5, Ass'y Docs. 1845.

Report of Canal Commissioners; Doc. 15, vol. 1, Senate Docs. 1846.

JESSE HOLLISTER.

Report of Canal Board; Doc. 152, vol. 5, Ass'y Docs. 1846.

Report of Canal committee; Doc. 62, vol. 2, Ass'y Docs. 1849.

HOMŒOPATHY.

Mr. Backus' report on proposed college; Doc. 108, vol. 4, Senate Docs. 1846.

Mr. Long's report on same; Doc. 125, vol. 4, Ass'y Docs. 1846.

Homœopathy illustrated, an address by Dr. Thomas W. Blatchford, before the State Medical Society, Albany, 1851; Doc. 125, (page 69,) vol. 4, Ass'y Docs. 1851.

HOMESTEAD EXEMPTION.

Mr. Alling's majority report Doc. 203, vol. 7, Ass'y Docs. 1847.

Mr. Bascom's report; Doc. 233, vol. 8, Ass'y Docs. 1849.

Mr. Bowie's report; Doc. 78, vol. 3, Ass'y Docs. 1848.

Mr. Winsor's report; Doc. 123, vol. 5, Ass'y Docs. 1850.

Mr. Caleb Lyon's report; Doc. 130, vol. 4, Ass'y Docs. 1851.

HONEOYE LAKE.

Report of Canal Board in relation to supply of water; Doc. 40, vol. 1, Senate Docs. 1850.

JAMES H. HOOKER.

Mr. McCarty's report, claims, in relation to loss of canal boat; Doc. 152, vol. 5, Ass'y Docs. 1848.

Mr. T. S. Williams' report; Doc. 32, vol. 2, Senate Docs. 1849.

Mr. Hale's report; Doc. 16, vol. 1, Ass'y Docs. 1849.

Report of committee on claims; Doc. 118, vol. 5, Ass'y Docs. 1850.

SANFORD A. HOOPER.

Mr. Hopkins' report, claims; Doc. 111, vol. 3, Senate Docs. 1843.

Mr. Jackson's report, claims; Doc. 125, vol. 5, Ass'y Docs. 1843.

Mr. Gorham's report, claims; Doc. 39, vol. 3, Ass'y Docs. 1844.

Attorney General Chatfield's report on lost note; Doc. 85, vol. 4, Ass'y Docs. 1853.

JAMES HOPE, NATHANIEL JOHNSON.

Mr. Griffin's report on the legality of their acts in court martial; Doc. 39, vol. 2, Ass'y Docs. 1842.

GILBERT HOPKINS.

Mr. Richard S. Williams' report; Doc. 39, vol. 1, Senate Docs. 1850.

JOHN G. HOPPER.

Mr. N. B. Smith's report; Doc. 134, vol. 4, Ass'y Docs. 1847.

HOPS.

Report of inspection at Albany; Doc. 145, vol. 4, Ass'y Docs. 1845.

Mr. N. J. Beach's report on the compulsory feature of the inspection laws, as respects this article; Doc. 92, vol. 4, Ass'y Docs. 1846.

ALLEN W. HORTON.

Mr. Gilbert's report, claims; Doc. 31, vol. 2, Ass'y Docs. 1852.

Mr. Barrow's report, claims; Doc. 27, vol. 1, Ass'y Docs. 1854.

GEORGE W. HORTON.

Report of Canal Board; Doc. 68, vol. 3, Ass'y Docs. 1844.

HORSE RACING.

Mr. Orville Clark's report on bill to prevent horse racing on the Albany and Troy McAdam road; Doc. 58, vol. 3, Senate Docs. 1845.

WILLIAM H. C. HOSMER.

Mr. Fiske's report on claim for compensation as witness on the trial of Alexander McLeod, at Utica; Doc. 89, vol. 5, Ass'y Docs. 1850.

HOSPITALS—*In Europe.*

Sketch by James H. Armsby; Doc. 85, vol. 2, Ass'y Docs. 1852.

In America.

Sketch by James H. Armsby; Doc. 67, (page 137,) vol. 3, Ass'y Docs. 1853.

HOSPITAL—*New-York.*

Annual report of Governors; Doc. 60, vol. 3, Senate Docs. 1842. Doc. 95, vol. 5, Ass'y Docs. 1842.

Annual report; Doc. 41, vol. 1, Senate Docs. 1843. Doc. 147, vol. 5, Ass'y Docs. 1843.

Annual report; Doc. 86, vol. 2, Senate Docs. 1844. Doc. 81, vol. 3, Ass'y Docs. 1844.

Annual report; Doc. 44, vol. 1, Senate Docs. 1845. Doc. 176, vol. 5, Ass'y Docs. 1845.

Annual report; Doc. 62, vol. 2, Senate Docs. 1846. Doc. 121, vol. 4, Ass'y Docs. 1846.

Annual report; Doc. 73, vol. 2, Ass'y Docs. 1847.

Annual report; Doc. 77, vol. 3, Senate Docs. 1848. Doc. 194, vol. 6, Ass'y Docs. 1848.

Annual report; Doc. 226, vol. 5, Ass'y Docs. 1849.

do do 178, vol. 8, do 1850.

do do 80, vol. 3, Senate Docs. 1849.

Mr. Truslow's report, concerning amendment of charter; Doc. 15, vol. 1, Ass'y Docs. 1850.

Annual report; Doc. 116, vol. 3, Senate Docs. 1850.

do do 58, vol. 2, do 1853.

Table of patients admitted and discharged from February 1, 1792, to December 31, 1849; Doc. 67, (page 156) vol. 3, Ass'y Docs. 1853.

HORACE HOTCHKISS, WM. P. SMITH.

Memorial in relation to their claim against agent of Sing Sing State prison; Doc. 85, vol. 2, Ass'y Docs. 1849.

Report of committee on claims; Doc. 96, vol. 4, Ass'y Docs. 1851.

Mr. W. Clark's report; Doc. 75, vol. 2, Senate Docs. 1854.

FRANKLIN B. HOUGH.

Mr. Dewey's report in relation to historical enquiries; Doc. 111, vol. 3, Ass'y Docs. 1854.

MICHAEL HONSEAUR.

Mr. W. A. Gilbert's report, claims; Doc. 98, vol. 5, Ass'y Docs. 1852.

DEAN S. HOWARD.

Mr. Caleb Lyons' report; Doc. 115, vol. 4, Ass'y Docs. 1851.

HUMPHREY HOWLAND.

Mr. Flagler's report; Doc. 17, vol. 2, Ass'y Docs. 1842.

Report of Canal Commissioners concerning lot 63, Tyre; Doc. 25, vol. 1, Senate Docs. 1843.

ALEX. HUBBARD.

Mr. Schoonmaker's report, claims; Doc. 52, vol. 2, Senate Docs 1850.

JONAS A. HUGHSTON.

Report of committee on claims, on petition asking compensation for services as district attorney of Delaware county, during 1845; Doc. 50, vol. 2, Ass'y Docs. 1845.

Mr. J. E. Beers' report, claims; Doc. 52, vol. 2, Ass'y Docs. 1847.

HUDSON.

Mr. Orville Clark's report—militia—on the subject of the payment of the guard of one hundred men for the protection of the jail of the city of Hudson, in the disturbances of 1845; Doc. 42, vol. 1, Senate Docs. 1845.

Mr. Fonda's report as to the probable expense of said guard; Doc. 86, vol. 4, Ass'y Docs. 1845.

Commissary General Storm's report as to expenses of said guard; Doc. 87, vol. 4, Ass'y Docs. 1845.

RICHARD HUDSON.

Mr. Beach's report; Doc. 128, vol. 5, Ass'y Docs. 1848.

HUDSON RIVER.

State Engineer, W. J. McAlpine's report on removing obstructions to navigation; Doc. 24, vol. 1, Senate Docs 1853.

Communication from C. W. Conrad, Secretary of war, to J. C. Wright, Comptroller, in relation to the appropriation made by Congress, Doc. 5, (page 115,) vol. 1, Ass'y Docs. 1853.

Communication from Jefferson Davis, Secretary of War, to Senator Erastus Brooks, with report of Col. J. G. Totten; Doc. 31, vol. 1, Senate Docs. 1854.

HUDSON AND DELAWARE CANAL.

Letter from John Wurts president, to Gov. Seward, respecting condition of company; Doc. 4, of Doc. 2, vol. 1, Senate Docs. 1842. Vol. 1, Ass'y Docs. 1842.

Report of condition; Doc. 109, vol. 5, Ass'y Docs. 1842.

VOLNEY HUGHES, CHARLES WOOLSTEN.

Mr. Sherman's report, claims; Doc. 47, vol. 3, Ass'y Docs. 1851.

Mr. N. Jones' report, claims; Doc. 38, vol. 1, Senate Docs. 1852.

CHARLES HULETT.

Report of committee on judiciary, in relation to transmission of bonds and mortgages; Doc. 18, vol. 1, Ass'y Docs. 1847.

DAVID HULSE, JONATHAN O. DUNNING.

Mr. W. A. Gilbert's report, claims; Doc. 59, vol. 2, Ass'y Docs. 1852.

CHARLES HUMPHREY.

Report of fees as clerk of the Supreme court; Doc. 24, vol. 1, Senate Docs. 1847.

MATTHEW HUNTINGTON.

Mr. Alvord's report, claims; Doc. 65, vol. 3, Ass'y Docs. 1844.

Mr. Lewis' report; Doc. 34, vol. 3, Ass'y Docs. 1850.

Mr. Jones' report, claims; Doc. 47, vol. 1, Senate Docs. 1852.

SETH HUNT.

Mr. S. Baldwin's report, claims; Doc. 90, Ass'y Docs. 1854.

WASHINGTON HUNT—(Comptroller.)

Report of expenses of commission on reform of practice and pleading; Doc. 33, vol. 1, Ass'y Docs. 1850.

Report of sums paid for printing; Doc. 47, vol. 2, Senate Docs. 1850.

Communication concerning failure of Hudson and Berkshire railroad company to pay the interest on the State loan; Doc. 6, vol. 1, Ass'y Docs. 1850.

Annual report; Doc. 8, vol. 1, Ass'y Docs. 1850.

Report in relation to the time of making annual report; Doc. 60, vol. 4, Ass'y Docs. 1850.

WASHINGTON HUNT—(Governor.)

Annual message; Doc. 2, vol. 1, Senate Docs. 1851. Doc. 2, vol. 1, Ass'y Docs. 1852.

Message at extra session; Doc. 75, vol. 3, Senate Docs. 1851. Doc. 137, vol. 5, Ass'y Docs. 1851.

Communication relative to the Washington National Monument.

Communication, with abstract of the seventh census; Doc. 157, vol. 6, Ass'y Docs. 1851.

Communication in relation to Colonial History; Doc. 66, vol. 3, Ass'y Docs. 1851.

Annual message, Doc. 1, vol. 1, Ass'y Docs. 1852. Doc. 2, vol. 1, Senate Docs. 1852.

Correspondence with Louis Kossuth; Doc. 84, vol. 2, Senate Docs. 1852.

List of reprieves, pardons, and restorations granted in 1852; Doc. 44, vol. 2, Ass'y Docs. 1853.

HYDROSTATIC SCALE, (Amsden's.)

Report of Canal Commissioner Nelson J. Beach, on powers; Doc. 225, vol. 5, Ass'y Docs. 1849.

Further report on same subject; Doc. 35, vol. 3, Ass'y Docs. 1850.

PETER HYNDS.

Mr. Hammond's report; Doc. 133, vol. 4, Ass'y Docs. 1847.

IDIOTS.

Mr. F. F. Backus' report on the Census; Doc. 23, vol 1, Senate Docs. 1848.

Mr. Backus' report as to the establishment of Asylum; Doc. 44, vol. 2, Senate Docs. 1847.

Annual report; Doc. 30, vol. 1, Senate Docs. 1852.

Report of Secretary of State, H. S. Randall, with an enumeration; Doc. 73, vol. 3, Senate Docs. 1853.

Annual report; Doc. 29, vol. 2, Ass'y Docs. 1853.

Mr. O. Hastings' report on appropriation; Doc. 68, vol. 3, Ass'y Docs. 1853.

IMPEACHMENT.

Mr. Week's report relative to the Assembly's power of impeachment; Doc. 123, vol. 6, Ass'y Docs. 1853.

Mr. Champlain's majority report; Doc. 130, vol. 6, Ass'y Docs. 1853.

Mr. T. C. Peters' minority report; Doc. 131, vol. 6, Ass'y Docs. 1853.

INCORPORATED COMPANIES.

Comptroller Flagg's seport as to taxes paid by them—real estate and capital stock; Doc. 98, vol. 3, Ass'y Docs. 1844.

INDEPENDENT TREASURY.

Memorial of John Hecker and others, for its adoption in the financial system of New-York; Doc. 85, vol. 5, Ass'y Docs. 1842.

INDIANA.

Resolutions of Legislature in favor of colonization and the suppression of the African slave trade; Doc. 91, vol. 2, Senate Docs. 1852.

INDIAN AFFAIRS.

Mr. Dixon's report; Doc. 92, vol. 4, Senate Docs. 1842.

Mr. Dixon's further report in relation to the St. Regis, Six Nations and Tuscaroras, and in respect to the tenure of their lands; Doc. 95, vol. 4, Senate Docs. 1842.

INDIVIDUAL LIABILITY.

Report of committee on banks, by Mr. J. M. Cook, upon so much of Governor Fish's message as relates to the constitutional requirement concerning the individual liability of stockholders in monied corporations; Doc. 42, vol. 2, Senate Docs. 1849.

INDUSTRIAL ASSOCIATIONS.

Mr. Allen's report, judiciary; Doc. 162, vol. 6, Ass'y Docs. 1844.

FREDERICK W. INGERSOLL.

Mr. Beach's report; Doc. 51, vol. 2, Ass'y Docs. 1848.

JONAS INGRAHAM, DANIEL BOLLES, SILAS INGRAHAM.

Report of Canal Commissioners on petition; Doc. 11, vol. 1, Senate Docs. 1843.

Report of judiciary committee; Doc. 19, vol. 1, Senate Docs. 1843.

Report of Canal Commissioners; Doc. 74, vol. 2, Senate Docs. 1844.

Report on petition; Doc. 13, vol. 1, Senate Docs. 1848.

JONAS INGRAHAM, SQUIRE L. CASE.

Report of Canal Board; Doc. 218, vol. 6, Ass'y Docs. 1845.

Report of Canal Commissioners; Doc. 138, vol. 4, Senate Docs. 1846.

Mr. Pitts' report, claims; Doc. 47, vol. 2, Ass'y Docs. 1846.

INSPECTION LAWS AND INSPECTORS.

Remonstrance of Peter Esquirrol, against their alteration; Doc. 69, vol. 3, Ass'y Docs. 1843.

Abstract of returns under, and furnished by Secretary of State, S. Young, with his report; Doc. 131, vol. 5, Ass'y Docs. 1843.

Mr. E. H. White's report, select committee, on their practical operation; Doc. 142, vol. 5, Ass'y Docs. 1843.

Abstract of returns, furnished by Secretary of State, S. Young; Doc. 81, vol. 2, Senate Docs. 1844.

REPORT OF SECRETARY OF STATE.

N. S. Benton, as to annual reports made to him; Doc. 53, vol. 2. Senate Docs 1845.

Abstracts of annual returns; Doc. 56, vol. 2, Senate Docs. 1845.

Mr. Bockee's report, manufactures, on the subject of compensation of inspectors; Doc. 69, vol. 2, Senate Docs. 1845.

Abstract of annual returns with accompanying report of Secretary of State, N. S. Benton; Doc. 82, vol. 3, Senate Docs. 1846.

INSPECTOR GENERAL.

Annual report, B. F. Bruce, Doc. 8, vol. 1, Ass'y Docs. 1852.

Annual report, B. F. Bruce, Doc. 19, vol 2, Ass'y Docs. 1853.

INSTITUTE—(American.)

Annual report; Doc. 101, vol. 4, Senate Docs. 1842.
do do 108, do 3, do 1843.
do do 124, do 4, do 1844.

Annual report, 1844, is in Doc. 85 (Transactions of State Agricultural Society), vol. 3, Senate Docs. 1845.

Annual report, 1845, is in Doc. 105, (Transactions of State Agricultural Society,) vol. 4, Senate Docs. 1846.

Annual report is also Doc. 200, vol. 6, Ass'y Docs. 1846.

Annual report;	Doc. 151,	vol. 6,	Ass'y Docs.	1847.
do	do 216,	do 7,	do	1848.
do	do 244,	do 7,	do	1849.
do	do 199,	do 9,	do	1850.
do	do 149,	do 5,	do	1851.
do	do 129,	do 7,	do	1852.
do	do 133,	do 6,	do	1853.
do	do 150,	do 5,	do	1854.

INSURANCE.

Mr. M. H. Buell's report, on the memorial of 17 insurance companies of New-York and Brooklyn, praying for increase of tax on agencies of companies chartered by other States and countries; Doc. 80, vol. 3, Ass'y Docs. 1845.

Mr. Edwards' minority report in favor of increasing the tax on foreign agencies; Doc. 105, vol. 4, Ass'y Docs. 1845.

Mr. S. Lawrence's report on unauthorised insurances; Doc. 72, vol. 3, Ass'y Docs. 1846.

Mr. Hadley's report on the taxation of foreign insurance companies; Doc. 251, vol. 8, Ass'y Docs. 1847.

Comptroller Fillmore's report, with abstract of returns of companies in the city of New-York; Doc. 41, vol. 2, Senate Docs. 1848.

Memorial of fire department of New-York, in relation to the tax on foreign insurance companies; Doc. 9, vol. 1, Senate Docs. 1849.

Comptroller Fillmore's report in relation to foreign insurance companies; Doc. 36, vol. 1, Senate Docs. 1849.

Mr. G. Underwood's report in examination of proposed amendments to the several laws; Doc. 99, vol. 5, Ass'y Docs. 1852.

Abstract of reports of companies having a stock capital; Doc. 5, (page 111,) vol. 1, Ass'y Docs. 1853.

List of companies under law of 1853; Doc. 19, vol. 1, Senate Docs. 1854.

Mr. Danforth's report on charter renewals; Doc. 20, vol. 1, Senate Docs. 1854.

Report of Secretary of State, E. W. Leavenworth, as to the filing of lists; Doc. 23, vol. 1, Senate Docs. 1854.

Report of Comptroller, James M. Cook, in relation to the condition of fire insurance companies; Doc. 95, vol. 3, Ass'y Docs. 1854.

INSURANCE COMPANIES.

ÆTNA.

Report of premiums received and taxes paid; Doc. 124, vol. 4, Ass'y Docs. 1845.

BOWERY.

Report of premiums received and taxes paid; Doc. 82, vol.4, Ass'y Docs. 1845.

BROOKLYN.

Report of premiums received and taxes paid; Doc. 142, vol. 4, Ass'y Docs. 1845.

CITY.

Report of premiums received and taxes paid; Doc. 115, vol. 4, Ass'y Docs. 1845.

CONTRIBUTIONSHIP.

Report of premiums received and taxes paid; Doc. 98, vol. 4, Ass'y Docs. 1845.

EAGLE.

Report of premiums received and taxes paid; Doc. 120, vol. 4, Ass'y Docs. 1845.

EAST RIVER.

Report of premiums received and taxes paid; Doc. 123, vol. 4, Ass'y Docs. 1845.

FIREMENS'.

Report of premiums received and taxes paid; Doc. 111, vol. 4, Ass'y Docs. 1845.

GREENWICH.

Report of premiums received and taxes paid; Doc. 106, vol. 4, Ass'y Docs. 1845.

GUARDIAN.

Report of premiums received and taxes paid; Doc. 119, vol. 4, Ass'y Docs. 1845.

Further report; Doc. 128, vol. 4, Ass'y Docs. 1845.

HOWARD.

Report of premiums received and taxes paid; Doc. 112, vol. 4, Ass'y Docs. 1845.

JEFFERSON.

Report of premiums received and taxes paid; Doc. 100, vol. 4, Ass'y Docs. 1845.

LONG ISLAND.

Report of premiums received and taxes paid; Doc. 144, vol. 4, Ass'y Docs. 1845.

MANHATTAN.

Report of premiums received and taxes paid; Doc. 116, vol. 4, Ass'y Docs. 1845.

MERCHANTS'.

Report of premiums received and taxes paid; Doc. 143, vol. 4, Ass'y Docs. 1845.

NATIONAL.

Report of premiums received and taxes paid; Doc. 137, vol. 4, Ass'y Docs. 1845.

NEW-YORK FIRE.

Report of premiums received and taxes paid; Doc. 127, vol. 4, Ass'y Docs. 1845.

NORTH AMERICAN.

Report of premiums received and taxes paid; Doc. 138, vol. 4, Ass'y Docs. 1845.

Mr. A. C. Hand's report on application for relief in taxation, on account of losses; Doc. 21, vol. 1, Senate Docs. 1846.

NORTH RIVER.

Report of premiums received and taxes paid; Doc. 108, vol. 4, Ass'y Docs. 1845.

TRUST.

Report of premiums received and taxes paid; Doc. 114, vol. 4, Ass'y Docs. 1845.

UNITED STATES.

Report of premiums received and taxes paid; Doc. 89, vol. 4, Ass'y Docs. 1845.

INTEMPERANCE.

Mr. Bokee's report, finance, against purchasing Dr. Sewell's pathology of drunkenness; Doc. 116, vol. 3, Senate Docs. 1843

Mr. Hibbard's report, select committee, on same subject; Doc. 33, vol. 2, Ass'y Docs. 1843.

Report relative to grog-shops on the line of the canals; Doc. 122, vol. 3, Senate Docs. 1843.

Mr. Burt's report on license question; Doc. 83, vol 3, Ass'y Docs. 1844.

Mr. Ashley Sampson's report on Dr. Sewell's plates of the causes of drunkenness; Doc. 102, vol. 5, Ass'y Docs. 1844.

Mr. Palmer's report, judiciary, on the question of making intemperance a good cause for divorce: Doc. 156, vol. 6, Ass'y Docs. 1844.

Mr. Garritson's report on license election law; Doc. 50, vol. 3, Ass'y Docs. 1845.

Report of Secretary of State, N. S. Benton, with the returns of the license elections of 3d Tuesday of 1846; Doc. 40, vol. 1, Ass'y Docs. 1844.

Mr. Chandler's majority report in favor of the repeal of the excise election law of 1845; Doc. 139, vol. 4, Ass'y Docs. 1847.

Mr. Curry's minority report against repeal; Doc. 140, vol. 4, Ass'y Docs. 1847.

Mr. Lee's report; Doc. 167, vol. 5, Ass'y Docs. 1848.

Remonstrance of the N. Y. State Temperance Society against legalizing traffic; 169, vol. 5, Ass'y Docs. 1848.

Mr. Crispell's report on prohibitory law; Doc. 220, vol. 5, Ass'y Docs. 1849.

Mr. C. C. Noble's minority report; Doc. 230, vol. 5, Ass'y Docs. 1849.

Memorial for prohibitory law; Doc. 10, vol. 1, Senate Docs. 1850.

Mr. Albert Gilbert's majority report on a prohibitory law; Doc. 119, vol. 5, Ass'y Docs. 1850, with reports from the keepers of the several jails in State; Doc. 119, vol. 5, Ass'y Docs. 1850.

Mr. James F. Bush's minority report on same; Doc. 121, vol. 5, Ass'y Docs. 1850.

Charles J. Warren's appeal for a prohibitory act; Doc. 145, vol. 6, Ass'y Docs. 1850.

Mr. Chamberlain's report on "An act relating to excise;" Doc. 46, vol. 3, Ass'y Docs. 1851.

Mr. Fordyce's majority report on a prohibitory law; Doc. 110, vol, 4, Ass'y Docs. 1851.

Mr. A. Chamberlain's minority report on same subject; Doc. 111, vol. 4, Ass'y Docs. 1851.

Mr. J. Ryan's minority report on same subject; Doc. 118, vol. 4, Ass'y Docs. 1851.

Mr. Monroe's report; Doc. 26, vol. 1, Senate Docs. 1852.

Mr. E. L. Snow's majority report on same subject; Doc. 88, vol. 2, Ass'y Docs. 1852.

Mr. J. Rose, Jr's., minority report on same subject; Doc. 88, (page 17,) vol. 2, Ass'y Docs. 1852.

Mr. Bristol's report on prohibitory law; Doc. 21, vol. 1, Senate Docs 1852.

Mr. P. W. Rose's report on prohibitory law; Doc. 66, vol. 3, Ass'y Docs. 1853.

Mr. M. H. Clark's report from select committee, on prohibitory law; Doc. 17, vol. 1, Senate Docs. 1854.

Mr. M. H. Clark's majority report on so much of Governor Seymour's message, as relates to this subject; Doc. 37, vol 1, Senate Docs. 1854.

Mr. C. F. Crosby's minority report on same; Doc. 37, vol. 1, Senate Docs. 1854.

Mr. C. C. Leigh's majority report; Doc. 20, vol. 1, Ass'y Docs 1854.

Mr. Dewey's minority report; Doc. 20, vol. 1, Ass'y Docs. 1854.

Mr. Sessions' majority report; Doc. 112, vol. 3, Ass'y Docs. 1854.

Mr. Mallory's minority report; Doc. 112, vol. 3, Ass'y Docs. 1854.

Mr. Morris' minority report; Doc. 118, vol. 3, Ass'y Docs. 1854.

INTERNATIONAL EXCHANGES.

Communication from M. Alexander Vattemare; Doc. 185, vol. 5, Ass'y Docs. 1845.

Communication from Governor, John Young, with letters from Secretary of State, N. S. Benton; from M. Alexander Vattemare—from the Ministers of War—Public Instruction—Marine and Colonies—Finances — Interior—Agriculture and commerce—Arago, Secretary of the Royal Academy—with catalogue of donations made through Mr. Vattemare; Doc. 128, vol. 4, Senate Docs. 1847. Doc. 244, vol. 8, Ass'y Docs. 1847.

Mr. Lawrence Smith's report, with address of M. Vattemare; Doc. 226, vol. 7, Ass'y Docs. 1847.

Letter from M. Vattemare, suggesting a statistical document; Doc. 208, vol. 5, Ass'y Docs. 1849.

Second report of M. Vattemare, with communication from officers of the French government, and with catalogue of donations; Doc. 127, vol. 5, Ass'y Docs. 1850.

Communication from Gov. Fish, with letter from M. Vattemare; Doc. 192, vol. 8, Ass'y Docs. 1850.

Communication from Gov. Fish, with letter from Bishop John Hughes, relating to the donation by the Pope; Doc. 117, vol. 3, Ass'y Docs. 1849.

Communication from Gov. Fish, with letter from Mr. Vattemare; Doc. 201, vol. 5, Ass'y Docs. 1850.

INTRAMURAL INTERMENTS.

Mr. J. A. Cross' report on the prohibition; Doc. 81, vol. 3, Senate Docs. 1850.

IRON MANUFACTURE BY CONVICT LABOR.

Mr. Ransom Cook's report as commissioner on question of employment; Doc. 32, vol. 2, Ass'y Docs. 1843.

Remonstrance of citizens of Northern New-York; Doc. 129, vol. 5, Ass'y Docs. 1843.

Ransom Cook's answer to above; Doc. 155, vol. 5, Ass'y Docs. 1843.

Resolutions of Plattsburgh meeting; Doc. 157, vol. 5, Ass'y Docs. 1843.

Palmer Cleveland's memorial; Doc. 159, vol. 5, Ass'y Docs. 1843.

Mr. Suydam's report; Doc. 41, vol. 3, Ass'y Docs. 1844.

Ransom Cook's report; Doc. 16, vol. 1, Senate Docs. 1845.

Mr. Rowe's report on the result of the manufacture at Clinton prison; Doc. 62, vol. 2, Ass'y Docs. 1852.

IROQUOIS.

Petition to Gov. Bouck, in relation to their land; Doc. J., accompanying message, Doc. 2, vol. 1, Senate Docs. 1842. Doc. J. accompanying message, Doc. 2, vol. 1, Ass'y Docs. 1842.

Henry R. Schoolcraft's census and delineation; Doc. 24, vol. 1, Senate Docs. 1846.

Mr. Collins' proposition to extend to them the right of suffrage; Doc. 63, vol. 3, Ass'y Docs. 1846.

Mr. Folsom's report on aid to those who have emigrated westward; Doc. 70, vol. 2, Senate Docs. 1847.

JOHN B. IVES.

Report of Canal Board; Doc. 85, vol. 3, Ass'y Docs. 1844.

Mr. McCarty's report, claims; Doc. 119, vol. 3, Ass'y Docs. 1848.

ANDREW JACKSON.

Mr. Chamberlain's report, select committee, on subject of remission of fine; Doc. 56, vol. 2, Senate Docs. 1843.

Mr. Slingerland's report, select committee; Doc. 171, vol. 5, Ass'y Docs. 1843.

Mr. Clark's report, select committee; Doc. 9, vol. 1, Senate Docs. 1844.

ISAAC JACKSON.

Report of committee on claims; Doc. 69, vol. 3, Ass'y Docs. 1846.

OZIAS JACOBS.

Report of Commissioners of Land Office, in relation to lands purchased of Indians; Doc. 107, vol. 4, Ass'y Docs. 1847.

Mr. S. Morris' report; Doc. 141, vol. 4, Ass'y Docs. 1847.

WILLIAM JAMES, JOHN JAMES.

Report of Canal Commissioners; Doc. 140, vol. 4, Senate Docs. 1847.

DAVID JAMEISON, JOHN STRONG (heirs of Wm. Strong), STEPHEN A. DAGGETT, H. T. ALEXANDER (heirs of Abram Van Epps).

Mr. Treadwell's report, claims; Doc. 257, vol. 8, Ass'y Docs.

WILLIAM JEROME.

Mr. Ruger's report, claims; Doc. 59, vol. 3, Senate Docs. 1842.

HEZEKIAH JOHNSON, WILLIAM A. MILLS.

Mr. Hitchcock's report; Doc. 112, vol. 4, Ass'y Docs. 1847.

JOHN JOHNSON.

Mr. N. Jones' report, claims; Doc. 80, vol. 2, Senate Docs. 1852.

JEWS.

Mr. Joshua A. Spencer's report as to their day of worship; Doc. 131, vol. 4, Senate Docs. 1847.

STILES JOHNSON, NORMAN BUTLER.

Mr. W. A. Wheeler's report, claims; Doc. 101, vol. 5, Ass'y Docs. 1850.

Mr. Schoonmaker's report, claims, Doc. 109, vol. 5, Senate Docs. 1850.

Mr. Curtis's report; Doc. 51, vol. 2, Senate Docs. 1851.

Mr. Severance's report; Doc. 24, vol. 2, Ass'y Docs. 1851.

JOHNSTOWN.

Report of committee on judiciary, in relation to a reduction in the number of assessors; Doc. 44, vol. 2, Senate Docs. 1842.

CHARLES A JONES.

Mr. J. B. Williams' report, claims; Doc. 72, vol. 2, Senate Docs. 1852.

Mr. J. B. Williams' further report; Doc. 73, vol. 2, Senate Docs. 1852; with testimony.

DAVID JONES.

Report of Attorney-General Chatfield; Doc. 118, vol. 6, Ass'y Docs. 1853.

JOHN H. JONES.

Report of Canal Commissioners; Doc. 99, vol. 3, Senate Docs. 1844.

JONES' WOOD PARK.

Mr. James W. Beekman's majority report, with testimony; Doc. 22, vol. 3, Senate Docs. 1853.

Mr. Cooley's minority report; Doc. 83, vol. 3, Senate Docs. 1853.

Mr. Mark Spencer's report in favor of repeal of law of 1853, providing for Park, and Judge Rosevelt's opinion on law; Doc. 47, vol. 1, Senate Docs. 1854.

Mr. Barrow's report adverse to repeal of the law of 1853; Doc. 18, vol. 1, Ass'y Docs. 1854.

Mr. Cummings' report in favor of repeal; Doc. 21, vol. 1, Ass'y Docs. 1854.

JORDAN LEVEL, ERIE CANAL.

Report of Canal Commissioners, as to cost and damages; Doc. 129, vol. 4, Senate Docs. 1844.

Report of Canal Commissioners as to abandonment by contractors of sections 9, 10, 11, enlargement; Doc. 88, vol. 3, Ass'y Docs. 1846.

Report of Canal Commissioners as to draining; Doc. 49, vol. 4, Ass'y Docs. 1847.

JOSIAH E. JULIEN.

Mr. S. Baldwin's report, claims; Doc. 137, vol. 4, Ass'y Docs. 1854.

BETHEL JUDD.

Mr. Hopkin's report, claims; Doc. 33, vol. 1, Senate Docs. 1854.

JUDGE ADVOCATE 32ND. DIVISION OF INFANTRY.

Report of Comptroller Flagg; Doc. 29, vol. 1, Senate Docs. 1843.

JUDICIARY.

Mr. Arphaxed Loomis' report; Doc. 81, vol. 5, Ass'y Docs. 1842.

Mr. George A. Simmons' report, including proposed constitutional amendments; Doc. 120, vol. 5, Ass'y Docs. 1842.

Mr. A. C. Hand's report on organization under new constitution; Doc. 106, vol. 3, Senate Docs. 1847.

JUDICIAL DISTRICTS.

Mr. Hand's conference report on the bill for the division of the State into judicial districts; Doc. 71, vol. 2, Senate Docs. 1847.

Mr. Hadley's report on above bill; Doc. 117, vol. 4, Ass'y Docs. 1847.

Mr. Johnson's report on same; Doc. 86, vol. 3, Senate Docs. 1847.

Mr. Thomas Smith's second conference report; Doc. 138, vol. 4, Ass'y Docs. 1847.

Report of committee of conference on the same; Doc. 99, vol. 3, Senate Docs. 1847.

JURY TRIAL TO SLAVES.

Governor Seward's message concerning action of South Carolina and Virginia; Doc. 96, vol. 4, Senate Docs. 1842.

JUSTICE IN THE CITY OF NEW-YORK.

Mr. Hutchins' report on so much of Gov. Hunt's message as relates to the administration of justice in the city of New-York; Doc. 97, vol. 5, Ass'y Docs. 1852.

JUVENILE ASYLUM, (New-York.)

Mr. E. Pratt's report; Doc. 78, vol. 5, Ass'y Docs. 1850.

JUVENILE DELINQUENTS—(Society for Reformation in New-York.)

Report of condition; Doc. 120, vol. 4, Ass'y Docs. 1847.

Report as above; Doc. 224, vol. 5, Ass'y Docs. 1849.

Annual report; Doc. 190, vol. 5, Ass'y Docs. 1848.

Memorial of society for aid in erection of buildings; Doc. 17, vol. 1, Senate Docs. 1850.

Annual report; Doc. 172, vol. 6, Ass'y Docs. 1850.

JUVENILE DELINQUENTS—(House of Refuge in Western New-York.)

Mr. Case's report; Doc. 182, vol. 7, Ass'y Docs. 1842.

Mr. Blodgett's report; Doc. 93, vol. 4, Ass'y Docs. 1846.

Report of managers; Doc. 42, vol. 3, Ass'y Docs. 1850.

Memorial of managers for an additional wing; Doc. 115, vol. 5, Ass'y Docs. 1850.

Report of managers; Doc. 8, vol. 1, Senate Docs. 1851.

do do 31, do 2, Ass'y Docs. 1853.

Mr. Miller's report as to admissions; Doc. 49, vol. 2, Ass'y Docs. 1853.

Mr. Miller's report in relation to appropriation; Doc. 50, vol. 2, Ass'y Docs. 1853.

JOSEPH M. KASSON, HENRY CADY.

Mr. Putnam's report, claims; Doc. 36, vol. 1, Senate Docs. 1843.

Mr. Beach's report; Doc. 117, vol. 3, Ass'y Docs. 1848.

HELENA R. KEARNEY.

Mr. T. E. Clark's report, claims; Doc. 75, vol. 3, Senate Docs. 1849.

JOSIAH S. KELLOGG.

Mr. H. G. Root's report; Doc. 97, vol. 5, Ass'y Docs. 1850.

Mr. Schoonmaker's report, claims; Doc. 85, vol. 3, Senate Docs. 1850.

Mr. Schoonmaker's minority report; Doc. 23, vol. 2, Senate Docs. 1851.

Mr. Severance's report, claims; Doc. 11, vol. 1, Ass'y Docs. 1851.

S. KELLOGG.

Mr. McCarty's report, claims; Doc. 33, vol. 2, Ass'y Docs. 1848.

KENTUCKY.

Resolutions of Legislature concerning soldiers of the Revolution; Doc. 96, vol. 5, Ass'y Docs. 1842. Same; Doc. 26, vol. 2, Senate Docs. 1842.

Resolutions of Legislature concerning obligations of States to preserve their public faith; Doc. 51, vol. 3, Ass'y Docs. 1842.

Resolutions of same, respecting certain resolutions of Massachusetts, concerning free Representatives, and in relation to the district system of electing members of Congress; Doc. 194, vol. 7, Ass'y Docs. 1844.

AMASA KELSON'S ESTATE.

Mr. S. J. Wilkins' report on the claim to the estate of the deceased, who was a mulatto, he having died intestate; Doc. 70, vol. 2, Senate Docs. 1849.

JAMES H. KING, AMOS B. KING.

Report of Canal Board; Doc. 28, vol. 1, Ass'y Docs. 1844.

Mr. Alvord's report, claims; Dec. 141, vol. 6, Ass'y Docs. 1844.

Report of Canal Commissioner, Jonas Earll, jr.; Doc. 154, vol. 6, Ass'y Docs. 1844.

Mr. McCarty's report, claims; Doc. 112, vol. 3, Ass'y Docs. 1848.

Mr. Hale's report, claims; Doc. 75, vol. 2, Ass'y Docs. 1849.

JOHN KING.

Mr. Reamer's report; Doc. 166, vol. 5, Ass'y Docs. 1848.

AMOS KINGSLEY, JOHN NILES, ARCHIBALD CAMPBELL.

Mr. Alvord's report, claims; Doc. 201, vol. 7, Ass'y Docs. 1844.

AVERY L. KINGSLEY.

Mr. Hale's report; Doc. 17, vól. 1, Ass'y Docs. 1849.

KINGSTON POLICE JUSTICE.

Mr. H. Putnam's report, judiciary; Doc. 117, vol. 3, Senate Docs. 1845.

KINGSTON AND MIDDLETOWN TURNPIKE.

Mr. Schermerhorn's report; Doc. 20, vol. 1, Senate Docs. 1850.

GEORGE KINSELLA.

Mr. McCarty's report, claims; Doc. 158, vol. 5, Ass'y Docs. 1848.

Mr. E. Ward's report, claims; Doc. 56, vol. 2, Senate Docs. 1852.

AARON KNAPP.

Mr. Hammond's report; Doc. 260, vol. 8, Ass'y Docs. 1847.

Mr. Floyd's report, claims; Doc. 72, vol. 3, Senate Docs. 1849.

Mr. Hale's report, claims; Doc. 68, vol. 2, Ass'y Docs. 1849.

Mr. N. Jones' report, claims; Doc. 76, vol. 2, Senate Docs. 1852.

Mr. Bradley's report, claims; Doc. 32, vol. 2, Ass'y Docs. 1852.

DANIEL KNIGHT.

Report of Canal Commissioners; Doc. 132, vol. 4, Senate Docs. 1846.

Mr. Dean's report; Doc. 56, vol. 2, Ass'y Docs. 1846.

JAMES KNIGHT.

Mr. Tupper's report, claims; Doc. 82, vol. 5, Ass'y Docs. 1842.

KOSSUTH.

The correspondence of Gov. Hunt, with Louis Kossuth; Doc. 85, vol. 5, Ass'y Docs. 1852.

LABORERS' WAGES.

Mr. Bowen's report; Doc. 173, vol. 5, Ass'y Docs. 1848.

JOHN LA FOY, J. W. CLEMENS.

Report of Canal Board; Doc. 132, vol. 4, Ass'y Docs. 1845.

Mr. H. G. Root's report, claims; Doc. 31, vol. 3, Ass'y Docs. 1846.

Mr. Swift's report, claims; Doc. 54, vol. 2, Ass'y Docs. 1852.

LANDS OF STATE.

Report of State Engineer, Chas. B. Stuart, with list and description; Doc. 104, vol. 3, Ass'y Docs. 1848.

Further report of State Engineer, Chas. B. Stuart, on same subject; Doc. 27, vol. 1, Senate Docs. 1849.

Report of State Engineer, H. S. Seymour, of unappropriated land, Oct. 1, 1849; Doc. 88, vol. 5, Ass'y Docs. 1850.

Report of State Engineer, H. S. Seymour, as to number of acres belonging to State, in the counties of Herkimer and Hamilton; Doc. 19, vol. 1, Senate Docs. 1851. This document contains a detailed statement of the lands belonging to General Fund—School Fund—Literature Fund—Canal Fund.

Statement of all the unsold lands—specifying tracts and counties—number of acres and the funds to which they belong; Doc. 105, vol. 5, Ass'y Docs. 1852.

Report of Commissioners of Land Office, giving list of land belonging to School Fund; Doc. 46, vol. 1, Senate Docs. 1854.

LANDS OF UNITED STATES.

Mr. John Cramer's majority report, in relation to the share of this State; Doc. 122, vol. 5, Ass'y Docs. 1842.

Mr. F. O. Pratt's minority report; Doc. 126, vol. 5, Ass'y Docs. 1842.

Mr. John A. Lott's majority report; Doc. 112, vol. 3, Senate Docs. 1843.

Mr. Gideon Hard's minority report; Doc. 117, vol. 3, Senate Docs 1843.

Governor Bouck's communication respecting additional shares of proceeds due from the United States; Doc. 120, vol. 3, Senate Docs. 1843.

Treasurer Farrington's communication respecting the payment of the share due New-York, into the State Treasury; Doc. 16, vol. 2, Ass'y Docs. 1843; Doc. 116, vol. 4, Ass'y Docs. 1843.

Further communication respecting compensation paid to agent; Doc. 17, vol. 3, Ass'y Docs. 1843.

Governor Wright's communication respecting the last instalment of proceeds; Doc. 88, vol. 4, Ass'y Docs. 1845.

Mr. Caleb Lyons' report; Doc. 130, vol. 4, Ass'y Docs. 1851.

Resolutions of Canal Board as to appropriations for canal enlargement; Doc. 13, vol. 1, Senate Docs. 1854.

LANDS UNDER WATER.

Report of Commissioners of Land Office in the case of the grant in Westfield, Staten Island, to James S. Libby, Dexter Fairbank, Dexter S. King, William S. Hill; Doc. 121, vol. 5, Ass'y Docs. 1852.

(This Document contains the provisions of law and rules of the Commissioners applicable to such grants.)

Report of John T. Clark, State Engineer, as to grants in harbor of New-York—the Ruggles grant, Doc. 12; Doc. 35, vol. 1, Senate Docs. 1834.

Mr. E. Brooks' majority report; Doc. 49, vol. 1, Senate Docs. 1854. (Includes opinion of Charles O'Conor, United States District Attorney, page 29; and of Professor Renwick, page 27.)

Mr. Hutchins' minority report; Doc. 49, vol. 1, Senate Docs. 1854. (Includes report of ferry commissioner, Samuel Cheever, and associates, page 53.)

Remonstrance of citizens of Brooklyn, against the appointment of commissioners in relation to piers and bulkheads; Doc. 44, vol. 1, Senate Docs. 1854.

Report of Attorney-General, Ogden Hoffman, in relation to grants at the harbor of New-York; Doc. 105, vol. 3, Ass'y Docs. 1854.

LANSINGBURGH.

Report of committee on roads and bridges, in relation to power to build bridges over the Hudson and Mohawk river; Doc. 77, vol. 2, Ass'y Docs. 1852.

GEORGE J. E. LASHER.

Mr. Johnson's report, claims; Doc. 51, vol. 2, Senate Docs. 1846.

JACOB LAWSON.

Mr. Hopkins' report, claims; Doc. 115, vol. 3, Senate Docs. 1843.

Mr. Bentley's report, militia; Doc. 114, vol. 4, Ass'y Docs. 1843.

Mr. Turner's report, militia; Doc. 35, vol. 3, Ass'y Docs. 1844.

JOHN G. LEAKE, JAMES HAY.

Mr. Daly's report, select committee, on history of the claim to estate, and favorable to claim of orphan asylum; Doc. 74, vol. 3, Ass'y Docs. 1844.

Mr. Edward Sanford's report, favorable to orphan asylum; Doc. 126, vol. 5, Ass'y Docs. 1844.

Mr. S. A. Brown's majority report, aliens, adverse to orphan asylum; Doc. 210, vol. 6, Ass'y Docs. 1845.

Mr. C. F. Crosby's minority report, favorable to orphan asylum; Doc. 215, vol. 6, Ass'y Docs. 1845.

Mr. Wakeman's report; Doc. 87, vol. 5, Ass'y Docs. 1850.

Mr. Levi Harris' report; Doc. 101, vol. 4, Ass'y Docs. 1851.

Mr. Boyd's report on petition of James Hay; Doc. 93, vol. 3, Ass'y Docs. 1854.

LEAKE AND WATTS ORPHAN HOUSE.

Mr. D. E. Wheeler's report, as to the rules for binding out orphans; Doc. 223, vol. 6, Ass'y Docs. 1845.

LEARNED AND JOHNSON.

Report of Canal Board; Doc. 154, vol. 5, Ass'y Docs. 1846.

E. W. LEAVENWORTH, (Secretary of State.)

Report of criminal statistics; Doc. 54, vol. 1, Senate Docs. 1854.

ISAAC LEDYARD, JOHN B. MATTHEWS.

Report of Canal Board; Doc. 201, vol. 6, Ass'y Docs. 1842.

Mr. Teffts' report, claims; Doc. 226, vol. 6, Ass'y Docs. 1845.

Mr. Cornwell's report; Doc. 159, vol. 6, Ass'y Docs. 1847.

Mr. McCarty's report, claims; Doc. 100, vol. 3, Ass'y Docs. 1848.

LEGAL NOTICES.

Report of Chief Justice Bronson, as to the notices which can be omitted for publication in the State paper; Doc. 85, vol. 3, Senate Docs. 1846.

Report of Chancellor Walworth, on same subject; Doc. 96, vol. 3, Senate Docs. 1846.

Mr. Lott's report, judiciary, on the same; Doc. 113, vol. 4, Senate Docs. 1846.

Mr. A. G. Chatfield's report, on the same, Doc. 77, vol. 3, Ass'y Docs. 1846.

Comptroller Flagg's report as to notices and bond under act of 1846; Doc. 13, vol. 1, Senate Docs. 1847.

LEGAL REFORM.

Memorial of members of the bar of New-York, for reform in legal practice; Doc. 48, vol. 2, Ass'y Docs. 1847.

Communication of Arphaxed Loomis, David Graham, David Dudley Field, in relation to their progress; Doc. 146, vol. 4, Senate Docs. 1847.

Communication from Nicholas Hill, jr., resigning his place as commissioner; Doc. 197, vol. 7, Ass'y Docs. 1847.

Report of Messrs. Graham and Loomis, as to progress and plan; Doc. 201, vol. 7, Ass'y Docs. 1847.

Report of Messrs. Graham, Loomis and Field, in relation to the probable time of making their report, Doc. 235, vol. 8, Ass'y Docs. 1847.

Report of same commissioners in relation to the rate of allowances for cost; Doc. 211, vol. 6, Ass'y Docs. 1848.

Mr. S. G. Raymond's report; Doc. 183, vol. 5, Ass'y Docs. 1848.

Report of commissioners, Loomis, Field, Graham, concerning plans and progress; Doc. 6, vol. 1, Senate Docs. 1849.

Mr. Fuller's report on the second, third and fourth reports of commissioners; Doc. 67, vol. 2, Senate Docs. 1849.

Mr. Bagley's report on the bill to continue in office the commissioners; Doc. 47, vol. 2, Ass'y Docs. 1849.

Mr. White's report on same subject; Doc. 167, vol. 3, Ass'y Docs. 1849.

Mr. Ellwood's report on same bill; Doc. 51, vol. 2, Ass'y Docs. 1849.

Comptroller Fillmore's report as to expenses of commission; Doc. 69, vol. 2, Ass'y Docs. 1849.

Comptroller Washington Hunt's report on expense of commission; Doc. 33, vol. 1, Senate Docs. 1850.

Report of codes complete, by commissioners Loomis, Graham, Field; Doc. 16, vol. 2, Ass'y Docs. 1850.

Dissent of commissioner, David Graham, jr., from certain parts of the Code of Civil Procedure, as reported by the commissioners; Doc. 17, vol. 2, Ass'y Docs. 1850.

Code of Criminal Procedure; Doc. 18, vol. 3, Ass'y Docs. 1850.

Special acts accompanying the report; Doc. 19, vol. 3, Ass'y Docs. 1850.

Mr. W. J. Bacon's report; Doc. 149, vol. 6, Ass'y Docs. 1850.

Copy of an act to establish a Code of Civil Procedure; Doc. 55, vol. 3, Ass'y Docs. 1853.

Legislative committee for examination of accounts of Treasury and Canal Departments.

Report of Senator Laurens Hull, Assemblymen, Michael Hoffman, Edmund J. Porter; Doc. 4, vol. 1, Ass'y Docs. 1842.

Report of same committee on the accounts of Banking Department; Doc. 7, vol. 1, Ass'y Docs. 1842.

Report of committee; Doc. 13, vol. 1, Ass'y Docs. 1843.

Further report; Doc. 18, vol. 2, Ass'y Docs. 1843.

Annual report; Doc. 9, vol. 1, Ass'y Docs. 1844.

do do 36, do 1, Senate Docs. 1845. Doc. 4, vol. 1, Ass'y Docs. 1845.

Annual report; Doc. 7, vol. 1, Ass'y Docs. 1845.

Report on the account of Benjamin Enos, treasurer, Doc. 116, vol. 4, Ass'y Docs. 1846.

Annual report; Doc. 21, vol. 1, Ass'y Docs. 1847.

do	do	65,	do	3,	do	1848.
do	do	83,	do	2,	do	1849.
do	do	7,	do	1,	do	1850.
do	do	23,	do	2,	do	1851.
do	do	14,	do	1,	do	1852.
do	do	8,	do	1,	do	1853.
do	do	25,	do	1,	do	1854.

LEGISLATURE.

Comptroller Wright's communication that the appropriation for their payment is exhausted; Doc. 128, vol. 6, Ass'y Docs. 1853.

DAVID A. LEIGHTON, IRA M. DELAMATER.

Report of Commissioners of Land Office; Doc. 78, vol. 2, Senate Docs. 1847.

DE HURON LENT.

Mr. N. Jones' report, claims; Doc. 48, vol. 2, Senate Docs. 1833.

LE ROY.

Mr. Bockee's report, finance, as to the plan of collecting taxes; Doc. 122, vol. 4, Senate Docs. 1844.

MOSES W. LESTER.

Mr. Mitchell's report; Doc. 30, vol. 1, Ass'y Docs. 1854.

FRANKLIN J. LE VALLEY, JOSHUA WORRELL.

Mr. N. Jones' report, claims; Doc. 53, vol. 2, Senate Docs. 1852.

Mr. Gilbert's report, claims; Doc. 18, vol. 1, Ass'y Docs. 1852.

JAMES S. LIBBY, AND ASSOCIATES.

Report of Commissioners of Land Office concerning grant of land under water at Staten Island; Doc. 121, vol. 5, Ass'y Docs. 1852. Memorial, (page 8,) remonstrance, (page 10.)

LIBERIA.

Memorial for an appropriation to aid emigration; Doc. 19, vol. 1, Senate Docs. 1852.

Mr. Barrow's report, claims; Doc. 100, vol. 3, Ass'y Docs. 1854.

LIBRARY, STATE.

Annual report of trustees; Doc. 6, vol. 1, Senate Docs. 1842.

Mr. Furman's report, joint library committee; Doc. 104, vol. 4, Senate Docs. 1842.

Annual report of trustees; Doc. 50, vol. 1, Senate Docs. 1844.

Report of trustees, as to funds; Doc. 114, vol. 3, Senate Docs. 1844.

Mr. Davezac's minority report, joint library committee; Doc. 176, vol. 7, Ass'y Docs. 1844.

Annual report of trustees; Doc. 10, vol 1, Senate Docs. 1845.

Report on subject of purchasing the "Warden library;" Doc. 11, vol. 1, Ass'y Docs. 1845.

Annual report of trustees; Doc. 4, vol. 1, Senate Docs. 1846.

Annual report; Doc. 21, vol. 1, Senate Docs. 1847.

Report as to donations received through M. Alexander Vattemare; Doc. 129, vol. 4, Senate Docs. 1847; Doc. 227, vol. 8, Ass'y Docs. 1847.

Annual report; Doc. 21, vol. 1, Senate Docs. 1848.

Annual report; Doc. 21, vol. 1, Senate Docs. 1849.

Mr. Bailey's report; Doc. 67, vol. 2, Ass'y Docs. 1849.

Mr. J. W. Beekman's report; Doc. 131, vol. 3, Ass'y Docs. 1849.

Annual report; Doc. 29, vol. 1, Senate Docs. 1850.

Annual report; Doc. 25, vol. 3, Senate Docs. 1851.

Annual report of trustees; Doc. 93, vol. 3, Senate Docs. 1852.

Report of State officers in relation to new building; Doc. 42, vol. 2, Ass'y Docs. 1852.

Annual report of trustees; Doc. 25, vol. 1, Senate Docs. 1853.

Report of trustees in relation to new building; Doc. 92, vol. 3, Ass'y Docs. 1854.

Annual report of trustees; Doc. 138, vol. 4, Ass'y Docs. 1854.

LICENTIOUSNESS.

Mr. Simmons' report, judiciary committee, on suppression, Doc. 159, vol. 7, Ass'y Docs. 1842.

Report of select committee; Doc. 134, vol. 5, Ass'y Docs. 1843.

Mr. Allen's report, judiciary; Doc. 63, vol. 3, Ass'y Docs. 1844.

Mr. Israel Huntington's report; Doc. 23, vol. 1, Ass'y Docs. 1845.

Mr. Van Schoonhoven's report; Doc. 68, vol 2, Senate Docs. 1847.

LIEUTENANT GOVERNOR.

Mr. Talcott's majority report on the bill to provide for the election; Doc. 115, vol. 4, Senate Docs. 1847.

Mr. Joshua A. Spencer's minority report on same subject; same document.

LIFE INSURANCE.

Report of committee on insurance companies, on the proposed amendment of the general law; Doc. 111, vol. 5, Ass'y Docs. 1852.

Memorial of Edmund Blunt; Doc. 121, vol. 6, Ass'y Docs. 1853.

Communication from Morris Franklin, New-York Life Insurance company; Doc. 85, vol. 3, Senate Docs. 1853.

LIGATION OF ARTERIES.

William H. Van Buren's treatise; Doc. 67, (page 27,), Ass'y Docs. 1853.

CORNELIA LILIE, EBEN A. HALL.

Mr. J. A. Lott's report adverse to divorce; Doc. 125, vol. 4, Senate Docs. 1846.

LITERATURE FUND.

Mr. Hillard's report in relation to its distribution; Doc. 135, vol. 5, Ass'y Docs. 1844.

LITTLE FALLS.

Report of Canal Board, relative to a bridge at Bellinger street; Doc. 157, vol. 6, Ass'y Docs. 1844.

Mr. Hand's report, cities and villages, on the act to authorize the inhabitants to borrow money; Doc. 114, vol. 3, Senate Docs. 1845.

Mr. Bokee's report on changing the name of Little Falls; Doc. 74, vol. 3, Senate Docs. 1848.

LIVERPOOL.

Report of Canal Board, on the side cut from the Oswego Canal; Doc. 99, vol. 3, Senate Docs. 1845.

LOAN COMMISSIONERS.

Comptroller Flagg's report as to compensation; Doc. 32, vol. 1, Senate Docs. 1847.

LOANS OF 1792, 1808.

Report of Comptroller Fillmore, as to the time of their expiration; Doc. 176, vol. 3, Ass'y Docs. 1849.

WILLIAM LOGAN, WILLIAM BARNES, WILLIAM STEWART.

Mr. Fisk's report, claims; Doc. 133, vol. 3, Ass'y Docs. 1489.

Mr. Schoonmaker's report, claims; Doc. 67, vol. 2, Senate Docs. 1850.

JOHN LOCHENTELLY, DAVID LEMONIER.

Mr. Gleason's report; Doc. 33, vol. 1, Ass'y Docs. 1854.

LOCKS ON ERIE CANAL.

Report of the Canal Commissioners, in answer to a resolution of enquiry, as to length and width of enlarged locks—size and form of boats—form and capacity of the prism of enlarged canal; Doc. 50, vol. 2, Senate Docs. 1849.

Report of State Engineer, H. C. Seymour, on lengthening; Doc. 67, vol. 3, Ass'y Docs. 1851.

LOCKS—(at Lockport)

Report of Canal Commissioner, Bissell; Doc. 98, vol. 3, Senate Docs. 1843.

Report of Canal Board with copies of contracts; Doc. 130, vol. 4, Senate Docs. 1844.

Report of Canal Commissioner Bissell; Doc. 131, vol. 5, Ass'y Docs. 1844.

Report of Canal Commissioners; Doc. 35, vol. 2, Ass'y Docs, 1846.

Mr. Bishop Perkins' report as to the removal of material; Doc. 185, vol. 5, Ass'y Docs. 1846.

ELIZABETH LUDWICK—(an Indian.)

Mr. Folsom's report; Doc. 137, vol. 4, Senate Docs. 1846.

LUNATIC ASYLUM—STATE.

Report of commissioners, W. H. Sherman, T. S. Faxon, James Platt, to the Governor; Doc. E., of Doc. 2, vol. 1, Senate Docs. 1842.

Same in vol. 1, Ass'y Docs. 1842.

Report of trustees; Doc. 20, vol. 1, Senate Docs. 1842. (Containing statistics and descriptions of other Institutions and examinations of their mode of treatment.)

Report of secretary, Doc. B., accompanying Doc. 2, Senate Docs. 1843. Doc. B., Doc 3, vol. 1, Ass'y Docs. 1843.

Report of managers; Doc. 50, vol. 3, Ass'y Docs. 1843.

Mr. Barlow's majority report, medical societies; Doc. 127, vol. 4, Senate Docs. 1844.

Mr. Backus' minority report, same committee; Doc. 128, vol. 4, Senate Docs. 1844.

Annual report of managers; Doc. 21, vol. 1, Ass'y Docs. 1844. (This contains Miss Dix's exhibit of the condition of the insane, in the various poor houses in the State.)

Mr. Rossman's minority report, select committee; Doc. 94, vol. 3, Ass'y Docs. 1844.

Mr. Ashley Sampson's majority report; select committee; Doc. 95, vol. 3, Ass'y Docs. 1844.

Annual report; Doc. 29, vol. 1, Ass'y Docs. 1845.

Mr. T. F. Bockee's report; Doc. 12, vol. 1, Senate Docs. 1845.

Annual report; Doc. 25, vol. 1, Senate Docs. 1846.

Mr. Barlow's report; Doc. 56, vol. 2, Senate Docs. 1846.

Annual report; Doc. 30, vol. 1, Senate Docs. 1847.

Annual report of managers; Doc. 20, vol. 1, Senate Docs. 1848.

Annual report; Doc. 90, vol. 2, Ass'y Docs. 1849.
do do 57, do 2, Senate Docs. 1850.
do do 42, do 2, do 1851.

Annual report; Doc. 46, vol. 1, Senate Docs. 1852.
do do 27, do 1, do 1853.
do do 76, do 3, Ass'y Docs. 1854.

LUNATICS IN PRISONS.

Mr. J. A. Yard's report; Doc. 41, vol. 3, Ass'y Docs. 1850.

ELAM LYNDS.

Memorial of, as late keeper of Sing Sing prison; Doc. 91, vol. 2, Senate Docs. 1844.

Mr. H. Putnam's report, select committee, Doc. 135, vol. 4, Senate Docs. 1844.

REUBEN LYON.

Mr. Severance's report, claims; Doc. 35, vol. 2, Ass'y Docs. 1851.

W. J. McALPINE—(State Engineer and Surveyor.)

Report in relation to the clerical force in his department; Doc. 18, vol. 1, Senate Docs. 1853.

Report in relation to the improvement of the navigation of the Hudson river; Doc. 23, vol. 1, Senate Docs. 1853.

Report in relation to railway turnouts and switches; Doc. 31, vol. 1, Senate Docs. 1853.

Report of the freight carried on the railways of the State; Doc. 59, vol. 2, Senate Docs. 1853.

Report as to the cost of finishing the canals; Doc. 64, vol. 2, Senate Docs. 1853.

Report on the railways of the State; Doc. 10, vol. 1, Ass'y Docs. 1853.

Report on the canals of the State; Doc. 28, vol. 2, Ass'y Docs. 1853.

Report in relation to the improvement of the outlet of the Owasco lake; Doc. 37, vol. 2, Ass'y Docs. 1853.

Report on the number of engineers employed; Doc. 70, vol. 3, Ass'y Docs. 1853.

Report on railroad statistics; Doc. 120, vol. 3, Ass'y Docs. 1854.

ROBERT McBRIDE

Report of Canal Board in relation to work on canal at Rochester; Doc. 215, vol. 6, Ass'y Docs. 1848.

Mr. Stevenson's report; Doc. 193, vol. 3, Ass'y Docs. 1849.

Report of committee on claims; Doc. 64, vol. 4, Ass'y Docs. 1850.

JAMES McCABE.

Mr. Schoonmaker's majority report, claims; Doc. 60, vol. 2, Senate Docs. 1850.

Report of committee on claims; Doc. 15, vol. 1, Ass'y Docs. 1851.

WILLIAM McCRACKEN.

Mr. Schoonmaker's report; Doc. 62, vol. 2, Senate Docs. 1850.

A. P McDONALD, JOHN H. NICHOLLS, CHARLES J. DE GRAW, HENRY DE GRAW.

Mr. Ward's report, claims; Doc. 36, vol. 1, Senate Docs. 1852.

ALEXANDER McGHEE.

Mr. N. Jones' report, claims; Doc. 22, vol. 1, Senate Docs. 1852.

CHARLES McKNIGHT'S HEIRS.

Attorney General Van Buren's report; Doc. 63, vol. 2, Senate Docs. 1845.

Mr. Porter's report, claims; Doc. 79, vol. 2, Senate Docs. 1845.

Attorney General Van Buren's report; Doc. 196, vol. 5, Ass'y Docs. 1846.

WILLLIAM McLACHLIN, (or Laughin.)

Report of Canal Board; Doc. 109, vol. 5, Ass'y Docs. 1844.

Mr. Johnson's report, claims; Doc. 12, vol. 1, Senate Docs. 1845. Doc. 26, vol. 1, Senate Docs. 1845.

ALEXANDER McLEOD.

Correspondence of President Tyler, Governor Seward, Daniel Webster, the British Minister, Mr. Fox, Attorney-Generals, I. J. Crittenden, and Willis Hall, Judge Nelson, concerning arrest and trial; Doc. C., Doc. 2, vol. 1, Senate Docs. 1842. Same in vol. 1, Ass'y Docs. 1842.

ZALMON J. McMASTER, JACOB S. MERRITT.

Mr. Lawrence's report, claims; Doc. 46, vol. 1, Senate Docs. 1844.

Mr. N. Jones' report, claims; Doc. 45, vol. 2, Senate Docs. 1853.

M. William Clark's report; Doc. 15, vol. 1, Senate Docs. 1854.

Further report, W. Clark; Doc. 42, vol. 1, Senate Docs. 1854.

JAMES McNAIR.

Mr. McNamara's report; Doc. 253, vol. 8, Ass'y Docs. 1847.

Mr. Miller's report, claims; Doc. 107, vol. 3, Ass'y Docs. 1854.

MADISON UNIVERSITY.

Mr. Burchard's report; Doc. 158, vol. 6, Ass'y Docs. 1847.

Mr. Pruyn's report; Doc. 111, vol. 3, Ass'y Docs. 1848.

Memorial of Daniel Haskill, B. W. Babcock, and others; Doc. 37, vol. 2, Senate Docs. 1849.

Remonstrance of Friend Humphrey, Ira Harris and others; Doc. 52, vol. 2, Senate Docs. 1849.

Report of condition made to Regents of the University; Doc. 77, (page 116) vol. 2, Senate Docs. 1854.

MAINE.

Resolutions of Legislature in relation to limitation of office of President to one term; Doc. 28, vol. 2, Ass'y Docs. 1842.

Resolutions relative to the imprisonment of citizens of that State in other States; Doc. 87, vol. 3, Senate Docs. 1843.

Resolutions for the abolition of the Military Academy at West Point; Doc. 115, vol. 4, Ass'y Docs. 1843.

MAIN AND HAMBURGH-STREET CANAL.

Report of Canal Commissioners; Doc. 207, vol. 6, Ass'y Docs. 1845.

Report of Canal Board; Doc. 152, vol. 6, Ass'y Docs. 1847.

PAUL P. MAINE, S. CHAPMAN.

Report of Attorney-General Barker, in relation to lot 38, north west part of Oneida Reservation; Doc. 58, vol. 3, Ass'y Docs. 1843.

GEORGE W. MANCHESTER.

Mr. Fitzhugh's report; Doc. 52, vol. 2, Ass'y Docs. 1849.

JANE MANDEVILLE.

Mr. Boardman's report; Doc. 87, vol. 3, Ass'y Docs. 1849.

JAMES R. MANLEY.

Biographic sketch in transactions of State Medical Society; Doc. 88, (page 51,) vol. 2, Ass'y Docs. 1852.

MALONE VILLAGE, (Arsenal Green.)

Mr. Guinnip's report on sale of lot; Doc. 14, vol. 1, Senate Docs 1851.

JOHN JACOB MANG. (Thomas Wheeler, administrator.)

Report of Mr. Johnson, claims, on petition of administrators, Thomas Wheeler, Harvey Alvord; Doc. 98, vol. 3, Senate Docs. 1845.

Mr. G. Stevens' report; Doc. 28, vol. 2, Ass'y Docs. 1851.

GARRET MANN.

Mr. Mitchell's report, claims, Doc. 140, vol. 4, Ass'y Docs. 1854.

MANOR LAND TILES.

Mr. Simmons' report, judiciary; Doc. 177, vol. 7, Ass'y Docs. 1842.

Mr. Loomis' report, judiciary; Doc. 181, vol. 7, Ass'y Docs. 1842.

Mr. W. F. Allen's report, judiciary; Doc. 183, vol. 7, Ass'y Docs. 1844. (This contains a copy of the patent.)

Mr. Whipple's report, select committee; Doc. 189, vol. 7, Ass'y Docs. 1844. (This contains a copy of the lease.)

Mr. Constant's majority report; Doc. 222, vol. 6, Ass'y Docs. 1845. (Contains letters from S. Van Rensselaer and John A. King.)

Report of committee on claims, on Jonas A. Hughston's petition for compensation for services as district attorney of Delaware Co., during 1845; Doc. 50, vol. 2, Ass'y Docs. 1845.

Mr. Ira Harris' minority report on the relations between landlord and tenant; Doc. 247, vol. 7, Ass'y Docs. 1845.

Mr. Joshua A. Spencer's majority report, on the same; Doc. 92, vol. 3, Senate Docs. 1846.

Mr. Van Schoonhoven's minority report on same; Doc. 107, vol. 4, Senate Docs. 1846.

Mr. Joshua A. Spencer's report, finance, on the taxation of leasehold estates; Doc. 115, vol. 4, Senate Docs. 1846.

Mr. Porter's report, finance, on the taxation of leasehold estates; Doc. 135, vol. 4, Senate Docs. 1846.

Mr. Beer's report on the act to equalize taxation; Doc. 139, vol. 4, Senate Docs. 1846.

Mr. Beer's report on the act to abolish distress for rent; Doc. 140, vol. 4, Senate Docs. 1846.

Mr. Lott's report, judiciary, on the petition for pardon of persons convicted of offences growing out of the relation of landlord and tenant; Doc. 142, vol. 4, Senate Docs. 1846.

Mr. Bishops Perkins' resolutions relative to leasehold estates; Doc. 12, vol. 1, Ass'y Docs. 1846.

Mr. S. J. Tilden's report; Doc. 156, vol. 5, Ass'y Docs. 1846.

Mr. Ira Harris' resolutions; Doc. 159, vol. 5, Ass'y Docs. 1846.

Mr. Worden's report as to rent charges; Doc. 223, vol. 6, Ass'y Docs. 1846.

Memorial of Stephen Van Rensselaer, setting forth the operation of the law for equalizing taxation; Doc. 47, vol. 2, Senate Docs. 1847.

Mr. J. E. Beers' report, claims, on Jonas A. Hughston's memorial for services as district attorney of Delaware, during 1845; Doc. 52, vol. 2, Ass'y Docs. 1847.

Blandina Dudley's memorial, on same subject; Doc. 56, vol. 2, Senate Docs. 1847.

Report of sums paid by State for maintaining laws in Delaware and Columbia counties; Doc. 99, vol. 2, Ass'y Docs. 1847.

Mr. Allaben's majority report on leasehold estates and the difficulties between landlord and tenant; Doc. 162, vol. 6, Ass'y Docs. 1847.

Mr. Bowdish's report on leasehold estates; Doc. 261, vol. 8, Ass'y Docs. 1847.

Mr. Hammond's report on same subject; Doc. 263, 8, vol. Ass'y Docs. 1847.

Mr. Johnson's resolutions in relation to grants of lands from the crown of Great Britain, to the colonial government of New-York; Doc. 31, vol. 2, Senate Docs. 1848.

Mr. J. L. Lawrence's report in regard to title of Pulteney and Hornby estate; Doc. 61, vol. 2, Senate Docs. 1848.

Mr. Treadwell's resolution in relation to grants of lands from the crown of Great Britain, to the colonial government of New-York; Doc. 29, vol. 1, Senate Docs. 1848.

Mr. Myer's minority report on the relation of landlord and tenant; Doc. 126, vol. 5, Ass'y Docs. 1848.

Mr. Willett's majority report on same subject; Doc. 125, vol. 3, Ass'y Docs. 1848.

Mr. Coe's report, on expenses incurred in Ulster county; Doc. 175, vol. 5, Ass'y Docs. 1848.

Attorney-General Chatfield's report, on progress of suits; Doc. 21, vol. 1, Senate Docs. 1850.

Mr. Joel B. Nott's report on the state of the suits brought by the Attorney-General; Doc. 24, vol. 3, Ass'y Docs. 1850.

Mr. E. Pratt's report; Doc. 80, vol. 5, Ass'y Docs. 1850.

Mr. James Monroe's report in relation to the expenses incurred by Delaware and Ulster; 111, vol. 5, Ass'y Docs. 1850.

Mr. Carroll's resolutions, with staistics, in relation to Rensselaerwick; Doc. 84, vol. 3, Senate Docs. 1850.

Mr. Schoonmaker's report on the bill to stay proceedings in certain cases; Doc. 9, vol. 1, Senate Docs. 1851.

Attorney-General Chatfield's report on the condition of the suit brought by the State; Doc. 27, vol. 2, Senate Docs. 1851.

Mr. Schoonmaker's minority report on the bill to provide for the extinguishment of feudal tenures; Doc. 96, vol. 3, Senate Docs. 1851.

Mr. Gleason's majority report in relation to the bill to stay proceedings; Doc. 132, vol. 5, Ass'y Docs. 1851.

Mr. Maurice's minority report on the same subject; Doc. 133, vol. 5, Ass'y Docs. 1851.

Mr. Sayles' report; Doc. 92, vol. 5, Ass'y Docs. 1852.

Attorney-General Chatfield's report on the Indian title to the manor lands; Doc. 59, vol. 3, Ass'y Docs. 1853.

Mr. Stewarts' report on the same subject; Doc. 79, vol. 3, Ass'y Docs. 1853.

Communication from Gov. Seymour, in relation to resistance of service of process; Doc. 119, vol. 6, Ass'y Docs. 1853.

Mr. A. B. Rose's majority report, against claims of the Mohawk and Stockbridge Indians to manor lands; Doc. 106, vol. 3, Ass'y Docs. 1854.

Mr. Jesse E. Willis, minority report, in favor of the claim; Doc. 106, vol. 3, Ass'y Docs. 1854.

MANUFACTURING INCORPORATIONS.

Attorney-General Van Buren's report on constitutionality; Doc. 59, vol. 2, Senate Docs. 1845.

Mr. Barlow's report on general law; Doc. 13, vol. 1, Senate Docs. 1845.

Mr. Barlow's report, (Seth S. Jones' application for a manufacturing corporation at Rochester); Doc. 65, vol. 2, Senate Docs 1846.

Mr. Barlow's report on the provisions of the new constitution; Doc. 53, vol. 2, Senate Docs. 1847.

Mr. Barlow's conference report on the bill for general incorporation; Doc. 116, vol. 4, Senate Docs. 1847.

Mr. Denniston's further conference report; Doc. 143, vol. 4, Senate Docs. 1847.

Mr. Bascom's conference report; Doc. 240, vol. 8, Ass'y Docs. 1847.

The general act; Doc. 28, vol. 1, Senate Docs. 1848.

MAPS AND PLANS OF PUBLIC WORKS.

Mr. W. A. Bird's report, in relation to their preservation; Doc. 154, vol. 7, Ass'y Docs. 1843.

Communication of Surveyor-General, Nathaniel Jones, in relation to those on file, of such works as have received aid from the State; Doc. 41, vol. 3, Ass'y Docs. 1843.

ALBERT MARCELLUS.

Mr. Beach's report ; Doc. 123, vol. 3, Ass'y Docs. 1848.

Mr. McCarty's report, claims; Doc. 153, vol. 5, Ass'y Docs. 1848.

MARINE COURT.

Report of Justice Waterbury, as to fees received ; Doc. 215, vol. 6, Ass'y Docs. 1846.

Report of business ; Doc. 183, vol. 3, Ass'y Docs. 1849.

MARINERS' FAMILY INDUSTRIAL SOCIETY.

Report, Doc. 73, vol. 2, Senate Docs. 1854.

MARINE HOSPITAL.

Report of Comptroller Flagg in relation to Mariners' Fund; Doc. 29, vol. 1, Senate Docs. 1845.

Mr. Orville Clark's report relative to the management of the fund ; Doc. 95, vol. 3, Senate Docs. 1847.

Memorial of commissioners of health of New-York, concerning government; Doc. 196, vol. 7, Ass'y Docs. 1847.

Memorial of Commissioners of Emigration, soliciting appropriation; Doc. 46, vol. 2, Senate Docs. 1848.

Opinions of Justices McLean, Grier and Daniel, of the Supreme Court of the United States, on the unconstitutionality of the tax paid by merchants; Doc. 74, vol. 3, Senate Docs. 1849.

Comptroller Fillmore and Attorney-General Jordan, communication respecting the monies paid by merchants under protest; Doc. 206, vol. 5, Ass'y Docs. 1849.

Communication from Gov. Fish and Comptroller Fillmore as to funds ; Doc. 39, vol. 1, Ass'y Docs. 1849.

Communication of Gov. Fish, with statement of Dr. H. Campbell Stewart ; Doc. 154, vol. 6, Ass'y Docs. 1850.

Remonstrance of assistant physicians; Doc. 168, vol. 6, Ass'y Docs. 1850.

Mr. Wakeman's report in relation to the physician, with statements of commissioners ; Doc. 155, vol. 6, Ass'y Docs. 1851.

Mr. W. A. Wheeler's report on the subject of the moneys paid under protest ; Doc. 97, vol. 4, Ass'y Docs. 1851.

MARLETT AND DUNHAM.

Report of Canal Board; Doc. 56, vol. 3, Ass'y Docs. 1844.

Mr. Gorham's report, claims; Doc. 97, vol. 3, Ass'y Docs. 1844.

MARRIED WOMEN.

Mr. O'Sullivan's report, judiciary; Doc. 184, vol. 7, Ass'y Docs. 1842.

Mr. Allen's report, judiciary; Doc. 96, vol. 3, Ass'y Docs. 1844.

Mr. B. F. Coopers' majority report, judiciary; Doc. 219, vol. 6, Ass'y Docs. 1846.

AGNES MARTIN.

Mr. S. A. Brown's report, aliens; Doc. 172, vol. 5, Ass'y Docs. 1845.

MOSES L. MARTIN.

Mr. J. B. Nott's report; Doc. 124, vol 5, Ass'y Docs. 1850.

THOMAS MARVIN.

Mr. Schoonmaker's report, claims; Doc. 58, vol. 2, Senate Docs. 1850.

MARYLAND.

Resolution of general assembly, concerning abolition of slavery in District of Columbia; Doc. 149, vol. 7, Ass'y Docs. 1842.

Resolutions of same concerning the inteference of Congress with the domestic institutions of the States; Doc. 193, vol. 7, Ass'y Docs. 1844.

Resolutions of same concerning slavery; Doc. 194, vol. 8, Ass'y Docs. 1850.

MASSACHUSETTS.

Resolutions of State, relative to such an amendment of the Constitution of the United States, as would confine the basis of representation to free persons; Doc. 52, vol. 3, Ass'y Docs. 1844.

Resolutions of State, on the action of Virginia, in returning certain resolutions, heretofore passed by Massachusetts, concerning the representation of free persons alone; Doc. 170, vol. 7, Ass'y Docs. 1844.

Resolutions of State concerning admission of Texes; Doc. 175, vol. 7, Ass'y Docs. 1844.

Resolutions concerning French spoliations; Doc. 184, vol. 7, Ass'y Docs. 1844.

JOHN C. MATHER, (Canal Commissioner.)

Mr. Champlain's report from a select committee of investigation, presenting a resolution for impeachment; Doc. 103, vol. 4, Ass'y Docs. 1853. (In the appendix is contained the testimony.)

Communication in denial of the charges made, and remonstrating against the action of the committee; Doc 104, vol. 4, Ass'y Docs. 1853.

Communication in answer to the report and resolutions of impeachment of the select committee of the Assembly; Doc. 111, vol. 4, Ass'y Docs. 1853.

Report of Auditor Schoonmaker, in relation to draft drawn October 21st, 1853; Doc. 135, vol. 4, Ass'y Docs. 1854.

Further report on same subject; Doc. 141, vol. 4, Ass'y Docs. 1854.

SIMON MATTISON.

Mr. Jackson's report, claims; Doc. 127, vol. 5, Ass'y Docs. 1843.

Report of Canal Appraisers; Doc. 145, vol. 3, Ass'y Docs. 1849.

WESTFALL MAY.

Mr. A. C. Hand's report, grievances; Doc. 20, vol. 1, Senate Docs. 1846.

JOHN MEAD.

Mr. Mark's report, claims; Doc. 83, vol. 2, Ass'y Docs. 1847.

JAMES R. MEARS, WILLIAM A. MEARS.

Mr. W. A. Gilbert's report, claims; Doc. 24, vol. 1, Ass'y Docs. 1852.

MECHANIC LABOR IN STATE PRISONS.

Mr. Wier's report; Doc. 65, vol. 4, Ass'y Docs. 1842.

Report of committee on State prisons; Doc. 99, vol. 3, Senate Docs. 1843.

Resolutions of Albany meeting; Doc. 156, vol. 5, Ass'y Docs. 1843.

MECHANICS' STATE ASSOCIATION.

Report of Commissioners of the Land Office, on petition for a room in the State Hall; Doc. 163, vol. 5, Ass'y Docs. 1843.

MECHANICS' AND TRADERS' SAVINGS INSTITUTION, New-York.

Mr. Gale's minority report; Doc. 40, vol. 2, Ass'y Docs. 1852.

ALFRED MEDBURY AND BYRON POOLE.

Mr. Williams' report, claims; Doc. 33, vol. 1, Senate Docs. 1853.

MEDICAL MEN—(Society for the relief of widows and orphans.)

Mr. S. Ely's report; Doc. 53, vol. 2, Senate Docs. 1843.

MEDICAL COLLEGES.

Mr. Hubbard's report on appropriations; Doc. 136, vol. 5, Ass'y Docs. 1844.

Mr. Tefft's report on college of physicians and surgeons, New-York; Doc. 76, vol. 3, Ass'y Docs. 1845.

MEDICAL PRACTICE.

Mr. Williams' report, select committee, on the petitions for repeal of restrictions; Doc. 62, vol. 3, Ass'y Docs. 1843.

Mr. Lawrence's report, printing; Doc. 30, vol. 1, Senate Docs. 1844.

Mr. Scott's report, select committee; Doc. 31, vol. 1, Senate Docs. 1844.

Remonstrance of State Medical Society; Doc. 55, vol. 2, Senate Docs. 1844.

Amendments to a proposed bill; Doc. 63, vol. 2, Senate Docs. 1844.

Mr. Carpenter's report; Doc. 60, vol. 3, Ass'y Docs. 1844.

Mr. Tuthill's report in relation to bleeding; Doc. 148, vol. 5, Ass'y Docs. 1851.

Mr. Hooker's report on medical education, made to American Medical Association; Doc. 85, (page 93,) vol. 2, Ass'y Docs. 1852.

MEDICAL SOCIETY, STATE.

Communication in regard to collection of statictics of births, marriages and deaths; Doc. 80, vol. 3, Senate Docs. 1850.

Statement respecting publication of transactions; Doc. 173, vol. 6, Ass'y Docs. 1850.

Transactions of annual meeting of 1850, held at Albany; Doc. 174, vol. 6, Ass'y Docs. 1850.

Transactions of annual meeting of 1851, held at Albany; Doc. 125, vol. 4, Ass'y Docs. 1851.

Transactions of annual meeting of 1852, held at Albany; Doc. 85, vol. 2, Ass'y Docs. 1825.

Transactions of annual meeting of 1853, held at Albany; Doc. 67, vol. 3, Ass'y Docs. 1853.

Transactions of annual meeting of 1854, held at Albany; Doc. 133, vol. 4, Ass'y Docs. 1854.

MEMBERS OF LEGISLATURE ELECTED TO CONGRESS.

Mr. S. J. Wilkins' majority report on question whether any constitutional provision exists rendering a person, elected to the office of representative in Congress, disqualified to retain his seat in the Legislature; Doc. 48, vol. 2, Senate Docs. 1849.

Mr. J. Fine's minority report, on same question; Doc. 49, vol. 2, Senate Docs. 1849.

Mr. Carroll's resolutions in respect to the election of Marius Schoonmaker; Doc. 62, vol. 2, Senate Docs. 1851.

MERCHANDIZE, PROVISIONS, PRODUCE.

Abstract of returns of weighers, inspectors, measurers, prepared by the Secretary of State, Samuel Young; Doc. 139, vol. 7, Ass'y Docs. 1842.

MERCHANTS' AND MECHANICS' BANK, OSWEGO.

Report of D. B. St. John, Superintendent of Bank Department; Doc. 68, vol. 2, Senate Docs. 1854.

Mr. Sherrill's report; Doc. 95, vol. 2, Senate Docs. 1854.

JOHN MERRELL.

Report of committee on claims; Doc. 66, vol. 2, Ass'y Docs. 1852.

Mr. N. Jones' report, claims; Doc. 53, vol. 2, Ass'y Docs. 1853.

JOHN MERIAM, JOHN CARR, BENJAMIN D. UTTER, ISAAC WOOD.

Report of Canal Board; Doc. 138, vol. 5, Ass'y Docs. 1844.

Mr. Teffts' report; Doc. 74, vol. 3, Ass'y Docs. 1845.

Mr. Pitt's report, claims; Doc. 38, vol. 2, Ass'y Docs. 1846.

ELIJAH E. MERRILL, DANIEL P. MCDONALD, ZENAS BARNUM.

Mr. Tupper's report, claims; Doc. 111, vol. 5, Ass'y Docs. 1842.

SAMUEL MERRY'S Representatives, (JOHN DE WOLF, and associates.)

Report of Commissioners of Land Office on a forfeiture; Doc. 71, vol. 3, Ass'y Docs. 1844.

METROPOLITAN COLLEGE.

Mr. W. Taylor's minority report on incorporation; Doc. 87, vol. 2, 1852.

MEXICO.

Mr. Bokee's resolution in relation to war with Mexico; Doc. 3, vol. 1, Senate Docs. 1848.

Report of majority of select committee, on so much of Governor Young's message as relates to the war with Mexico; Doc. 19, vol. 1, Senate Docs. 1848.

Report of minority of same committee, on same subject; same Doc. and vol.

MICHIGAN.

Resolutions of Legislature concerning lake harbors and commerce; Doc. 103, vol. 4, Ass'y Docs. 1843.

CLARISSA MILLARD, CORNELIA MILLARD.

Mr. Tupper's report, claims; Doc. 112, vol. 5, Ass'y Docs. 1842.

JULIUS FREDERICK. KEILMAN MILLER.

Mr. Vanderbilt's report; Doc. 24, vol. 1, Senate Docs. 1852.

MARIA MILLER.

Report of committee on canals, with opinion of Attorney-General Chatfield, and other statements annexed; Doc. 95, vol. 4, Ass'y Docs. 1851.

MILITIA AND PUBLIC DEFENCE.

Communication from Governor Seward, respecting accounts between ordnance department of United States and this State; Doc. 27, vol. 2, Senate Docs. 1842.

Mr. Griffin's report; Doc. 97, vol. Ass'y Docs. 1842.

Mr. Erastus Root's report; Doc. vol. 3, Senate Docs. 1843.

Mr. F. E. Erwin's majority report; Doc. 42, vol. 3, Ass'y Docs. 1848.

Minority report; Doc. 54, vol. 3, Ass'y Docs. 1843.

Proceedings of State Military Convention, held at Albany, January 25, 1843; Doc. 46, vol. 3, Ass'y Docs. 1843.

Mr. McMurray's report; Doc. 175, vol. 2. Ass'y Docs. 1843.

Mr. John A. Lott's report as to Charles Baldwin and Hallock Stilwell, marshals of court martial; Doc. 83, vol. 2, Senate Docs. 1844.

Mr. C. M. Turner's report; Doc. 64, vol. 3, Ass'y Docs. 1844.

Mr. John Sweeny's minority report; Doc. 109, vol. 4, Ass'y Docs. 1845.

Mr. Fonda's majority report; Doc. 110, vol. 4, Ass'y Docs. 1845.

Memorial of a military convention of the 40th brigade for an efficient organization; Doc. 67, vol. 2, Senate Docs 1846.

Mr. W. S. Sherwood's resolutions for an efficient organization; Doc. 13, vol. 1, Ass'y Docs. 1846.

Mr. N. K. Hall's minority report; Doc. 211, vol. 6, Ass'y Docs. 1846.

Report of amount received for fines and commutations under act of May 3, 1846; Doc. 219, vol. 7, Ass'y Docs. 1847.

Mr. William Hall's report on reorganization of the 12th regiment of first division; Doc. 52, vol. 2, Senate Docs. 1848.

Mr. Levi Harris' report on organization and enrolment; Doc. 54, vol. 3, Ass'y Docs. 1851.

Mr. L. Harris' further report; Doc. 113, vol. 4, Ass'y Docs. 1851.

Report of General John Watts De Peyster, in relation to the militia in Europe; Doc. 74, vol. 3, Senate Docs. 1853.

Report of Z. T. Bentley, Lansing B. Swan and Adjutant-General, R. E. Temple, commissioners to codify and amend the militia laws; Doc. 66, vol. 2, Senate Docs. 1853.

Report of General Charles W. Sanford, in relation to fines and commutation; Doc. 30, vol. 2, Ass'y Docs. 1853.

Report of Attorney General, Ogden Hoffman, in relation to militia acts of Oct., 21st, 1814, and April 21st, 1818.

JOHN D. MILLINER.

Mr. Barrow's report, claims ; Doc. 81, Ass'y Docs. 1854.

JOHN MILLS.

Report of Willis Hall, select committee, in relation to interment in Capitol Park; Doc. 145, vol. 5, Ass'y Docs. 1843.

WARREN MILLS.

Mr. Cornwell's report in relation to payment for a lock in Chemung canal; Doc. 204, vol. 7, Ass'y Docs. 1847.

MINDEN—(Town of.)

Mr. McCarty's report, claims; Doc. 100. vol. 3, Ass'y Docs. 1848.

MINING AND SMELTING.

Mr. Palmer Cleveland's memorial respecting the employment of convicts; Doc. 96, vol. 3, Senate Docs. 1843.

MISSISSIPPI.

Resolutions of Legislature relative to the annexation of Texas; Doc. 199, vol. 7, Ass'y Docs. 1842. Doc. 202, vol. 7, Ass'y Docs. 1844.

Resolutions of Legislature concerning slavery; Doc. 179, vol. 8, Ass'y Docs. 1850.

Resolutions of same, in relation to the grant of land to the soldiers of the war with Mexico; Doc. 188, vol. 8, Ass'y Docs. 1850.

MISSOURI.

Resolutions of Legislature, relative to army of United States; Doc. 164, vol. 6, Ass'y Docs. 1847.

Resolutions of State in relation to slavery; Doc. 229, vol. 5, Ass'y Docs. 1849.

AGNES MITCHELL.

Mr. Tupper's report, claims; Doc. 22, vol. 22, Ass'y Docs. 1842.

Mr. Ruger's report, claims; Doc. 26, vol. 1, Senate Docs. 1843.

FERDINAND MONGIN, ASENATH MONGIN.

Mr. S. A. Brown's report, aliens; Doc. 169, vol. 5, Ass'y Docs. 1845.

ROBERT MONELL.

Report as clerk of Supreme court, Geneva, of office expenses; Doc. 50, vol. 2, Senate Docs. 1846.

MONTAUK LANDS.

Mr. Rose's report on incorporation of proprietors; Doc. 12, vol. Ass'y Docs. 1848.

MONTGOMERY MINING COMPANY.

Mr. Rumsey's report; Doc. 79, vol. 3, Ass'y Docs. 1851.

MONTEZUMA SALT SPRINGS.

Annual report of superintendent; Doc. 49, vol. 2, Senate Docs. 1842.

Mr. Furman's report, committee on manufactures; Doc. 91, vol. 4, Senate Docs. 1842.

Annual report; Doc. 19, vol. 1, Senate Docs. 1844.
do do 11, do 1, do 1845.
do do 41, do 2, do 1846.

Mr. Barlow's report, manufactures, as to regulations of superintendent; Doc. 70, vol. 2, Senate Docs. 1846.

Mr. Samuel Bell's report in relation to appropriation to rebuild reservoir; Doc. 56, vol. 2, Ass'y Docs. 1847.

Report of Commissioners of Land Office, as to general condition; Doc. 121, vol. 4, Senate Docs. 1847.

ZEBULON MOORE.

Report of committee on claims; Doc. 12, vol. 1, Senate Docs. 1849.

Mr. Orlando Allen's report; Doc. 73, vol. 4, Ass'y Docs. 1850.

JOHN MOOT.

Report of the Commissioners of the Land Office; Doc. 8, vol. 1, Senate Docs. 1846.

MORTGAGE SALES.

Mr. E. F. Warren's report; Doc. 89, vol. 3, Ass'y Docs. 1843.

CHRISTOPHER MORGAN, (Secretary of State.)

(The entries will be found at length under the head of the different subjects.)

SCHOOLS AND FREE SCHOOLS.

Doc. 98, vol. 3, Ass'y Docs. 1848. Doc. 14, vol. 1, Ass'y Docs. 1849. Doc. 20, vol. 2, Ass'y Docs. 1849. Doc. 202, vol. 5, Ass'y Docs. 1849. Doc. 50, vol. 4, Ass'y Docs. 1850. Doc. 21, vol. 1, Ass'y Docs. 1851.

POOR OF STATE.

Doc. 79, vol. 3, Senate Docs. 1848. Doc. 83, vol. 3, Senate Docs. 1849. Doc. 169, vol. 6, Ass'y Docs. 1850.

CRIME.

Doc. 193, vol. 6, Ass'y Docs. 1848. Doc. 242, vol. 5, Ass'y Docs. 1849. Doc. 195, vol. 8, Ass'y Docs. 1850. Doc. 140, vol. 5, Ass'y Docs. 1851.

BIRTHS, MARRIAGES AND DEATHS.

Doc. 73, vol. 3, Senate Docs. 1848, Doc. 86, vol. 3, Senate Docs. 1849.

NATURAL HISTORY.

Doc. 124, vol. 4, Ass'y Docs. 1851. Doc. 23, vol. 1, Ass'y Docs. 1852.

PARDONS.

Doc. 66, vol. 2, Senate Docs. 1848.

PRINTING.

Doc. 15, vol. 1, Senate Docs. 1849.

RAILROADS.

Doc. 132, vol. 5, Ass'y Docs. 1848. Doc. 182, vol. 3, Ass'y Docs. 1849.

REGISTER, (New-York.)

Doc. 77, vol. 3, Senate Docs. 1849.

ST. REGIS.

Doc. 27, vol., 3, Ass'y Docs. 1850.

SURROGATES.

Doc. 57, vol. 3, Ass'y Docs. 1848.

CAYUGA INDIANS.

Doc. 61, vol. 3, Ass'y Docs. 1848.

COLONIAL HISTORY.

Doc. 188, vol. 3, Ass'y Docs. 1849.

BENJAMIN BIRDSALL.

Doc. 162, vol. 3, Ass'y Docs. 1849.

DIGEST SCHOOL LAW.

Doc. 115, vol. 3, Ass'y Docs. 1848.

CLERK, (New-York.)

Doc. 78, vol. 3, Senate Docs. 1849. Doc. 152, vol. 6, Ass'y Docs. 1850.

GEOLOGICAL SURVEY.

Doc. 124, vol. 4, Ass'y Docs. 1851. Doc. 23, vol. 1, Ass'y Docs. 1852.

DAVIDSON MOSHER.

Mr. Ward's report; Doc. 113, vol. 3, Ass'y Docs. 1849.

DIGHTEN Z. MOSHER.

Mr. Develin's report, relative to the oath of office; Doc. 166, vol. 6, Ass'y Docs. 1847.

J. B. MOSS.

Report of Canal Commissioners; Doc. 185, vol. 7, Ass'y Docs. Docs. 1847.

REPORT OF CANAL BOARD.

Doc. 86, vol. 2, Senate Docs. 1850.

THOMAS MOTT'S HEIRS, (John W. Still, Elizabeth Still.)

Report of Mr. Ruger, claims; Doc. 107, vol. 3, Senate Docs. 1843.

Mr. Stratton's report; Doc. 79, vol. 4, Ass'y Docs. 1843.

Mr. Burham's report; Doc. 79, vol. 3, Ass'y Docs. 1844.

Mr. Tefft's report; claims; Doc. 134, vol. 4, Ass'y Docs. 1845.

Mr. Pitt's report, claims; Doc. 100, vol. 4, Ass'y Docs. 1846.

Mr. J. E. Beers' report, claims; Doc. 33, vol. 1, Ass'y Docs. 1847.

Mr. J. M. Cook's report, claims; Doc. 38, vol. 2, Senate Docs. 1848.

Mr. Thos. E. Clark's report; Doc. 17, vol. 1, Senate Docs. 1849.

WASHINGTON JEFFERSON MURRY.

Report of Canal Board; Doc. 49, vol. 3, Ass'y Docs. 1844.

WILLIAM AND JANE MUGGLESWORTH, and associates, next of kin to William Dunn, deceased.

Report of Commissioners of Land Office; Doc. 42, vol. 3, Ass'y Docs. 1844.

ALFRED MUNSON, MARTIN HART, JAMES SAYRE, ALANSON HOUSE.

Mr. Towers' report, claims; Doc. 78, vol. 4, Ass'y Docs. 1843.
Mr. Porter's report, claims; do 24, do 1, Senate Docs. 1844.
Mr. Johnson's do do 19, do 1, do 1846.

EBENEZER MURDOCH.

Comptroller Flagg's report; Doc. 77, vol. 3, Senate Docs. 1846.

Report of committee on claims; Doc. 62, vol. 2, Senate Docs. 1853.

DAUPHIN MURRAY.

Mr. H. Putnam's report, claims; Doc. 66, vol. 2, Senate Docs. 1843.

DAVID MURRAY.

Report of Canal Board; Doc. 28, vol. 1, Senate Docs. 1843.

Mr. Ruger's report, claims; Doc. 64, vol. 2, Senate Docs. 1843.

GEORGE W. MURRAY.

Mr. Hand's report, grievances; Doc. 22, vol 1, Senate Docs. 1846.

Comptroller Flagg's report, Doc. 17, vol. 1, Senate Docs. 1847.

Mr. Johnson's report, claims; Doc. 88, vol. 3, Senate Docs. 1847.

Mr. J. M. Cook's report, claims; Doc. 26, vol. 1, Senate Docs. 1848.

Report of committee on claims; Doc. 13, vol. 1, Senate Docs. 1849.

EDWARD MURRAY.

Mr. N. Jones' report, claims; Doc. 32, vol. 1, Senate Docs. 1852.

MARY MURRAY, and associates.

Report of Canal Board on memorial relative to damages occasioned by the construction of the Genesee Valley canal; Doc. 22, vol. 1, Ass'y Docs. 1844.

Mr. Gorham's report, claims; Doc. 51, vol. 3, Ass'y Docs.

Mr. Tefft's report, claims; Doc. 147, vol. 4, Ass'y Docs. 1845.

Mr. McLean's report, claims; Doc. 128, vol. 3, Ass'y Docs. 1849.

AMOS W. MUZZY

Mr. Emmon's report, claims; Doc. 36, vol. 1, Senate Docs. 1847.

Mr. McCarty's report, claims; Doc. 62, vol. 3, Ass'y Docs. 1848.

MUTUAL SAFETY INSURANCE COMPANY, (New-York.)

Communication from J. B. Collins, secretary, in answer to a resolution of the Senate; Doc. 25, vol. 1, Senate Docs. 1849.

JOHN MYERS.

Mr. Dix's report, canals—on petition; Doc. 179, vol. 7, Ass'y Docs. 1842.

Mr. Putnam's report; Doc. 27, vol. 1, Senate Docs. 1843.

MANUEL MYERS.

Mr. McMurry's report, aliens; Doc. 115, vol. 5, Ass'y Docs. 1842.

Report of Commissioners of Land Office; Doc. 78, vol. 3, Senate Docs. 1843.

MYRTLE AVENUE AND JAMAICA PLANK ROAD.

Mr. McBurney's report, in relation to increase of capital stock; Doc. 96, vol. 4, Ass'y Docs. 1853.

NAMES.

Mr. A. C. Hand's report in the case of E. D. Rawson Smith, examining the question of change of name; Doc. 114, vol. 4, Senate Docs. 1846.

NATURAL HISTORY.

Mr. Daly's report, select committee; Doc. 82, vol. 4, Ass'y Docs. 1843.

Secretary of State's, S. Young, report; Doc. 87, vol. 3, Ass'y Docs. 1843.

Communication of Secretary of State, S. Young; Doc. 6, vol. 1, Senate Docs. 1845.

Report of Secretary of State, N. S. Benton; Doc. 43, vol. 1, Senate Docs. 1845.

Mr. Bartlett's majority report, as to progress and cost; Doc. 123, vol. 3, Senate Docs. 1845.

Mr. Porter's minority report; Doc. 124, vol. 3, Senate Docs. 1845.

Mr. Lott's report, judiciary, on the communication of the Secretary of State, S. Young; Doc. 125, vol. 3, Senate Docs. 1845.

Carroll & Cook's contract for printing; Doc. 78, vol. 3, Ass'y Docs. 1845.

Report of Comptroller Flagg, as to expenses of printing, binding and engraving, under act of 1844; Doc. 153, vol. 5, Ass'y Docs. 1845.

Report of Governor Wright and Secretary Benton, on the disposal of the volumes; Doc. 41, vol. 2, Ass'y Docs. 1846.

Mr. C. Drake's report as to a new and cheap edition; Doc. 172, vol. 5, Ass'y Docs. 1846.

Mr. Folsom's report on popular character of work; Doc. 155, vol. 4, Senate Docs. 1847.

Professor Agassiz's communication on same subject; Doc. 155, vol. 4, Senate Docs. 1847.

Gov. Fish's communication in relation to completion; Doc. 154, vol. 3, Ass'y Docs. 1849.

Mr. G. J. Cornell's report; Doc. 179, vol. 3, Ass'y Docs. 1849.

Mr. G. J. Cornell's report of investigation with testimony; Doc. 9, vol. 1, Ass'y Docs. 1850.

Report of Christopher Morgan, Secretary of State, and T. Romeyn Beck, Secretary of the Regents of the University, as commissioners ot investigation into financial affairs; Doc. 124, vol. 4, Ass'y Docs. 1851.

Further report; Doc. 23, vol. 1, Ass'y Docs. 1852.

Report of commissioners of supervision, H. S. Randall, Secretary of State, T. Romeyn Beck, Secretary of the Regents of the University; Doc. 74, vol. 3, Ass'y Docs. 1853.

NAUTILUS INSURANCE COMPANY.

Mr. J. M. Cook's report in relation to management; Doc. 53, vol. 2, Senate Docs. 1849.

WILLIAM J. NELSON, IRA E. PHILLIPS,

Report of Canal Board; Doc. 107, vol. 5, Ass'y Docs. 1841.

Mr. S. Lawrence's majority report, claims; Doc. 26, vol. 1, Senate Docs. 1844.

Mr. W. Platt's minority report, claims; Doc. 27, vol. 1, Senate Docs. 1844.

Mr. Bockee's report; Doc. 44, vol 1, Senate Docs. 1844.

Report of Canal Board; Doc. 17, vol. 1, Ass'y Docs. 1844.

Further report of Canal Board; Doc. 70, vol. 3, Ass'y Docs. 1844.

Further report of Canal Board; Doc. 86, vol. 3, Ass'y Docs. 1844.

Mr. Johnson's report, claims; Doc. 107, vol. 5, Ass'y Docs. 1844.

Mr. Alvord's report, claims; Doc. 142, vol. 6, Ass'y Docs. 1844.

Mr. Schoonmaker's report, claims; Doc. 35, vol. 2, Senate Docs. 1851.

Mr. Backhouse's report; Doc. 103, vol. 4, Ass'y Docs. 1851.

NFVERSINK BRIDGE AT FALLSBURGH.

Mr. Curry's minority report; Doc. 67, vol. 2, Ass'y Docs. 1847.

NEW COUNTIES.

Attorney-General John Van Buren's opinion, as to the population necessary for a new county, and in relation to its withdrawal from those out of which the new county is to be formed; Doc. 122, vol. 4, Ass'y Docs. 1846.

SCHUYLER, (old project.)

From Erie, Cattaraugus Chautauque.

Mr. Bockee's report; Doc. 43, vol. 2, Senate Docs. 1842.

Memorial of democratic convention of Chautauque county against; Doc. 178, vol. 5, Ass'y Docs. 1843.

Mr. S. C. Johnson's majority report; Doc. 30, vol. 1, Senate Docs. 1845.

Attorney-General John Van Buren's opinion, as to constitutionality; Doc. 66, vol. 2, Senate Docs. 1845.

HARRISON,

Delaware, Greene, Schoharie.

Mr. D. R. Floyd Jones' report, adverse; Doc. 49, vol. 2, Senate Docs. 1846.

Mr. Pardee's favorable report; Doc. 135, vol. 3, Ass'y Docs. 1849.

Remonstrance of citizens of Greene county; Doc. 172, vol. 3, 1849.

Mr. A. H. Bailey's report, adverse; Doc. 174, vol. 3, Ass'y Docs. 1849.

UNADILLA.

Delaware, Otsego, Chenango.

Mr. J. T. Raymond's minority report, favorable; Doc. 107, vol. 4, Ass'y Docs. 1845.

Mr. J. Brook's report; Doc. 174, vol. 5, Ass'y Docs. 1845.

Attorney-General Jordan's report on constitutionality; Doc. 123, vol. 3, Ass'y Docs. 1846.

Mr. Philips' majority report, favorable; Doc. 97, vol. 4, Ass'y Docs. 1846.

CANISTEO,

Steuben and Allegany,

Mr. Pardee's report, favorable; Doc. 136, vol, 3, Ass'y Docs. 1849.

Mr. Noble's report, judiciary; Doc. 138, vol. 3, Ass'y Docs. 1849.

MARSHALL,

Erie, Cattaraugus, Chautauque.

Mr. B. Huntington's report, adverse; Doc. 70, vol. 2, Senate Docs. 1852.

Mr. J. K. Gardner's favorable report; Doc. 57, vol. 3, Ass'y Docs. 1853.

SCHUYLER,

Tompkins, Chemung, Steuben.

Mr. J. Cook's report; Doc. 110, vol. 3, Ass'y Docs. 1844.

Mr. Hazleton's minority report, adverse; Doc. 105, vol. 4, Ass'y Docs. 1846.

LA FAYETTE.

(Chemung, Steuben, Yates and Tompkins.)

Mr. Hazleton's majority report, adverse; Doc. 109, vol. 4, Ass'y Docs. 1846.

Mr. Treadwell's majority report, favorable; Doc. 62, vol. 2, Ass'y Docs. 1847.

Mr. Chandler's minority report, adverse; Doc. 81, vol. 2, Ass'y Docs. 1847.

PATTERSON.

(Delaware, Broome, Chenango and Otsego.)

Mr. Hale's report favorable, Doc. 152, vol. 3, Ass'y Docs. 1849.

NEW HAMPSHIRE.

Resolutions of State respecting postage; Doc. 19, vol. 2, Ass'y Docs. 1843.

Resolutions of State, concerning the arrest and fine of General Jackson; Doc. 191, vol. 7, Ass'y Docs. 1844.

NEW JERSEY.

Resolutions of Legislature concerning tariff; Doc. 53, vol. 2, Senate Docs. 1842.

Resolutions relative to repudiation; Doc. 86, vol. 3, Senate Docs. 1843.

GEORGE W. NEWELL.

Report as to extra allowances made on canal contracts; Doc. 23, vol. 1, Senate Docs. 1852.

Report in relation to estimates for ordinary expenses; Doc. 116, vol. 5, Ass'y Docs. 1852.

Report in relation to the expenditures on the canals; Doc. 125, vol. 5, Ass'y Docs. 1852.

Report in relation to the Champlain canal; Doc. 29, vol. 1, Senate Docs. 1853.

Report of reasons why certain claims were not charged to Canal Debt Sinking Fund; Doc. 51, vol. 2, Senate Docs. 1853.

Report in relation to Smith A. Waterman, David Barrett, Thomas Greenly. To this the proceedings of Canal Board, and the testimony taken in investigation before them, are appended. Doc. 71, vol. 3, Senate Docs. 1853.

Report in relation to the appropriations for the canals; Doc. 84, vol. 3, Senate Docs. 1853.

Report to Commissioners of Canal Fund, of the canal finances; Doc. 15, vol. 2, Ass'y Docs. 1853.

Report in relation to unauthorised claims; Doc. 56, vol. 3, Ass'y Docs. 1853.

Report of compensation and travel of resident and division engineers; Doc. 73, vol. 3, Ass'y Docs 1853.

Report of the tolls, trade and tonnage; Doc. 107, vol. 4, Ass'y Docs. 1853.

Communication in relation to canal appropriations for 1853; Doc. 126, vol. 6, Ass'y Docs. 1853.

Report of expenditures on the canals; Doc. 105, vol. 4, Ass'y Docs. 1853.

Report of finances of canal made to Commissioners of Canal Fund; Doc. 1, vol. 10, Ass'y Docs. 1854.

Report of expenditures on the canals; Doc. 146, vol. 5, Ass'y Docs. 1854.

Report in relation to mileage of George Cole, an engineer; Doc. 122, vol. 6, Ass'y Docs. 1853.

NEW YORK LIFE INSURANCE COMPANY.

Communication from Morris Franklin; Doc. 85, vol. 3, Senate Docs. 1853.

NEW ROCHELLE BANK.

Answer of president to resolution; Doc. 217, vol. 5, Ass'y Docs. 1849.

NIAGARA COUNTY.

Report on refusal of supervisors to divide the county into Assembly districts; Doc. 170, vol. 6, Ass'y Docs. 1847.

NIAGARA FALLS SHIP CANAL COMPANY.

Mr. Martin's report; Doc. 157, vol. 6, Ass'y Docs. 1850.

Mr. E. G. West's minority report, in favor of an incorporation; Doc. 76, vol. 3, Ass'y Docs. 1853.

Mr. Clapp's majority report against special corporation; Doc. 77, vol. 3, Ass'y Docs. 1853.

NIAGARA FALLS HYDRAULIC COMPANY.

Mr. Denniston's report; Doc. 30, vol. 1, Senate Docs. 1846.

JAMES NICHOLS.

Report of Canal Board; Doc. 170, vol. 5, Ass'y Docs. 1848.

NICHOLAS NICKERSON.

Mr. A. C. Hand's report; Doc. 94, vol. 3, Senate Docs. 1846.

NICHOLAS NICHOLSON, JONATHAN COLTON.

Report of Canal Commissioners; Doc. 71, vol. 3, Senate Docs. 1843.

JOHN NILES.

Mr. J. E. Beer's report, claims; Doc. 31, vol. 1, Ass'y Docs. 1847.

Mr. McLean's report, claims; Doc. 36, vol. 1, Ass'y Docs. 1849.

RICHARD NILES, JAMES W. PATTEN.

Mr. Hopkin's report, claims; Doc. 22, vol. 1, Senate Docs. 1844.

Mr. Pettingill's report, claims; Doc. 124, vol. 6, Ass'y Docs. 1853.

WILLIAM W. NILES.

Report of the committee on grievances, in relation to his claim for compensation for destruction of property at Astoria; Doc. 19, vol. 2, Ass'y Docs. 1848.

Wessel S. Smith's report; Doc. 161, vol. 5, Ass'y Docs. 1848.

Mr. James Brooks' minority report; Doc. 164, vol. 5, Ass'y Docs. 1848.

Mr. Wessel S. Smith's report; Doc. 186, vol. 5, Ass'y Docs. 1848.

Mr. Hawley's report; Doc. 31, vol. 2, Senate Docs. 1849.

Mr. Stone's majority report, with communication from John C. Spencer; Doc. 82, vol. 3, Senate Docs. 1850.

Attorney General Chatfield's report; Doc. 61, vol. 2, Senate Docs. 1850.

NON-RESIDENT TAXES.

Report of Comptroller Flagg; Doc. 13, vol. 1, Senate Docs. 1843.

Mr. John Porter's report as relates to the city of New-York; Doc. 109, vol. 4, Senate Docs. 1846.

Report of Comptroller, W. Hunt, Secretary of State, C. Morgan, Attorney General, L. S. Chatfield, in respect to their collection; Doc. 39, vol. 3, Ass'y Docs. 1850.

Report of Comptroller, James M. Cook; Doc. 101, vol. 3, Ass'y Docs. 1854.

NORMAL SCHOOL.

Mr. Hubbard's report in relation to its establishment; Doc. 135, vol. 5, Ass'y Docs. 1844.

Report of Secretary of State, S. Young, as Superintendent of Common Schools, and Peter Wendell, Chancellor of the Regents of the University; Doc. 24, vol. 1, Senate Docs. 1845.

Report of executive committee; Doc. 32, vol. 1, Senate Docs. 1845.

Report of executive committee as to salaries; Doc. 168, vol. 5, Ass'y Docs. 1846.

Annual report of executive committee; Doc. 31, vol. 1, Senate Docs. 1847.

Annual report of executive committee; Doc. 18, vol. 1, Senate Docs. 1848.

Mr. S. J. Wilkins' report on condition; Doc. 49, vol. 2, Senate Docs. 1848.

Annual report of executive committee; Doc. 8, vol. 1, Senate Docs. 1849.

Annual report of executive committee; Doc. 56, vol. 2, Senate Docs. 1850.

Annual report of executive committee; Doc. 12, vol. 1, Ass'y Docs. 1851.

Annual report of executive committee; Doc. 34, vol. 1, Senate Docs. 1852.

Mr. H. L. Webb's report in relation to the safety of the building, and the propriety of having two schools; Doc. 119, vol. 5, Ass'y Docs. 1852.

Annual report of executive committee; Doc. 20, vol. 2, Ass'y Docs. 1853.

Annual report of executive committee; Doc. 30, vol. 1, Senate Docs. 1854.

NORMAN NORTHRUP.

Mr. G. W. Jermain's report; Doc. 91, vol. 5, Ass'y Docs. 1850.

NORTHERN RIVERS.

Mr. McNamara's majority report in relation to jurisdiction over and ownership in rivers not navigable; Doc. 223, vol. 7, Ass'y Docs. 1847.

Mr. Hammond's minority report on same subject; same document.

Report of select committee relative to improving upper waters; Doc. 103, vol. 5, Ass'y Docs. 1849.

HENRY NORTON, CALEB S. CHURCH.

Mr. Flagler's report; Doc. 44, vol. 2, Ass'y Docs. 1842.

OAK ORCHARD BRIDGE, (across Oneida river.)

Mr. Lewis' report relative to a draw; Doc. 49, vol. 3, Ass'y Docs. 1850.

JOHN O'BRIEN.

Mr. Richard's majority report; Doc. 39, vol. 1, Ass'y Docs. 1854.

OBSERVATORY.

Mr. Folsom's report on the establishment of an astronomical observatory; Doc. 45, vol. 2, Senate Docs. 1847.

MORDECAI OGDEN, JOHN DURFEE, ISAAC JACKSON.

Report of Canal Commissioners; Doc. 136, vol. 4, Senate Docs. 1846.

OGDENSBURGH ACADEMY.

Mr. Foster's report, literature; Doc. 32, vol. 1, Senate Docs. 1843.

OIL.

Mr. Thomas Burch's report in relation to the frauds in manufacture; Doc. 34, vol. 2, Senate Docs. 1849.

OLD FORTIFICATION BLOCK, No. 2, West Oswego.

Mr. Allen's report, ways and means, in relation to purchasers; Doc. 101, vol. 4, Ass'y Docs. 1843.

Mr. Alvord's report, claims; Doc. 59, vol. 3, Ass'y Docs. 1844.

Report of Commissioners of Land Office; Doc. 111, vol. 5, Ass'y Docs. 1844.

Mr. Van Schoonhoven's report; Doc. 41, vol. 2, Senate Docs. 1847.

Report of Commissioners of Land office, on petition of Alvah Bronson; Doc. 121, vol. 3, Ass'y Docs. 1848.

JANE OLIVER.

Mr. Davis' report, aliens; Doc. 47, vol. 3, Ass'y Docs. 1844.

JOHN O'NIEL.

Report of the committee on the judiciary, Mr Foster, on the petition of Mary E. O'Niel, Andrew Parsons, John G. Blauvelt, executors and executrix; Doc. 72, vol. 3, Senate Docs. 1842.

ONEIDA CREEK FEEDER.

Report of Canal Commissioners; Doc. 45, vol. 3, Ass'y Docs. 1843.

ONEIDA INDIANS.

Mr. S. C. Johnson's report in case of W. A. Stone; Doc. 6, vol. 1, Senate Docs. 1845.

Communication from Commissioners of Land office, in relation to their lands in this State; Doc. 215, vol. 7, Ass'y Docs. 1847.

Report of Commissioners of Land Office, on petition of First Christian Party, concerning lands near Wood Creek; Doc. 216, vol. 7, Ass'y Docs. 1847.

Mr. William Samuel Johnson's report, concerning memorial of chiefs and headmen of First Christian Party, residing at Duck Creek, in Wisconsin; Doc. 46. vol. 2, Senate Docs. 1849.

Mr. Malburn's report on claims for compensation; Doc. 80, vol. 3, Ass'y Docs. 1853.

ONEIDA LAND PURCHASERS.

Mr. Allen's report, ways and means, on petition of O. F. Root, and others; Doc. 81, vol. 4, Ass'y Docs. 1843.

Mr. Bockee's report, finance; Doc. 58, vol. 2, Senate Docs. 1845.

Report of Commissioners of Land Office, on petition of Peter Baird, and others; Doc. 18, vol. 1, Ass'y Docs. 1845.

Report of Commissioners of Land Office, on proper construction of the act of April 14, 1845, for relief; Doc. 9, vol. 1, Senate Docs. 1845.

Report of Commissioners of Land Office, upon the petition of purchasers of the second purchase; Doc. 34, vol. 2, Ass'y Docs. 1846.

Mr. Miller's report as to purchasers of second purchase; Doc. 87, vol. 3, Ass'y Docs. 1846.

Report of Commissioners of Land Office; Doc. 43, vol. 1, Ass'y Docs 1847.

Further report of Commissioners of Land Office, (William Cramer's petition,) Doc. 45, vol. 1, Ass'y Docs. 1847.

Mr. Morris' report, John Dunlop's petition; Doc. 104, vol. 4, Ass'y Docs. 1847.

Mr. S. Morris' further report; Doc. 144, vol. 4, Ass'y Docs. 1847.

Report of Commissioners of Land Office as to rebate of interest; Doc. 191, vol. 7, Ass'y Docs. 1847.

Mr. Hoyt's roport; Doc. 76, vol. 2, Ass'y Docs. 1849.

Mr. Bowne's report, Dexter Hubbard's petition; Doc. 32, vol. 3, Ass'y Docs. 1850.

Mr. W. A. Gilbert's report, claims; Doc. 61, vol. 2, Ass'y Docs. 1852.

ONONDAGA INDIANS.

Remonstrance of a portion of the chiefs against the action of David Hill; Doc. 124, vol. 4, Ass'y Docs. 1847.

Mr. Tillinghast's report as to *per capita* distribution of annuities; Doc. 128, vol. 4, Ass'y Docs. 1847.

Report of Commissioners of Land Office, in relation to their land in this State; Doc. 215, vol. 7, Ass'y Docs. 1847.

ONONDAGA SALT SPRINGS.

Communication to Governor, of superintendent relative to manufacture of salt; Doc. F. in Doc. 2, vol., 1, Senate Docs. 1842.

Same in vol. 1, Ass'y Docs. 1842.

Annual report of superintendent; Doc. 8, vol. 1, Senate Docs. 1842.

Same, Doc. 11, vol. 1, Ass'y Docs. 1842.

Communication at extra session from superintendent; Doc. E. accompanying Governor Seward's extra session message; Doc. 106, vol. 4, Senate Docs. 1842; Doc. E. accompanying Doc. 195, vol. 7, Ass'y Docs. 1842.

Annual report; Doc. 7, vol. 1, Senate Docs. 1843. Doc. 6, vol. 1, Ass'y Docs' 1843.

Communication from Commissioners of Land Office, relative to reservation; Doc. 39, vol. 2, Ass'y Docs. 1843.

Mr. McCarty's report; Doc. 111, vol. 4, Ass'y Docs. 1843.

Petition of citizens of Salina, and manufacturers, in relation to the extension of the market; Doc. 133, vol. 5, Ass'y Docs. 1843.

Report of Commissioners of the Land Office; Doc. 156, vol. 5, Ass'y Docs. 1843.

Annual report of superintendent, Rial Wright; Doc. 13, vol. 1, Ass'y Docs. 1844.

Report of Commissioners of Land Office, on the exchange of certain salt lands; Doc. 155, vol. 6, Ass'y Docs. 1844.

Report of superintendent, Rial Wright, as to men employed; Doc. 39, vol. 1, Senate Docs. 1845.

Annual report of superintendent, Rial Wright; Doc. 10, vol. 1, Ass'y Docs. 1845.

Mr. A. Wood's report on Calvin Guiteau's patent; Doc. 57, vol. 2, Ass'y Docs. 1846.

Annual report, Enoch Marks'; Doc. 9, vol. 1, Ass'y Docs. 1846.

Mr. A. Wood's report on abolition of office of inspector, and reduction of fees of superintendent; Doc. 79, vol. 3, Ass'y Docs. 1846.

Mr. John Porter's report on the act giving bounty to the transportation of coal, salt and lead; Doc. 47, vol. 2, Senate Docs. 1846.

Report of Commissioners of Land Office, in relation to sale of land; Doc. 108, vol. 3, Senate Docs. 1847.

Annual report of superintendent, E. Marks; Doc. 11, vol. 1, Ass'y Docs. 1847.

Statement of revenue for 1846; Doc. 118, vol. 4, Senate Docs. 1847.

Annual report superintendent, E. Marks; Doc. 23, vol. 2, Ass'y Docs. 1848.

Report of State Engineer, C. B. Stuart; Doc. 130, vol. 3, Ass'y Docs. 1849.

Annual report of superintendent, R. Gere; Doc. 19, vol. 1, Ass'y Docs. 1849.

Annual report of superintendent, Robert Gere; Doc. 36, vol. 3, Ass'y Docs. 1850.

Mr. Leavenworth's report on the reduction of the tolls on foreign salt; Doc. 184, vol. 8, Ass'y Docs. 1850.

Mr. Orlando Allen's report in relation to lots in Geddes; Doc. 135, vol. 5, Ass'y Docs. 1850.

Mr. McLean's report in relation to tolls on foreign and domestic salt; Doc. 165, vol. 6, Ass'y Docs. 1850.

State Engineer, H. C. Seymour's report as to State lands; Doc. 19, vol. 1, (page 19, of Doc.) Senate Docs. 1851.

Annual report of superintendent, Robert Gere; Doc. 25, vol. 2, Ass'y Docs. 1851.

Annual report of superintendent, Harvey Rhoades; Doc. 43, vol. 2, Ass'y Docs. 1852.

Mr. Conger's minority report in relation to abuses and frauds in manufacture; Doc. 86, vol. 3, Senate Docs. 1853.

Annual report of superintendent, Harvey Rhoades; Doc. 78, vol. 3, Ass'y Docs. 1853. To this is appended a report by Professor George M. Cook.

Communication of George M. Cook, to Regents of the University; page 79, of Doc. 50, of vol. 1, Senate Docs. 1854.

Mr. D. P. Wood's report; Doc. 132, vol. 4, Ass'y Docs. 1854.

HENRY B. OPP.

Mr. McCarty's report, claims; Doc. 48, vol. 2, Ass'y Docs. 1848.

OREGON TERRITORY.

Resolutions in relation to occupation by Great Britain; Doc. 39, vol. 1, Senate Docs. 1844.

Mr. Fullerton's resolutions; Doc. 24, vol. 1, Ass'y Docs. 1849.

ORPHAN ASYLUMS.

Mr. J. E. Beers' majority report in relation to the appropriation of the common school moneys to the Albany and St. Joseph's orphan asylums; Doc. 217, vol. 7, Ass'y Docs. 1847.

Mr. Watson's minority report on same subject; Doc. 259, vol. 8, Ass'y Docs. 1847.

Mr. Burchard's report on appropriations; Doc. 234, vol. 8, Ass'y Docs. 1847.

ABIJAH OSBORN.

Mr. Soper's report, claims; Doc. 64, vol. 2, Ass'y Docs. 1847.

Report of Canal Board; Doc. 209, vol. 7, Ass'y Docs. 1847.

Mr. Jones' report, claims; Doc. 16, vol. 1, Senate Docs. 1852.

Report of committee on claims; Doc. 108, vol. 4, Ass'y Docs. 1851.

J. C. OSGOOD, DANIEL KELLOGG.

Report of Canal Board; Doc. 58, vol. 2, Senate Docs. 1844. Doc. 59, vol. 2, Senate Docs. 1844.

OSSINSING.

Mr. J. A. Lott's report as to election of town officers; Doc. 90, vol. 3, Senate Docs. 1846.

OSWEGATCHIE RIVER.

Mr. Smith's report on the bill for the improvement; Doc. 93, vol. 5, Ass'y Docs. 1852.

OSWEGO.

Mr. Lott's report, judiciary, on the subject of the abolition of the office of police justice in (village) Oswego; Doc. 93, vol. 3, Senate Docs. 1846.

Mr. Geddes' report in relation to bridge; Doc. 36, vol. 2, Senate Docs. 1848.

OSWEGO CANAL.

Report of Canal Commissioners, and petitions relative to alleged unhealthiness of certain structures at Oswego Falls and the Horse Shoe; Doc. 167, vol. 7, Ass'y Docs. 1842.

Further report; Doc. 93, vol. 4, Ass'y Docs. 1843.

Memorial of New-York chamber of commerce concerning increase of tolls; Doc. 61, vol. 2, Senate Docs. 1845.

Report of Canal Board in relation to side cut at Liverpool; Doc. 99, vol. 3, Senate Docs. 1845.

Memorial of citizens of Western New-York on same subject; Doc. 81, vol. 4, Ass'y Docs. 1845.

Remonstrance of citizens of Oswego, on same subject; Doc. 85, vol. 4, Ass'y Docs. 1845.

Mr. Sears' majority report, canals, adverse to discriminating tolls; Doc. 189, vol. 5, Ass'y Docs. 1845.

Mr. Coe's minority report, in favor of such discrimination; Doc. 190, vol. 5, Ass'y Docs. 1845.

Report of Commissioners of Land Office, on land ceded by, to this State in purchase, 1830, 1834, 1841, May and June, 1842; Doc. 103, vol. 3, Ass'y Docs. 1849.

Mr. Geddes' report; Doc. 59, vol. 2, Senate Docs. 1851.

Mr. Severance's report on the claims of contractors; Doc. 31, vol. 2, Ass'y Docs. 1851.

Mr. Orlando Allen's report on enlargement; Doc. 129, vol. 4, Ass'y Docs. 1851.

OWASCO LAKE.

Mr. Graves' report on improvement of outlet, by agent of Auburn State Prison; Doc. 231, vol. 8, Ass'y Docs. 1847.

Report of State Engineer, W. J. McAlpine, in relation to improvement of outlet; Doc. 37, vol. 3, Ass'y Docs. 1853.

PACAMA AND BEAVERKILL SWAMPS LANDS.

Mr. Gay's report; Doc. 34, vol. 2, Ass'y Docs. 1848.

DENAS PAGE.

Mr. Hatch's report, claims; Doc. 60, vol. 3, Ass'y Docs. 1851.

JOHN KEYES PAIGE.

Report as clerk Supreme Court, in relation to fees; Doc. 81, vol. 3, Senate Docs. 1843.

Report; Doc. 98, vol. 4, Ass'y Docs. 1843.

WM. PAIGE.

Report of Canal Board, on petition; Doc. 164, vol. 7, Ass'y Docs. 1842.

Mr. Hopkins' report, claims; Doc. 121, vol. 3, Senate Docs. 1843.

Mr. Jackson's report, claims; Doc. 123, vol. 5, Ass'y Docs. 1843.

Mr. Lawrence's report, claims; Doc. 25, vol. 1, Senate Docs. 1844.

ABIEL PAINE.

Mr. Nicoll's report, claims; Doc. 99, vol. 4, Ass'y Docs. 1843.

Mr. Haight's report, grievances; Doc. 160, vol. 5, Ass'y Docs. 1843.

Mr. Alvord's majority report, claims; Doc. 37, vol. 3, Ass'y Docs. 1844.

Mr. Brunell's report, claims; Doc. 26, vol. 1, Ass'y Docs. 1846.

PALATINE AND FULTON ROAD.

Report of Mr. Geddes, Doc. 67, vol. 2, Senate Docs. 1848.

Mr. Treadwell's minority report on same subject; Doc. 70, vol. 2, Senate Docs. 1848.

PANAMA RAILROAD COMPANY.

Mr. Mowry's report; Doc. 35, vol. 1, Ass'y Docs. 1849.

LUTHER PARDEE.

Report of Canal Commissioners; Doc. 101, vol. 5, Ass'y Docs. 1842.

Mr. Jackson's report, claims; Doc. 132, vol. 5, Ass'y Docs. 1843.

PARDONS.

Report of pardons granted since January 1, 1840; Doc. 198, vol. 5, Ass'y Docs. 1846.

Report of Secretary of State, Christopher Morgan, with list of pardons granted by Governors' of New-York, commencing with De Witt Clinton, 1825; Doc. 66, vol. 2, Senate Docs. 1848.

List of reprieves, pardons, and restorations, granted by Gov. Hunt, in 1852; Doc. 44, vol. 2, Ass'y Docs. 1853.

HORACE PARMELEE.

Report of Canal Board; Doc. 44, vol. 3, Ass'y Docs. 1844.

SOLOMON PARMELEE, ROBERT C. KENYON, SANDS C. KENYON.

Mr. Schoonmaker's report, claims; Doc. 43, vol. 2, Senate Docs. 1851.

PAR-REDEMPTION OF BANK NOTES.

Mr. Corning's report, banks; Doc. 89, vol. 3, Senate Docs. 1845.

Mr. S. Lawrence's report, banks; Doc. 131, vol. 4, Ass'y Docs. 1846.

Mr. N. K. Hall's minority report; Doc. 145, vol. 5, Ass'y Docs. 1846.

Memorial of Oneida bank; Doc. 66, vol. 3, Ass'y Docs. 1848.

Memorial of Mohawk Valley bank; Doc. 86, vol. 3, Ass'y Docs. 1848.

Mr. Horton's report; Doc. 185, vol. 8, Ass'y Docs. 1850.

Memorial of Oneida bank; Doc. 24, vol. 1, Senate Docs. 1850.

PARTNERS OF JUDGES.

Mr. J. A. Lott's report, as to the rule proper to be followed; Doc. 17, vol. 1, Senate Docs. 1846.

PARTNERS AND JOINT DEBTORS.

Mr. Dodge's report on subject of relief; Doc. 112, vol. 3, Ass'y Docs. 1849.

PATENTS.

Communication from Secretary of State, Samuel Young, in relation to the digest of patents, 1790 to 1839, issued by the government of the United States; Doc. 123, vol. 5, Ass'y Docs. 1842.

PATENTS FOR LAND.

Reports of Commissioners of Land Office in relation to records; Doc. 22, vol. 1, Senate Docs. 1845.

PASSENGERS ON CANAL.

Report of Comptroller Flagg, concerning tolls upon; Doc. 21, vol. 1, Senate Docs. 1843.

PATENT MEDICINES.

Mr. Hurd's report; Doc. 20, vol. 2, Ass'y Docs. 1848.

Mr. Willard's report; Doc. 184, vol. 3, Ass'y Docs. 1849.

Dr. J. G. Sewall's address before State Medical Society; Doc. 125, (page 173,) vol. 4, Ass'y Docs. 1851.

ALBERT PATTEN, FRANKLIN J. PATTEN.

Mr. Sherman's report, claims; Doc. 100, vol. 4, Ass'y Docs. 1851.

Mr. Hitchcock's report, claims; Doc. 76, vol. 2, Senate Docs. 1854.

JOHN L. PEAKE,

Mr. McCarty's report, claims; Doc. 40, vol. 4, Ass'y Docs. 1848.

IRA PEARSON, IRA PEARSON, Jr.

Mr. Gorham's report, claims; Doc. 20, vol. 1, Ass'y Docs. 1844.

Mr. Teffts' report, claims; Doc. 52, vol. 3, Ass'y Docs. 1845.

LUCIEN T. PECKHAM.

Mr. N. Jones' report, claims; Doc. 50, vol. 2, Senate Docs. 1853.

PEEKSKILL AND TOWNER'S ROAD.

Mr. S. Miller's report; Doc. 103, vol. 3, Senate Docs. 1850.

H. P. PEET.

Report on the European institutions for the instruction of the deaf and dumb; Doc. 112, (page 83,) vol. 5, Ass'y Docs. 1852.

PEOPLE'S COLLEGE.

Mr. S. S. Smith's minority report; Doc. 38, vol. 2, Ass'y Docs. 1853.

Mr. Peters' report; Doc. 42, vol. 2, Ass'y Docs. 1853.

JOSEPH PERRINE.

Mr. McCarty's report, claims; Doc. 156, vol. 5, Ass'y Docs. 1848.

PERTH.

Report in relation to the enlargement of the town; Doc. 34, vol. 2, Senate Docs. 1842.

HENRY T. PETERS, RICHARD HUGHES.

Mr. G. R. Babcock's report; Doc. 18, vol. 1, Senate Docs. 1850.

PHARMACY, COLLEGE OF

Mr. Snow's report on appropriation; Doc. 67, vol. 2, Senate Docs. 1852.

Report of committee on medical societies; Doc. 71, vol. 3, Senate Docs. 1842.

Mr. F. F. Backus' report; Doc. 32, vol. 1, Senate Docs. 1845.

PHYSICIANS AND SURGEONS COLLEGE NEW-YORK.

Mr. Teffts' report on appropriation; Doc. 76, vol. 3, Ass'y Docs. 1845.

Mr. C. Drake's report on appropriation; Doc. 44, vol. 2, Ass'y Docs. 1846.

PHYSICIANS AND SURGEONS, NATIONAL COLLEGE.

Mr. Sprague's report against a special corporation; Doc. 65, vol. 3, Ass'y Docs. 1853.

PIER AT ALBANY.

Report of proprietors, in relation to tolls collected; Doc. 142, vol. 5, Ass'y Docs. 1848.

Mr. E. S. Willett's report on wharfage; Doc. 145, vol. 5, Ass'y Docs. 1848.

PILOTS AND PILOTAGE.

Message from Governor Wright respecting New-York pilots; Doc. 25, vol. 1, Senate Docs. 1845.

Mr. Floyd Jones' report, commerce and navigation; Doc. 40, vol. 1, Senate Docs. 1845.

Mr. T. R. Lee's report on the Governor's message; Doc. 186, vol. 5, Ass'y Docs. 1845.

Mr. J. D. Stevenson's report and memorial of New-York pilots; Doc. 104, vol. 4, Ass'y Docs. 1846.

Mr. Phœnix's report; Doc. 27, vol. 2, Ass'y Docs. 1848.

MATTHEW S. PITCHER.

Report of Canal Commissioners; Doc. 124, vol. 4, Senate Docs. 1847.

Mr. Ward's report, claims, Doc. 70, vol. 2, Ass'y Docs. 1849.

PLANK ROAD.

Mr. Simmons' report, roads and bridges, on the incorporation of companies to construct; Doc. 197, vol. 7, Ass'y Docs. 1844.

Mr. Burnham's report on general law; Doc. 50, vol. 2, Senate Docs. 1847.

Mr. Gay's report; Doc. 163, vol. 5, Ass'y Docs. 1848.

Secretary Morgan's report; Doc. 74, vol. 2, Senate Docs. 1850.

Mr. McBurney's report; Doc. 88, vol. 4, Ass'y Docs. 1853.

PLEURO-PNEUMONIA.

Samuel Shumway's treatise before State medical society; Doc. 85, (page 67,) vol. 2, Ass'y Docs. 1852.

POLICE IN NEW-YORK.

Mr. Develin's minority report; Doc. 174, vol. 5, Ass'y Docs. 1846.

OLIVER POOLE.

Mr. W. A. Gilbert's report, claims; Doc. 84, vol. 2, Ass'y Docs. 1852.

SAMUEL POOLE, WILLIAM POOLE.

Report of Commissioners of Land Office; Doc. 70, vol. 2, Ass'y Docs. 1847.

MEDAD POMEROY.

Mr. Ruger's report, claims; Doc. 89, vol. 3, Senate Docs. 1843.

Report of Canal Board; Doc. 90, vol. 3, Senate Docs. 1843.

Mr. Ward's report, claims; Doc. 29, vol. 1, Senate Docs. 1852.

POOR OF THE STATE.

Annual report of Secretary of State, S. Young, in relation to the paupers in the State; Doc. 121, vol. 5, Ass'y Docs. 1842.

Annual report of Secretary of State, S. Young; Doc. 38, vol. 2, Ass'y Docs. 1843.

Annual report of Secretary of State, S. Young; Doc. 73, vol. 2, Senate Docs. 1844.

Annual report of the Secretary of State, N. S. Benton; Doc. 197, vol. 5, Ass'y Docs. 1845.

Annual report of the Secretary of State, N. S. Benton; Doc. 199, vol. 5, Ass'y Docs. 1846.

Annual report of the Secretary of State, N. S. Benton; Doc. 100, vol. 3, Senate Docs. 1847.

Annual report of the Secretary of State, Christopher Morgan; Doc. 79, vol. 3, Senate Docs. 1848.

Annual report of the Secretary of State, Christopher Morgan; Doc. 83, vol. 3, Senate Docs. 1849.

Report of Secretary of State, C. Morgan, with abstracts of the reports of county superintendents; Doc. 169, vol. 6, Ass'y Docs. 1850.

Report of Secretary of State, C. Morgan, with abstracts of the reports of county superintendents; Doc. 147, vol. 5, Ass'y Docs. 1851.

Communication from Secretary of State, H. S. Randall, in relation to the publication of the poor laws; Doc. 14, vol. 1, Ass'y Docs. 1853.

Report of Secretary of State, H. S. Randall, with statistics; Doc. 120, vol. 6, Ass'y Docs. 1853.

Report of Secretary of State, E. W. Leavenworth, with statistics; Doc. 144, vol. 4, Ass'y Docs. 1854.

Communication from Comptroller Hunt and Attorney-General Jordan, as to the measures necessary to protect the people of this State, from the introduction among them of disease and pauperism from foreign countries, and from public burdens consequent upon such introduction; Doc. 76, vol. 3, Senate Docs. 1849.

PORT BYRON LEVEL.

Report of Canal Commissioners; Doc. 52, vol. 2, Ass'y Docs. 1846.

POSTAGE AND FRANKING.

Mr. Flagler's report; Doc. 165, vol. 7, Ass'y Docs. 1842.

Resolutions relating to reduction; Doc. 3, vol. 1, Senate Docs. 1844.

Mr. Carroll's report; Doc. 55, vol. 2, Senate Docs. 1850.

POT AND PEARL ASHES.

Report of Inspector, at New-York; Doc. 65, vol. 2, Senate Docs. 1845.

POTSDAM AND WATERTOWN.

Mr. Bartlett's report, on deficiency in organization; Doc. 63 vol. 2, Senate Docs. 1852.

JOHN PRATT.

Report of Commissioners of the Land Office; Doc. 105, vol. 8, Senate Docs. 1844.

EBENEZER PRESCOTT.

Mr. W. A. Gilbert's report, claims; Doc. 59, vol 2, Ass'y Docs. 1852.

Mr. Mitchell's report; Doc. 36, vol. 1, Ass'y Docs. 1854.

ISAAC PRICE—(Silas H. Marks, Alonzo Webber, Daniel Price, assignees.)

Mr. Carpenter's report in relation to temporary occupancy of lands at Lockport; Doc. 181, vol. 7, Ass'y Docs. 1847.

Mr. McCarty's report, claims; Doc. 157, vol. 5, Ass'y Docs. 1848.

RODERICK PRICE.

Mr. Coe's report upon lease of surplus waters of the Erie canal; Doc. 152, vol. 5, Ass'y Docs. 1845.

PRINTING OF STATE.

Gov. Seward's veto of bill concerning; Doc. 172, vol. 7, Ass'y Docs. 1842.

Comptroller Flagg's report concerning; Doc. 3, vol. 1, Senate Docs. 1843.

Comptroller Flagg's further report, embracing statements from 1823; Doc. 12, vol. 1, Senate Docs. 1843.

Report of State printer (T. Weed); Doc. 14, vol. 1, Senate Docs. 1843.

Report of committee on printing, on number of documents for distribution; Doc. 28, vol. 2, Ass'y Docs. 1843.

Report of State printer (E. Croswell); Doc. 37, vol. 1, Senate Docs. 1844.

Attorney General Barker's report, as to printing done for his department; Doc. 68, vol. 2, Senate Docs. 1844.

Surveyor General Jones' report of printing for his department; Doc. 75, vol. 2, Senate Docs. 1844.

Secretary of State, S. Young, report as to printing done for his department; Doc. 79, vol. 2, Senate Docs. 1844.

Report of Commissioners of Canal Fund on the same; Doc. 80, vol. 2, Senate Docs. 1844.

Report of Treasurer, T. Farrington, on the same; Doc. 82, vol. 2, Senate Docs. 1844.

Report of Comptroller, A. C. Flagg, on the same; Doc. 94, vol. 5, Senate Docs. 1844.

Mr. Sherman's report on prices paid; Doc. 31, vol. 1, Senate Docs. 1845.

E. Croswell's report of receipts as State printer; Doc. 34, vol. 3, Ass'y Docs. 1845.

Comptroller Flagg's statement of payments made for printing since 19th February, 1844; Doc. 56, vol. 2, Senate Docs. 1846.

Mr. E. Croswell's report of receipts as State printer; Doc. 68, vol. 2, Senate Docs. 1846.

Comptroller Flagg's report as to printing for executive departments; Doc. 75, vol. 3, Ass'y Docs. 1846.

Report of committee on printing on the bill to provide for the public printing; Doc. 86, vol. 3, Ass'y Docs. 1846.

Comptroller Flagg's report of amount paid for 1845; Doc. 91, vol. 4, Ass'y Docs. 1846.

Mr. Townsend's report on printing the Comptroller's report on the expenditures on the canals; Doc. 94, vol. 4, Ass'y Docs. 1846.

Mr. J. R. Thompson's minority report on same; Doc. 95, vol. 4, Ass'y Docs. 1846.

Report of E. & S. Croswell, as to charges made for publication of legal notices; Doc. 60, vol. 2, Senate Docs. 1847.

Comptroller Flagg's report as to sums paid for printing; Doc. 130, vol. 4, Ass'y Docs. 1847.

Mr. Mersereau's report; Doc. 228, vol. 8, Ass'y Docs. 1849.

Mr. Kennedy's report; Doc. 162, vol. 5, Ass'y Docs. 1848.

Report of Secretary of State, Christopher Morgan, with copies of contracts made; Doc. 15, vol. 1, Senate Docs. 1849.

Comptroller Hunt's report, amount paid for printing from 30th September, 1838; Doc. 47, vol. 1, Senate Docs. 1850.

Comptroller Fuller's report; Doc. 56, vol. 2, Senate Docs. 1851.

Comptroller Wright's report of cost of printing and engraving Documentary History; Doc. 5, vol. 1, Senate Docs. 1851.

Contracts for printing Colonial History; Doc. 5, (page 108,) vol. 1, Ass'y Docs. 1853.

Contract for State printing with C. Van Benthuysen; Doc. 5, (page 128,) vol. 1, Ass'y Docs. 1853.

PRISON ASSOCIATION.

Mr. A. G. Thompson's report on incorporation; Doc. 96, vol. 4, Ass'y Docs. 1845.

Report of the executive committee; Doc. 225, vol. 8, Ass'y Docs. 1847. (This contains a review of the condition of the various State prisons in the Union, and of county jails.)

Memorial in relation to the repeal of the charter of association; Doc. 256, vol. 8, Ass'y Docs. 1847.

Annual report; Doc. 243, vol. 6, Ass'y Docs. 1849.

do	do	120,	do 4,	do	1851.
do	do	123,	do 5,	do	1852.
do	do	103,	do 4,	do	1853.
do	do	143,	do 4,	do	1854.

PRISON DISCIPLINE SOCIETY.

Communication and statèment concerning; Doc. 80, vol. 2, Senate Docs. 1842.

PRIVATE RIGHTS OF OWNERSHIP.

Mr. A. C. Hand's report, as to how far the State may interfere; Doc. 47, vol. 2, Senate Docs. 1847.

PULTENEY ESTATE.

Report of Attorney-General Barker, on the petitions for investigation of title; Doc. 145, vol. 6, Ass'y Docs. 1844.

Mr. W. S. Smith's report on the petitions relative to title; Doc. 121, vol. 4, Ass'y Docs. 1847.

Mr. J. L. Lawrence's report on title; Doc. 60, vol. 2, Senate Docs. 1848.

Attorney General Chatfield's report; Doc. 26, vol. 1, Senate Docs. 1850.

Mr. Bowne's report; Doc. 197, vol. 8, Ass'y Docs. 1850.

PUNISHMENT IN STATE PRISONS.

Mr. F. F. Backus' report on the abolition of the whip, as an instrument of punishment in State prisons; Doc. 120, vol. 4, Senate Docs. 1846.

Mr. Hand's report on the same; Doc. 121, vol. 4, Senate Docs. 1846.

Report of Inspectors of Auburn State Prison, in relation to the punishment of the convict Plumb; Doc. 83, vol. 3, Ass'y Docs. 1846.

Report of Inspectors of same prison in relation to their prunitive regulations; Doc. 137, vol. 4, Ass'y Docs. 1846.

Report of Ransom Cook, agent of Clinton State Prison, on same subject; Doc. 138, vol. 4, Ass'y Docs. 1846.

Report of Inspectors of Sing Sing State Prison, on same subject; Doc. 139, vol. 4, Ass'y Docs. 1846.

Further report on same subject, from Inspectors of Auburn State Prison; Doc. 226, vol. 6, Ass'y Docs. 1846.

Report on same subject from Inspectors of Sing Sing Prison; Doc. 160, vol. 6, Ass'y Docs. 1847.

ABRAHAM V. PUTNAM.

Report of canal appraisers; Doc. 98, vol. 2, Ass'y Docs. 1847.

QUARANTINE AT STATEN ISLAND.

Mr. T. R. Lee's report, judiciary, on the laws relating to the port of New-York; Doc. 243, vol. 7, Ass'y Docs. 1845.

Mr. D. E. Wheeler's report, from a select committee, with testimony; Doc. 60, vol. 3, Ass'y Docs. 1846. (This contains the testimony of medical gentlemen, ship owners, mariners and savans, in relation to contagion, and other subjects connected with Quarantine.)

Mr. John L. Lawrence's majority report, against removal; Doc. 61, vol. 2, Senate Docs. 1848.

Mr. Floyd's minority report, in favor of removal; Doc. 62, vol. 2, Senate Docs. 1848.

Report of the Commissioners of the Land Office, relative to the establishment of a hospital at Sandy Hook; Doc. 96, vol. 3, Senate Docs. 1852.

Resolution of New-York Chamber of Commerce against removal from Staten Island; Doc. 40, vol. 2, Senate Docs. 1849.

Remonstrance of W. R. Townsend, in relation to above resolution; Doc. 144, vol. 3, Ass'y Docs. 1849.

Mr. J. L. Lawrence's majority report, adverse; Doc. 51, vol. 2, Senate Docs. 1849.

Mr. J. G. Floyd's minority report, favorable; Doc. 57, vol. 2, Senate Docs. 1849.

Communication from Governor Fish and Comptroller Fillmore, as to funds tor marine hospital; Doc. 39, vol. 1, Ass'y Docs. 1849.

Mr. Wessel S. Smith's report, after examination of the proposed change by a select committee, with the evidence taken; Doc. 60, vol. 2, Ass'y Docs. 1849.

Communication from Dr. Alexander H. Stevens; Doc. 146, vol. 3, Ass'y Docs. 1849.

Memorial of Health officer, Alexander B. Whiting; Doc. 191, vol. 3, Ass'y Docs. 1849.

Report of Commissioners of Land Office, as to purchase of land at Sandy Hook; Doc. 57, vol. 2, Senate Docs. 1853.

QUACK MEDICINES.

Address by Dr. John G. Sewall, before the State Medical Society, Albany, 1851, on the pernicious influences of nostrums or secret remedies upon the morals and health of the community; Doc. 125, (page 173) vol. 4, Ass'y Docs. 1851.

BENJAMIN D. QUIGG.

Mr. Barstow's report, claims, in relation to charges for arrest of fugitives; Doc. 131, vol. 4, Ass'y Docs. 1847.

Mr. McCarty's report, claims; Doc. 13, vol. 1, Ass'y Docs. 1848.

QUIT RENTS.

Comptroller Flagg's report as to taxation; Doc. 228, vol. 6, Ass'y Docs. 1845.

TALLMAN AND NOYES.

Report of Canal Board; Doc. 46, vol. 3, Ass'y Docs. 1844.

TARIFF.

Mr. D. S. Wright's resolutions; Doc. 143, vol. 7, Ass'y Docs. 1842.

Mr. G. Hard's resolutions; Doc. 93, vol. 3, Senate Docs. 1844.

WILLIAM RADFORD.

Report of Inspectors of State prisons, in relation to claim Doc. 23, vol. 1, Senate Docs. 1849.

Comptroller Fillmore's report; Doc. 92, vol. 2, Ass'y Docs. 1849.

RAILROADS.

Mr. Allen's report, select committee, and petitions for law to regulate; Doc. 85, vol. 4, Ass'y Docs. 1843.

Remonstrance of railroad companies, Buffalo to Schenectady, against proposed regulation law; Doc. 106, vol. 4, Ass'y Docs. 1843.

Remonstrance of railroad companies from Albany to Attica, against being compelled to run in the winter; against the appointment of a railroad commissioner; against the reduction of their fare; Doc 194, vol. 5, Ass'y Docs. 1845.

Mr. R. M. Morrison's report on above subjects; Doc. 224, vol. 6, Ass'y Docs. 1845.

Mr. Beven's report on the petitions for a repeal of the law opening the Utica and Schenectady road to the carrying of freight; Doc. 236, vol. 6, Ass'y Docs. 1845.

Report of Commissioners of Canal Fund, as to tolls on railway freight; Doc. 78, vol. 3, Senate Docs. 1846.

Mr. Tefft's report on the proposed charter for the south side Mohawk river route; the east side of the Hudson route, and a reduction of fare and freight charges, from Schenectady to Buffalo; Doc. 51, vol. 2, Ass'y Docs. 1846.

Report of Secretary of State, N. S. Benton, as to whether the several companies make their reports; Doc. 66, vol. 3, Ass'y Docs. 1846.

Mr. J. T. Bush's report, as to the carriage of freight without payment of tolls; Doc. 192, vol. 5, Ass'y Docs. 1846.

Mr. Hard's report as to the expediency of a general railway law; Doc. 64, vol. 2, Senate Docs. 1847.

Mr. Beekman's report as to expediency of consolidation of the various roads between Albany and Buffalo; Doc. 104, vol. 3, Senate Docs. 1847.

Annual report of Secretary of State, with statistics for the year; Doc. 102, vol. 4, Ass'y Docs. 1847.

Mr. R. H. Williams' report on propriety of consolidation of roads between Albany and Buffalo; Doc. 149, vol. 4, Senate Docs 1847.

Mr. Johnson's majority report on the formation of a general law; Doc. 33, vol. 2, Senate Docs. 1848.

Mr. Geddes' report on minority of same subject; Doc. 33, vol. 2, 1848.

Mr. Cornwell's report on general law; Doc. 15, vol. 1, Senate Docs. 1848.

Mr. E. C. Benedict's report on a general railroad law; Doc. 105, vol. 3, Ass'y Docs. 1848.

Report of Secretary of State, C. Morgan, with abstracts of reports of companies; Doc. 132, vol. 5, Ass'y Docs. 1848.

Mr. Britton's report, on general law; Doc. 207, vol. 5, Ass'y Docs. 1849.

Report of Secretary of State, Christopher Morgan, with statistics; Doc. 182, vol. 3, Ass'y Docs. 1849.

Report of State Engineer, Charles B. Stuart, with abstract of reports of companies; Doc. 84, vol. 3, Senate Docs. 1849.

Report of Hezekiah C. Seymour, State Engineer, with returns of the several companies in State; Doc. 92, vol. 5, Ass'y Docs. 1850.

Mr. Lewis' report in relation to the removal of tolls on railway freight; Doc. 131, vol. 5, Ass'y Docs. 1850.

Mr. E. D. Morgan's report on the same subject; Doc. 95, vol. 3, Senate Docs. 1850.

Report of Hezekiah C. Seymour, State Engineer, with returns of the several companies in State; Doc. 12, vol. 1, Senate Docs. 1851.

Mr. S. H. Johnson's report in favor of imposing canal tolls on the Erie and Northern railroads; Doc. 38, vol. 2, Senate Docs. 1851.

Mr. C. A. Mann's report against the imposition of tolls on railroads; same Document.

Mr. Schoonmaker's report in favor of the continuance of tolls on the Central line, the imposition on the Northern, but adverse to tolls on the Erie; same Document.

Mr. Geddes' report on the subject of removing the tolls from railways; Doc. 86, vol. 3, Senate Docs. 1851.

Mr. J. B. Varnum's minority report on tickets; Doc. 98, vol. 4, Ass'y Docs. 1851.

Mr. J. B. Varnum's report on reduction of fare; Doc. 88, vol. 3, Ass'y Docs. 1851.

Report of Wm. J. McAlpine, State Engineer, with returns of different companies; Doc. 27, vol. 1, Ass'y Docs. 1852.

Report of committee of investigation, State Engineer, W. J. McAlpine, Senator H. E. Bartlett, in relation to accidents; Doc. 13, vol. 1, Senate Docs. 1853.

Mr. D. B. Taylor's report, upon accidents, their causes and prevention; Doc. 117, vol. 6, Ass'y Docs. 1853.

Report of State Engineer, W. J. McAlpine, as to freight carried in this State; Doc. 59, vol. 2, Senate Docs. 1853.

Opinion of Comptroller Wright and Judge Amasa J. Parker, as to the rule of taxation of railways; Doc. 5, (page 107,) vol. 1, Ass'y Docs. 1853.

Annual report of State Engineer, W. J. McAlpine, of the condition of the several roads; Doc. 10, vol. 1, Ass'y Docs. 1853.

Memorial of New-York Chamber of Commerce against the imposition of tolls; Doc. 100, vol. 4, Ass'y Docs. 1854.

ALBANY AND COHOES.

Mr. Johnson's report, on the incorporation; Doc. 33, vol. 2, Senate Docs. 1848.

Mr. Cornwell's report on incorporation; Doc. 15, vol. 1, Senate Docs. 1848.

ALBANY AND GOSHEN.

Report of James Seymour; Doc. 108, vol. 5, Ass'y Docs. 1842.

ALBANY AND SCHENECTADY.

Report of business; Doc. 138, vol. 4, Senate Docs. 1847.

Report of agreement of associate roads between Schenectady and Buffalo; Doc. 68, vol. 3, Ass'y Docs. 1848.

Report in relation to selling emigrant tickets; Doc. 143, vol. 3, Ass'y Docs. 1849.

Report of committee on railroads, to preserve a fair competition between Albany and Schenectady, and Schenectady and Troy railroads; Doc. 159, vol. 3, Ass'y Docs. 1849.

Mr. Cornwell's report on same bill; Doc. 79, vol. 3, Senate Docs. 1849.

ALBANY AND WEST STOCKBRIDGE.

Report of condition; Doc. 86, vol. 5, Ass'y Docs. 1842.

Mr. Tefft's report on alleged refusal to transport the mail; Doc. 39, vol. 4, Ass'y Docs. 1846.

Mr. Leaven's report in relation to the transportation of freight; Doc. 103, vol. 4, Ass'y Docs. 1847.

ATTICA AND BUFFALO.

Remonstrance of Buffalo, against power to fix route through city; Doc. 44, vol. 3, Ass'y Docs. 1843.

Report of business; Doc. 135, vol. 4, Senate Docs. 1847.

Report of committee on railroads on consolidation with Tonawanda; Doc. 58, vol. 4, Ass'y Docs. 1850.

AUBURN AND BINGHAMTON.

Mr. Cornwell's majority report on bill to declare public use; Doc. 54, vol. 2, Senate Docs. 1849.

AUBURN AND ROCHESTER.

Report of condition; Doc. 191, vol. 7, Ass'y Docs. 1842.

Report of list of stockholders; Doc. 194, vol. 7, Ass'y Docs. 1842.

Report of list of stockholders; Doc. 64, vol. 2, Senate Docs. 1846.

Report of business; Doc. 136, vol. 4, Senate Docs. 1847.

Report of financial condition; Doc. 147, vol. 4, Senate Docs. 1847.

Report in relation to dividends paid; Doc. 149, vol. 3, Ass'y Docs. 1849.

Memorial respecting application for the direct road between Rochester and Syracuse; Doc. 13, vol. 1, Ass'y Docs. 1850.

AUBURN AND SYRACUSE.

Report of Commissioners of Canal Fund, as to omission to pay tolls on freight; Doc. 106, vol. 4, Senate Docs. 1846.

Report of business; Doc. 139, vol. 4, Senate Docs. 1847.

Communication in regard to agreement with Albany and Schenectady railroad; Doc. 73, vol. 3, Docs. 1848.

Report in relation to agent at Albany; Doc. 79, vol. 3, Ass'y Docs. 1848.

Report of dividend, capital and interest; Doc. 118, vol. 3, Ass'y Docs. 1849.

Memorial respecting application for direct road between Rochester and Syracuse; Doc. 13, vol. 1, Ass'y Docs. 1850.

BUFFALO AND BATAVIA.

Mr. Lee's report on petition for incorporation; Doc. 156, vol. 7, Ass'y Docs. 1842.

BUFFALO AND BLACK ROCK.

Mr. Orlando Allen's report; Doc. 59, vol. 3, Ass'y Docs. 1851.

CANANDAIGUA AND CORNING

Mr. C. A. Mann's report, on constitutionality of proposed amendment to charter; Doc. 37, vol. 1, Senate Docs. 1850.

CANAJOHARIE AND CATSKILL.

Report of condition; Doc. 118, vol. 5, Ass'y Docs. 1842.

CAYUGA AND SUSQUEHANNA.

Annual report of condition; Doc. 86, vol. 2, Ass'y Docs. 1847.

DIVISION AVENUE.

Mr. T. P. St. John's report; Doc. 62, vol. 3, Ass'y Docs. 1853.

ERIE, NEW-YORK AND.

Report to Governor of the actual condition; Doc. G., of Doc. 2, vol. 1, Senate Docs. 1842. Same in vol. 1, Ass'y Docs. 1842.

Petition of, for aid in construction; Doc. 18, vol. 1, Senate Docs. 1842.

Petition of, respecting line in Sullivan and Broome counties; Doc. 58, vol. 3, Senate Docs. 1842. Same, Doc. 92, vol. 5, Ass'y Docs. 1842.

Report of Senate committee on railroads, Mr. Scott, on route through valley of Delaware river; Doc. 74, vol. 3, Senate Docs. 1842.

Letter from James Bowen, president, accompanied by communication from Gov. Seward, in relation to condition; Doc. 113, vol. 5, Ass'y Docs. 1842.

Report of committee of investigation, Chatfield, Graham, Maclay, on affairs of road; Doc. 50, vol. 3, Ass'y Docs. 1842.

Report of condition; Doc. 141, vol. 7, Ass'y Docs. 1842.

Report of assignment; Doc. 38, vol. 1, Senate Docs. 1843.

Petition of directors for aid; Doc. 12, vol. 1, Ass'y Docs. 1843.

Report, with list of stockholders and of indebtedness; Doc. 76, vol. 3, Ass'y Docs. 1843.

Mr. Hillard's resolutions of enquiry; Doc. 94, vol. 4, Ass'y Docs. 1843.

Mr. Lee's resolution of enquiry; Doc. 95, vol. 4, Ass'y Docs. 1843.

Report of Wm. Baker, railroad commissioner, under act of 18th April, 1843, of condition; Doc. 6, vol. 1, Ass'y Docs. 1844.

Resolutions of board of directors, as to report of Major Baker; Doc. 31, vol. 1, Ass'y Docs. 1844.

Mr. Faulkner's report, railroads, on condition and act for relief; Doc. 109, vol. 3, Senate Docs. 1845.

Mr. Van Valkenburgh's report, railroads, on the petition for a surrender of the State lien; Doc. 31, vol. 3, Ass'y Docs. 1845.

Mr. Van Valkenburgh's report, railroads, on the subject of the route through Pike and Susquehanna counties, Pennsylvania; Doc. 58, vol. 5, Ass'y Docs. 1845.

Annual report of Wm. Baker, railroad commissioner, under act of April 18, 1843; Doc. 63, vol. 3, Ass'y Docs. 1845.

Proposed joint resolution, Mr. Morrison, authorising the adoption of the Pike and Susquehanna county route, Pennsylvania; Doc. 122, vol. 4, Ass'y Docs. 1845.

Same resolution, amended, defining the point of crossing the Delaware; Doc. 133, vol. 4, Ass'y Docs. 1845.

Same resolution further amended; Doc. 149, vol. 4, Ass'y Docs. 1845.

Remonstrance against altering the route into Pennsylvania; Doc. 182, vol. 5, Ass'y Docs. 1845.

Attorney General Van Buren's report, as to whether the act for a change of route requires a two-third vote; Doc. 204, vol. 6, Ass'y Docs. 1845.

Mr. Titus' majority report on the Pennsylvania route; Doc. 142, vol. 5, Ass'y Docs. 1846.

Mr. Blodgett's minority report against said route; Doc. 157, vol. 5, Ass'y Docs. 1846.

Act of the State of Pennsylvavia, Feb'y 16, 1841, as to the New-York and Erie railroad; Doc. 170, vol. 5, Ass'y Docs. 1846.

Report of commissioners, John B. Jervis, Horatio Allen, James

Wilson, William Dewey, appointed to determine in relation to location, in conflicting routes; Doc. 25, vol. 1, Ass'y Docs. 1847.

Report of minority of commissioners, Frederick Whittlesey, Orville W. Childs, Job Pierson, on same subject: Doc. 46, vol. 2, Ass'y Docs. 1847.

Mr. Leaven's majority report on location of route; Doc. 118, vol. 4, Ass'y Docs. 1847.

Mr. W. B. Wright's minority report on same subject; Doc. 119, vol. 4, Ass'y Docs. 1847.

Mr. Leaven's majority report against bill adverse to decision of commissioners; Doc. 122, vol. 4, Ass'y Docs. 1847.

Mr. S. H. Johnson's report in favor of imposing tolls; Doc. 38, vol. 2, Senate Docs. 1851.

Mr. Schoonmaker and Mr. C. A. Mann's report adverse to such imposition; Doc. 38, vol. 2, Senate Docs. 1851.

Mr. J. B. Varnum, Jr's., report on the Piermont route; Doc. 131, vol. 4, Ass'y Docs. 1851.

Mr. A. B. Conger's memorial, as chairman of a committee of citizens of Rockland county, adverse to legalizing the route by Sufferns; Doc. 131, vol. 4, Ass'y Docs. 1851.

Report in relation to agreement with other companies in New-Jersey; Doc. 83, vol. 4, Ass'y Docs. 1853.

HARLAEM.

Report of condition; Doc. 193, vol. 7, Ass'y Docs. 1843.

Mr. Van Valkenburgh's report, railroads, and amendment of charter; Doc. 44, vol. 3, Ass'y Docs. 1845.

Report as to agreement with Hudson River road, in relation to rate of fare; Doc. 26, vol. 1, Senate Docs. 1854.

HUDSON AND BERKSHIRE.

Report of condition ; Doc. 151, vol. 7, Ass'y Docs. 1842.

Mr. J. S. Gould's report on petition to grant authority to create a lien prior to that of the State; Doc. 116, vol. 4, Ass'y Docs. 1847.

Communication from Washington Hunt, Comptroller, concerning non-payment of interest on State loan; Doc. 6, vol. 1, Ass'y Docs. 1854.

Communication to J. C. Wright, Comptroller, notifying him of inability to meet the payment of interest; Doc. 5, (page 105,) vol. 1, Ass'y Docs. 1853.

HUDSON RIVER.

Mr. Scott's report, railroads, on incorporation; Doc. 104, vol. 3, Senate Docs. 1843.

Mr. Tefft's majority report, favorable to charter; Doc. 51, vol. 2, Ass'y Docs. 1846.

Mr. J. T. Bush's minority report, adverse; Doc. 53, vol. 2, Ass'y Docs. 1846.

Attorney General Jordan's report in relation to the location of the road through the Sing Sing Prison; Doc. 64, vol. 2, Senate Docs. 1848.

Mr. Story's report on amendment of charter; Doc. 11, vol. 1, Ass'y Docs. 1850.

Report as to agreement with Harlaem railroad as to rate of fare; Doc. 27, vol. 1, Senate Docs. 1854.

ITHACA AND OWEGO.

Report as to condition; Doc. 138, vol. 7, Ass'y Docs. 1843.

Further report; Doc. 144, vol. 7, Ass'y Docs. 1842.

LOCKPORT AND NIAGARA FALLS.

Mr. Story's report on the act for the relief of the creditors; Doc. 48, vol. 3, Ass'y Docs. 1850.

LONG ISLAND.

Report of condition; Doc. 163, vol. 7, Ass'y Docs. 1842.

Mr. Van Valkenburgh's report in relation to pecuniary condition, with the reply of the company to series of interrogatories; Doc. 203, vol. 6, Ass'y Docs. 1845.

Mr. Leaven's report on the petition of E. H. Wells, asking redress from acts of company; Doc. 123, vol. 4, Ass'y Docs. 1847.

MOHAWK AND HUDSON.

Report of condition; Doc. 192, vol. 7, Ass'y Docs. 1842.

Report as to freight transported; Doc. 82, vol. 3, Senate Docs. 1847.

NEW-YORK AND ALBANY.

Report of condition; Doc. 28, vol. 2, Senate Docs. 1842.

Report to Secretary of State; Doc. 35, vol. 2, Senate Docs. 1842.

Communication from president to Governor Bouck; Doc. D, accompanying Doc. 2, vol. 1, Senate Docs. 1843. Doc. 3, vol. 1, Ass'y Docs. 1843.

Mr. R. Denniston's resolutions of enquiry; Doc. 73, vol. 3, Senate Docs. 1843.

Report in answer to above; Doc. 110, vol. 3, Senate Docs. 1843.

Memorial, with Mr. E. F. Johnson's statement respecting the comparative merits of the river and inland route; Doc. 87, vol. 4, Ass'y Docs. 1843.

Mr. Beekman's report; Doc. 73, vol. 2, Senate Docs. 1845.

OGDENSBURGH AND LAKE CHAMPLAIN.

Mr. Redington's majority report, on construction by State; Doc. 127, vol. 5, Ass'y Docs. 1842.

Engineer William R. Casey's report; Doc. 70, vol. 4, Ass'y Docs. 1842.

Mr. Hard's report as to change of route; Doc. 144, vol. 4, Senate Docs. 1847.

Mr. R. H. Williams' report on same subject; same Document.

Mr. Fine's report; Doc. 24, vol. 1, Senate Docs. 1848.

Mr. S. H. Johnson's report in favor of imposing tolls; Doc. 38, vol. 2, Senate Docs. 1851.

Mr. Schoonmaker's report in favor of same; Doc. 38, vol. 2, Senate Docs. 1851.

RENSSELAER AND SARATOGA.

Report of condition; Doc. 117, vol. 5, Ass'y Docs. 1842.

Report of names and residence of stockholders; Doc. 43, vol. 2, Senate Docs. 1846.

SACKETTS HARBOR AND SARATOGA.

Mr. William Samuel Johnson's report; Doc. 39, vol. 2, Senate Docs. 1848.

Mr. Horton's report in relation to the amendment of the incorporation; Doc. 93, vol. 4, Ass'y Docs. 1851.

Mr. Peter's majority report in relation to change of route; Doc. 88, vol. 3, Ass'y Docs. 1854.

Mr. Randall's minority report in relation to change of route; Doc. 88, Ass'y Docs. 1854.

SARATOGA AND SCHENECTADY.

Report of condition; Doc. 130, vol. 5, Ass'y Docs. 1842.

SARATOGA AND WASHINGTON.

Mr. Hard's report on petition for repeal of charter; Doc. 152, vol. 4, Ass'y Docs. 1847.

SENECA LAKE AND ERIE.

Mr. Faulkner's report; Doc. 91, vol. 3, Senate Docs. 1845.

SOUTH SIDE OF MOHAWK.

Mr. R. H. Williams' majority report, on the proposition to allow the Schenectady and Troy railway to extend their road to Utica, on the south side of the Mohawk; Doc. 122, vol. 4, Senate Docs. 1846.

Mr. J. P. Beekman's minority report on the same; Doc. 123, vol. 4, Senate Docs. 1846.

Memorial of A. B. Johnson, and other citizens of Utica, for the same; Doc. 36, vol. 2, Ass'y Docs. 1846.

Mr. Tefft's adverse report; Doc 51, vol. 2, Ass'y Docs. 1846.

SYRACUSE AND UTICA.

Report of condition; Doc. 78, vol. 4, Ass'y Docs. 1842.

Report as to use of cars in bringing persons to attend a political meeting; Doc. 103, vol. 3, Senate Docs. 1846.

Report of Commissioners of Canal Fund, as to the omission to pay toll on freight; Doc. 106, vol. 4, Senate Docs. 1846.

Report of business; Doc. 137, vol. 4, Senate Docs. 1847.

Report of financial condition; Doc. 154, vol. 4, Senate Docs. 1847.

Memorial against reduction of railroad fare; Doc. 69, vol. 3, Ass'y Docs. 1848.

Communication in relation to agreement with Albany and Schenectady railroad company; Doc. 92, vol. 3, Ass'y Docs. 1848.

Report in relation to transportation expenses; Doc. 144, vol. 5, Ass'y Docs. 1848.

TIOGA COAL, IRON MINING AND MANUFACTURING COMPANY.
(Corning and Blossburgh.)

Mr. W. S. Allen's report on the suspension of the sale of road in default of payment of interest; Doc. 152, vol. 5, Ass'y Docs. 1844.

TONAWANDA.

Mr. Blodgett's report on the reduction of the price of freight; Doc. 58, vol. 2, Ass'y Docs. 1847.

Report of business; Doc. 133, vol. 4, Senate Docs. 1847.

Report in relation to contract with Albany and Schenectady company; Doc. 77, vol. 3, Ass'y Docs. 1848.

Report of committee on railroads in relation to the consolidation with Attica and Buffalo; Doc. 58, vol. 4, Ass'y Docs. 1850.

TROY AND GREENBUSH.

Mr. Hard's report on incorporation; Doc. 86, vol. 3, Senate Docs. 1845.

Report of relations with New-York and Albany railroad company; Doc. 68, vol. 3, Ass'y Docs. 1845.

Testimony taken before the railroad committee; Doc. 118, vol. 4, Ass'y Docs. 1845.

TROY AND RUTLAND.

Memorial and statistics in relation to; Doc. 151, vol. 3, Ass'y Docs. 1849.

TROY AND SCHENECTADY.

Attorney-General Van Buren's report as to the sale of the road; Doc. 167, vol. 5, Ass'y Docs. 1846.

Report as to freight transported; Doc. 84, vol. 3, Senate Docs. 1847.

Mr. Miner's report; Doc. 191, vol. 8, Ass'y Docs. 1850.

UTICA AND BINGHAMTON.

Mr. Peters' report in relation to town subscription; Doc. 80, Ass'y Docs. 1854.

UTICA AND SCHENECTADY.

Report of condition; Doc. 76, vol. 4, Ass'y Docs. 1842.

Report as to freight transported; Doc. 83, vol. 3, Senate Docs. 1847.

Report of business; Doc. 134, vol. 4, Senate Docs. 1847.

Report in relation to action of agent at Albany; Doc. 74, vol. 3, Ass'y Docs. 1848.

Report in relation to use of Utica and Schenectady cars; Doc. 80, vol. 3, Ass'y Docs. 1848.

Report in relation to the sale of emigrant tickets; Doc. 143, vol. 3, Ass'y Docs. 1849.

RAILROAD STATISTICS.

Report of Secretary of State, S. Young, with abstracts of the several reports made to his office; Doc. 123, vol. 5, Ass'y Docs. 1844.

Report of Secretary of State, N. S. Benton, with abstracts of the several reports; Doc. 129, vol. 4, Ass'y Docs. 1845.

Report of Secretary of State, N. S. Benton, with abstracts of the several reports; Doc. 80, vol. 3, Ass'y Docs. 1846.

Report of Secretary of State, N. S. Benton, with abstracts of the several reports; Doc. 102, vol. 4, Ass'y Docs. 1847.

Report of the Secretary of State, Christopher Morgan, with abstracts of the several reports; Doc. 132, vol. 5, Ass'y Docs. 1848.

Report of Secretary of State, Christopher Morgan, with abstracts of reports of companies; Doc. 182, vol. 3, Ass'y Docs. 1849.

Report of State Engineer, Charles B. Stuart, with abstracts of reports of companies; Doc. 84, vol. 3, Senate Docs. 1849.

Report of State Engineer, Hezekiah C. Seymour, with abstracts of reports of companies; Doc. 92, vol. 5, Ass'y Docs. 1850.

Report of State Engineer, Hezekiah C. Seymour, with abstracts of reports of companies; Doc. 12, vol. 1, Senate Docs. 1851.

Report of State Engineer, Wm. J. McAlpine, with abstracts of reports of companies; Doc. 27, vol. 1, Ass'y Docs. 1852.

Report of State Engineer, Wm. J. McAlpine, with abstracts of reports of companies; Doc. 10, vol. 1, Ass'y Docs. 1853.

Report of State Engineer, Wm. J. McAlpine, with abstracts of reports of companies; Doc. 120, vol. 3, Ass'y Docs. 1854.

HENRY S. RANDALL, (Secretary of State.)

Report on registration of births, marriages and deaths; Doc. 50, vol. 1, Senate Docs. 1852.

Report in reference to publication of Session Laws, Doc. 11, vol. 1, Ass'y Docs. 1852.

Report in relation to Colonial History; Doc. 43, vol. 2, Senate Docs. 1853.

Report in relation to clerical force in his office; Doc. 53, vol. 2, Senate Docs. 1853.

Report in relation to general statutes; Doc. 72, vol. 3, Senate Docs. 1853.

Report in relation to idiots; Doc. 73, vol. 3, Senate Docs. 1853.

Annual report of Superintendent of Common Schools; Doc. 4, vol. 1, Ass'y Docs. 1853.

JOHN RANDEL, JR.

Report of C. B. Stuart, State Engineer; Doc. 209, vol. 5, Ass'y Docs. 1849.

Mr. McCarty's report, claims; Doc. 181, vol. 5, Ass'y Docs. 1848.

READING OF BILLS.

Mr. Hand's report as to the proper time when a bill shall be read for the last time; Doc. 15, vol. 1, Senate Docs. 1847.

JOSHUA READ.

Report of Canal Board; Doc. 156, vol. 5, Ass'y Docs. 1845.

RAQUETTE AND MOOSE RIVERS.

Mr. Henry J. Raymond's report on the improvement; Doc. 68, vol. 4, Ass'y Docs. 1850.

Report of commissioners of improvement; Doc. 5, (page 138) vol. 1, Ass'y Docs. 1853.

JEROME B. RANSOM.

Mr. Upham's report, Doc. 46, vol. 2, Senate Docs. 1850.

HENRY RECTOR.

Mr. Burhans' majority report, claims; Doc. 119, vol. 5, Ass'y Docs. 1844.

Mr. Gorham's minority report; Doc. 143, vol. 6, Ass'y Docs. 1844.

Mr. Tefft's report, claims; Doc. 97, vol. 4, Ass'y Docs. 1845.

Mr. J. E. Beers' report, claims; Doc. 188, vol. 7, Ass'y Docs. 1847.

Mr. Floyd's report, claims; Doc. 16, vol. 1, Senate Docs. 1848.

Mr. Hale's report, claims; Doc 71, vol. 2, Ass'y Docs. 1849.

Mr. Severance report, claims; Doc 72, vol. 3, Ass'y Docs. 1851.

Report of committee on claims; Doc. 53, vol. 2, Ass'y Docs. 1852.

Report of committee on claims; Doc. 102, vol. 3, Ass'y Docs. 1854.

RED JACKET, (Town.)

Mr. Irish's report on the action of the supervisors of Erie county, in relation to the erection of this town; Doc. 167, vol. 6, Ass'y Docs. 1850.

JAMES R. REES.

Mr. Burrough's report; Doc. 159, vol. 6, Ass'y Docs. 1850.

REGENTS OF THE UNIVERSITY.

Annual report; Doc. 55, vol. 3, Senate Docs. 1842.

Correspondence of Harmanus Bleecker, with Holland government, in relation to gift of reports of Regents of the University; Doc. 108, vol. 4, Senate Docs. 1842.

Annual report; Doc. 57, vol. 2, Senate Docs. 1843.

do 78, do 2, do 1844.

Report of Dr. Beck, Secretary, as to scholars; Doc. 113, vol. 3, Senate Docs. 1844.

Report that the seat of John C. Spencer, is vacant; Doc. 131, vol. 4, Senate Docs. 1844.

Report in relation to the consolidation of school districts in Avon with Avon academy; Doc. 108, vol. 3, Senate Docs. 1845.

Annual report; Doc. 51, vol. 2, Senate Docs. 1845.

Annual report; Doc. 71, vol. 2, Senate Docs. 1846.

Report on condition of Cabinet Natural History; Doc. 91, vol. 3, Senate Docs. 1846.

Annual report, Doc. 101, vol. 3, Senate Docs. 1847.

Communication concerning appropriations to Academies and State Library; Doc. 35, vol. 1, Ass'y Docs. 1847.

Annual report; Doc. 71, vol. 3, Senate Docs. 1848.

Report on condition of Cabinet Natural History; Doc. 20, vol. 1, Senate Docs. 1849.

Annual report; Doc. 55, vol. 2, Senate Docs. 1849. (The Documents are not with this.)

Report on historical archives in State Library; Doc. 148, vol. 3, Ass'y Docs. 1849, (with list of manuscripts.)

Annual report; Doc. 78, vol. 3, Senate Docs. 1849.

Annual report; Doc. 113, vol. 3, Senate Docs. 1850.

Annual report on State Cabinet Natural History and antiquarian collection; Doc. 75, vol. 2, Senate Docs. 1850.

Annual report on State Cabinet of Natural History and antiquarian collection; Doc. 30, vol. 2, Senate Docs. 1851.

Annual report; Doc. 72, vol. 3, Senate Docs. 1851.

do 92, do 2, do 1852.

Annual report on the condition of the Cabinet of Natural History, illustrated with colored engravings; Doc. 122, vol. 5, Ass'y Docs. 1852.

Annual report on the condition of the Cabinet of Natural History; Doc. 1, vol. 16, Senate Docs. 1853.

Annual report; Doc. 70, vol. 2, Senate Docs. 1853.

Report in relation to their power to incorporate colleges; Doc. 22, vol. 2, Ass'y Docs. 1853.

Annual report; Doc. 77, vol. 2, Senate Docs. 1854.

REGISTER OF NEW-YORK.

Report of Secretary of State, Christopher Morgan, of fees received; Doc. 77, vol. 3, Senate Docs. 1849.

REGISTRY LAW—(City of New-York.)

Mr. Grant's report in favor of repeal; Doc. 13, vol. 1, Ass'y Docs. 1842.

Message from Gov. Seward, communicating his approval of repeal; Doc. 87, vol. 5, Ass'y Docs. 1842.

RENSSELAER COUNTY.

Mr. McElwain's report; Doc. 4, vol. 1, Senate Docs. 1853.

ROBERT RENWICK, ZEBINA WILSON, ZEBINA WILSON, JR.

Mr. Gorham's report, claims; Doc. 160, vol. 6, Ass'y Docs. 1844.

ROBERT RENWICK, JR., HENRY TRACY.

Report of Canal Board; Doc. 179, vol. 5, Ass'y Docs. 1848.

RE-PAYMENT OF TAXES.

Report of Commissioners of Land Office; Doc. 183, vol. 7, Ass'y Docs. 1843.

Report of Commissioners of Land Office; Doc. 8, vol. 1, Senate Docs. 1843.

REPUDIATION.

Mr. H. A. Foster's resolutions; Doc. 76, vol. 3, Senate Docs. 1843.

Mr. E. Rhodes' substitutory resolutions; same Document.

Resolutions concerning; Doc. 91, vol. 3, Senate Docs. 1843.

RETRENCHMENT.

Mr. E. C. Church's report; Doc. 113, vol. 4, Ass'y Docs. 1843.

Mr. Talcott's report; Doc. 79, vol. 3, Senate Docs. 1846.

Mr. Nathaniel Coe's report; Doc. 134, vol. 4, Ass'y Docs. 1846.

Mr. Pitt's report; Doc. 143, vol. 5, Ass'y Docs. 1846.

Mr. N. Coe's further report; Doc. 206, vol. 6, Ass'y Docs. 1846.

REVISED STATUTES.

Report in relation to the purchase of, by the Assembly; Doc. 16, vol. 1, Ass'y Docs. 1851.

JEMIMA REXFORD, CYRUS W. REXFORD.

Mr. Dixon's report, judiciary; Doc. 17, vol. 1, Senate Docs. 1843.

JOHN REYNOLDS.

Report on claims; Doc. 126, vol. 5, Ass'y Docs. 1843.

Mr. Lawyer's report, claims; Doc. 96, vol. 4, Ass'y Docs. 1846.

Mr. J. Beer's report, claims; Doc. 24, vol. 1, Ass'y Docs. 1847.

RHODE ISLAND.

Resolutions of General Assembly, relative to the election of presidential electors; Doc. 54, vol. 3, Ass'y Docs. 1842.

Resolutions of same, against any interference by Congress with the internal government and constitution of said State; Doc. 196, vol. 7, Ass'y Docs. 1844.

Communication from Governor Harris, for a manuscript volume of boundary line, Rhode Island and Massachusetts; Doc. 239, vol. 5, Ass'y Docs. 1849.

Communication from Governor Fish, in relation to above application; Doc. , vol. , Ass'y Docs. 1849.

Mr. J. W. Beekman's report on above application; Doc. 132, vol. 3, Ass'y Docs. 1849.

Resolutions of Legislature on subject of a board of agriculture; Doc. 180, vol. 8, Ass'y Docs. 1850.

Resolutions of thanks for a copy of the proceedings of boundary commissioners, transmitted by this State; Doc. 182, vol. 8, Ass'y Docs. 1850.

RICHARD D. RHODES.

Mr. Fitzhugh's report; Doc. 175, vol. 3, Ass'y Docs. 1849.

DAVID RICE.

Mr. Backhouse's report; Doc. 61, vol. 3, Ass'y Documents, 1857.

J. B. RICH.

Mr. Robinson's report on the incorporation of "Rich's Institute for Physical Training;" Doc. 99, vol 3, Senate Docs. 1850.

LYMAN RICH.

Mr. Lewis' report in relation to a farm bridge; Doc. 25, vol. 3, Ass'y Docs. 1850.

BENJAMIN RICHARDSON, JR.

Mr. Curtis' report in relation to Erieville reservoir; Doc. 16, vol. 1, Senate Docs. 1851.

CALVIN P. RICHARDSON, JOSIAH BRINTNALL, HIRAM BRINTNALL.

Report of Canal Board; Doc. 103, vol. 4, Ass'y Docs. 1846.

Mr. J. E. Beers' report, claims; Doc. 74, vol. 2, Ass'y Docs. 1847.

Mr. Ward's report; Doc. 134, vol. 3, Ass'y Docs. 1849.

PHINEAS RICHARDSON, DANIEL GROSS.

Mr. McCarty's report, claims; Doc. 154, vol. 5, Ass'y Docs. 1848.

Mr. Hale's report, claims; Doc. 124, vol. 3, Ass'y Docs. 1849.

RICHARD RICHARDSON.

Mr. Pettengill's report, claims; Doc. 101, vol. 4, Ass'y Docs. 1853.

SAMUEL S. RIDDLE, CONSTANT COOK, JOHN MAGEE, HORATIO R. RIDDLE.

Mr. Putnam's report, claims; Doc. 109, vol. 3, Senate Docs. 1843.

Mr. Porter's report, claims; Doc. 95, vol. 3, Senate Docs. 1844.

Mr. Porter's report, claims; Doc. 67, vol. 2, Senate Docs. 1845.

RIFLEMEN.

Mr. S. E. Church's report, in relation to the incorporation of company at New-York, Doc. 169, vol. 7, Ass'y Docs. 1842.

WILLIAM S. RILEY.

Mr. Alvord's report, claims; Doc. 72, vol. 3, Ass'y Docs. 1844.

BENJAMIN S. ROBERTS.

Mr. Nicole's report, claims; Doc. 122, vol. 5, Ass'y Docs. 1843.

DANIEL ROBERTS.

Mr. McMurray's report, aliens; Doc. 180, vol. 7, Ass'y Docs. 1842.

ANTHONY L. ROBERTSON,
(Commissioner of the Code.)

Report of Comptroller Fillmore, concerning salary; Doc. 42, vol. 2, Ass'y Docs. 1849.

Communication from, in relation to resolution of enquiry; Doc. 46, vol. 2, Ass'y Docs. 1849.

Communication from, resigning his office, and giving his views of a code of laws; Doc. 223, vol. 5, Ass'y Docs. 1849.

JABEZ ROBERTSON.

Report of committee on claims, Mr. Swartwout, on claim; Doc. 124, vol. 5, Ass'y Docs. 1842.

PETER ROBINSON.

Mr. Hitchcock's report; Doc. 57, vol. 2, Ass'y Docs. 1847.

ROCHESTER.

Mr. N. K. Hall's minority report, in favor of an additional savings bank; Doc. 68, vol. 3, Ass'y Docs. 1846.

Report ot Canal Board, as to bill for relief of citizens in relation to canal damages; Doc. 48, vol. 2, Senate Docs. 1848.

Report of Canal Board in relation to the diversion of the waters of the Genesee river, for canal purposes; Doc. 172, vol. 5, Ass'y Docs. 1848.

Mr. G. Underwood's report (Jacob Graves, and others), in relation to the diversion of the waters of the Genesee river, for the canal; Doc. 102, vol. 5, Ass'y Docs. 1852.

Mr. Moss' report in relation to Erie canal feeder; Doc. 109, vol. 5, Ass'y Docs. 1852.

Mr. Pettingill's report in relation to re-construction of feeder; Doc. 43, vol. 2, Ass'y Docs. 1853.

Mr. Pettingill's report on diversion of the waters of the Genesee river for Erie canal; Doc. 86, vol. 4, Ass'y Docs. 1853.

Mr. Mallory's report in relation to the claims of Jacob Graves, and others, mill owners, concerning the diversion of surplus waters; Doc. 104, vol. 3, Ass'y Docs. 1854.

ROCHESTER UNIVERSITY.

Memorial of trustees, asking for appropriation for library; Doc. 68, vol. 3, Ass'y Docs. 1851.

Report of condition made to Regents of the University; Doc. 77, (page 134) vol. 2, Senate Docs. 1854.

ANDREW ROCKWELL.

Report of Canal Board; Doc. 134, vol. 4, Senate Docs. 1846.

Mr. J. E. Beers' report, claims; Doc. 55, vol. 2, Ass'y Docs. 1847.

Mr. McCarty's report, claims; Doc. 38, vol. 2, Ass'y Docs. 1848.

Mr. Backhouse's report; Doc. 70, vol. 3, Ass'y Docs. 1851.

Mr. Bradley's report, claims; Doc. 78, vol. 2, Ass'y Docs. 1852.

JOHN R. B. RODGERS.

Report of Commissioners of Land Office; Doc. 49, vol. 1, Senate Docs. 1844.

PATRICK RODGERS.

Mr. Severance's report, claims; Doc. 52, vol. 3, Ass'y Docs. 1851.

DAVID ROGERS.

Mr. N. Jones's report; Doc. 13, vol. 1, Senate Docs. 1852.

SIMEON ROGERS.

Mr. J. G. Hopkins' report, clrims; Doc. 66, vol. 3, Senate Docs. 1842.

Report of committee on claims; Doc. 37, vol. 1, Ass'y Docs. 1846.

MORRISON ROLLS, WIBERT P. SANFORD.

Mr. Spaulding's report; Doc. 20, vol. 3, Ass'y Docs. 1848.

ROME.

Engineer Brodhead's report in relation to the enlarged Erie canal, and old and new line at this place; Doc. 110, vol. 3, Senate Docs. 1844.

Mr. Dickinson's report in relation to bringing into use the new line of canal at this place; Doc. 125, vol. 5, Ass'y Docs. 1844.

Report of Canal Commissioners, on same; Doc. 70, vol. 2, Senate Docs. 1845.

Report of Canal Board in relation to surplus waters of Rome level of Erie canal; Doc. 109, vol. 4, Ass'y Docs. 1847.

JOHN ROOF—(as heir of Captain John Roof.)

Mr. Boughton's report; Doc. 239, vol. 6, Ass'y Docs. 1845.

Attorney-General Van Buren's report, with examination of ancient patents; Doc. 240, vol. 7, Ass'y Docs. 1845.

Mr. W. J. Cornwell's report; Doc. 218, vol. 6, Ass'y Docs. 1846.

THOMAS ROSE, JOHN FLINT.

Report of Canal Board; Doc. 93, vol. 3, Ass'y Docs. 1844.

JOHN J. ROSS.

Mr. Hammond's report; Doc. 163, vol. 6, Ass'y Docs. 1847.

Mr. Joshua A. Spencer's report; Doc. 148, vol. 4, Senate Docs. 1847.

Mr. Feeter's report, claims: Doc. 125, vol. 2, Ass'y Docs. 1848.

MAHLON L. ROSS.

Mr. Barrow's report, claims; Doc. 77, vol. 3, Ass'y Docs. 1854.

ROUSE'S POINT BRIDGE.

Mr. John L. Lawrence's majority report, with testimony adverse; Doc. 24, vol. 1, Senate Docs. 1849.

Mr. J. G. Floyd's minority report, favorable; Doc. 56, vol. 2, Senate Docs. 1849.

Mr. Fitzhugh's report, favorable; Doc. 94, vol. 2, Ass'y Docs. 1849.

Testimony taken before committee; Doc. 87, vol. 3, Senate Docs. 1850.

Mr. Geddes' report from a committee of investigation; Doc. 20, vol. 1, Senate Docs. 1851.

Mr. Dart's report, same document.

Mr. Owens' report—same document.

To this, testimony and maps are annexed.

Mr. Geddes report, on extension of piers; Doc. 90, vol. 3, Senate Docs. 1851.

Mr. Lesley's minority report, adverse; Doc. 134, vol. 5, Ass'y Docs. 1851.

Mr. Lesly's majority report, adverse; Doc. 154, vol. 6, Ass'y Docs. 1851.

LEWIS SACOMBE.

Mr. C. P. Daly's report, select committee, on the application of French citizens of New-York, for the proceeds of Lewis Sacombe's estate; Doc. 181, vol. 5, Ass'y Docs. 1843.

BENJAMIN H. SAGE, WILLIAM B. WILLIAMS.

Report of Canal Board; Doc. 121, vol. 5, Ass'y Docs. 1844.

HEZEKIAH SAGE.

Mr. Schoonmaker's report, claims; Doc. 95, vol. 3, Senate Docs. 1851.

Mr. Backhouse's report, claims; Doc. 77, vol. 3, Ass'y Docs. 1851.

Mr. Van Valkenburgh's report, claims; Doc. 69, vol. 2, Ass'y Docs. 1852.

SAGE, CASLER & Co.

Mr. Dix's report, canals, on petition; Doc. 176, vol. 7, Ass'y Docs 1842.

Mr. Murray's report, canals; Doc. 80, vol. 4, Ass'y Docs. 1843.

SAGE, WAALRTH AND DUNHAM.

Report of Canal Board; Doc. 52, vol. 2, Senate Docs. 1844.

Mr. Porter's report, claims; Doc. 84, vol. 2, Senate Docs. 1844.

Mr. Newkirk's report, claims; Doc. 126, vol. 4, Ass'y Docs. 1845.

Mr. J. E. Beer's report, claims; Doc. 237, vol. 8, Ass'y Docs. 1847.

Mr. McCarty's report, claims; Doc. 88, vol. 3, Ass'y Docs. 1848.

Mr. H. G. Root's report, claims; Doc. 155, vol. 6, Ass'y Docs. 1850.

Mr. Schoonmaker's report, claims; Doc. 64, vol. 2, Senate Docs. 1851.

SAILOR'S SNUG HARBOR,

Annual report of treasurer; Doc. 32, vol. 2, Senate Docs. 1842.

Annual report of treasurer; Doc. 47, vol. 1, Senate Docs. 1844.

Annual report of treasurer; Doc. 91, vol. 4, Ass'y Docs. 1845.

Annual report of treasurer; Doc. 39, vol. 1, Senate Docs. 1847.

Annual report of treasurer; Doc. 195, vol. 6, Ass'y Docs. 1848.

Annual report of treasurer; Doc. 233, vol. 5, Ass'y Docs. 1849.

Annual report of treasurer; Doc. 104, vol. 3, Senate Docs. 1850.

Annual report of treasurer; Doc. 67, vol. 3, Senate Docs. 1851.

SANFORD AND EAGGLESTON.

Report of Canal Board; Doc. 69, vol. 3, Ass'y Docs. 1844.

Report of Canal Board; Doc. 78, vol. 3, Ass'y Docs. 1846.

Mr. Pitt's report, claims; Doc. 99, vol. 4, Ass'y Docs. 1846.

SANGERSFIELD PRESBYTERIAN CHURCH.

Mr. Orville Clark's report; Doc. 38, vol. 1, Senate Docs. 1844.

SARANAC RIVER.

Mr. Noble's report in relation to the improvement; Doc. 94, vol. 4, Ass'y Docs. 1854.

Report of commissioners to improve the navigation; Doc. 5, (page 117,) vol. 1, Ass'y Docs. 1853.

ISAAC SATTERLY.

Mr. Ward's report, claims; Doc. 15, vol. 1, Ass'y Docs. 1849.

Mr. Baldwin's report, claims; Doc. 118, vol. 3, Ass'y Docs. 1854.

SAVINGS BANKS.

Mr. S. Lawrence's report; Doc. 54, vol. 2, Ass'y Docs. 1846.

Mr. Ayrault's report on the policy of a general law; Doc. 59, vol. 2, Senate Docs. 1848.

Attorney-General Chatfield's report, as to whether they are for "banking purposes" within the meaning of the 4th section, 8th article, Constitution 1846; Doc. 28, vol. 3, Ass'y Docs. 1850.

Mr. Le Roy's majority report favorable to a general law for the incorporation; Doc. 39, vol. 2, Ass'y Docs. 1851.

Mr. J. J. Townsend's minority report against a general law; Doc. 40, vol. 2, Ass'y Docs. 1851.

Mr. Cooley's report on special corporations; Doc. 40, vol. 1, Senate Docs. 1852.

Report of Abram Wakeman and George Underwood, commissioners to ascertain the amount of unclaimed deposites and dividends in the several banks and savings banks; Doc. 127, vol. 7, Ass'y Docs. 1852.

ALBANY SAVINGS BANK.

Annual report; Doc. 63, vol. 4, Ass'y Docs. 1842.

Annual report as above; Doc. 202, vol. 5, Ass'y Docs. 1843.

Report of condition; Doc. 61, vol. 2, Senate Docs. 1844.

Annual report of condition; Doc. 88, vol. 2, Ass'y Docs. 1847.

BOWERY SAVINGS BANK.

Annual report; Doc. 55, vol. 4, Ass'y Docs. 1842. Doc. 37, vol. 2, Senate Docs. 1842.

Annual report; Doc. 197, vol. 5, Ass'y Docs. 1843.
do do 161, do 6, do 1844.
do do 115, do 3, Senate Docs. 1845. Doc. 187, vol. 5, Ass'y Docs. 1845.

Annual report; Doc. 196, vol. 6, Ass'y Docs. 1848.

BROOKLYN BANK, for savings.

Report; Doc. 54, vol. 4, Ass'y Docs. 1842.
do do 67, do 3, do 1843.
do do 51, do 2, do 1844.
do do 164, do 5, do 1845.
do do 173, do 6, do 1847.

BUFFALO SAVINGS BANK.

Report of condition; Doc. 223, vol. 8, Ass'y Docs. 1847.

Further report; Doc. 200, vol. 6, Ass'y Docs. 1848.

GREENWICH SAVINGS BANK.

Annual report; Doc. 46, vol. 2, Senate Docs. 1842.
do do 33, do 1, do 1844.
do do 120, do 3, do 1845.

ITHACA SAVINGS BANK.

Report of condition; Doc. 196, vol. 5, Ass'y Docs. 1843.
do do 148, do 4, do 1847.

NEW-YORK BANK for savings.

Annual report; Doc. 48, vol. 2, Senate Docs. 1842.
do do 64, do 3, Ass'y Docs. 1843.
do do 89, do 2, Senate Docs. 1844.
do do 121, do 3, do 1845.
do do 78, do 3, do 1848.

ONTARIO SAVINGS BANK.

Annual report; Doc. 122, vol. 3, Senate Docs. 1845.

SEAMENS' BANK FOR SAVINGS, New-York.

Annual report; Doc. 74, vol. 4, Ass'y Docs. 1842.
do do 188, do 5, do 1843.
do do 165, do 6, do 1844.
do do 167, do 5, do 1845.
do do 90, do 2, do 1847.
do do 198, do 6, do 1848.

SCHENECTADY SAVINGS BANK.

Annual report; Doc. 29, vol. 2, Senate Docs. 1842.
do do 32, do 1, do 1844.
do do 202, do 6, Ass'y Docs. 1848.

TROY SAVINGS BANK.

Annual report of unclaimed dividends and deposites; Doc. 25, vol. 2, Ass'y Docs. 1842.

Report of condition; Doc. 99, vol. 4, Senate Docs. 1842.

Annual report; Doc. 183, vol. 5, Ass'y Docs. 1843.

Annual report of condition; Doc. 168, vol. 6, Ass'y Docs. 1844.

Annual report of unclaimed dividends and deposites; Doc. 172, vol. 7, Ass'y Docs. 1844.

Annual report as above; Doc. 53, vol. 3, Ass'y Docs. 1845.

Annual report of condition; Doc. 213, vol. 6, Ass'y Docs. 1845.
do do do 201, do 6, do 1848.

UTICA SAVINGS BANK.

Annual report; Doc. 47, vol. 2, Senate Docs. 1842.
do do 171, do 7, Ass'y Docs. 1844.
do do 181, do 5, do 1845.
do do 87, do 2, do 1847.

MATTHEW SAYRE.

Mr. Alvord's report, claims; Doc. 66, vol. 3, Ass'y Docs. 1844.

Mr. McCarty's report, claims; Doc. 103, vol. 3, Ass'y Docs. 1848.

Report of committee on claims; Doc. 26, vol. 1, Ass'y Docs. 1849.

SCHENECTADY INDEPENDENT ARTILLERY COMPANY.

Mr. Erastus Root's report, militia; Doc. 113, vol. 3, Senate Docs. 1843.

SCHOOL DISTRICTS.

Mr. J. A. Lott's report as to taxing district No. 11, in Otselic; Doc. 100, vol. 4, Senate Docs. 1846.

Mr. A. C. Hand's report as to same; Doc. 14, vol. 1, Senate Docs. 1846.

SCHOOL LAWS.

Report of Samuel S. Randall, commissioner appointed by Gov. Hunt, to codify the laws of this State, relating to common schools, with the code, Doc. 21, vol. 1, Ass'y Docs. 1852.

HENRY R. SCHOOLCRAFT.

Census of the Iroquois; Doc. 24, vol. 1, Senate Docs. 1846.

MARIUS SCHOONMAKER, Senator.

Resolution in relation to election as Congressman; Doc. 62, vol. 2, Senate Docs. 1851.

NICHOLAS SCHUYLER.

Report of Canal Board; Doc. 98, vol. 4, Ass'y Docs. 1846.

Mr. Ward's report, claims; Doc. 168, vol. 3, Ass'y Docs. 1849.

SCHOHARIE CREEK AQUEDUCT.

Report of Canal Commissioners; Doc. 94, vol. 3, Senate Docs. 1843.

SCHOHARIE COURT HOUSE.

Mr. G. O. Chase's report on a change of location; Doc. 65, vol. 3, Ass'y Docs. 1846.

MARIUS SCHOONMAKER.

Report as to claim of Henry Hall; Doc. 41, vol. 1, Senate Docs. 1854.

Report as to the costs in the case of Phelps *vs.* Newell—Canal Law of 1851; Doc. 45, vol. 1, Senate Docs. 1854.

Report in the case of Merritt Clark, R. R. Clark, S. D. Wheeler; Doc. 72, vol. 2, Senate Docs. 1854.

Report as to funds advanced by G. W. Newell, to persons claiming to be superintendents of canal repairs; Doc. 63, vol. 2, Senate Docs. 1854.

Report as to tolls, trade and tonnage of the canals; Doc. 145, vol. 5, Ass'y Docs. 1854.

Report as to money paid to canal contractors, for damages and extra allowances from 1840, to 1853, inclusive; Doc. 148, vol. 5, Ass'y Docs. 1854.

Report in relation to a draft drawn by John C. Mather, Canal Commissioner, October 21, 1853; Doc. 135, vol. 4, Ass'y Docs. 1854.

Further report on same subject; Doc. 141, vol. 4, Ass'y Docs. 1854.

SCHOHARIE TURNPIKE ROAD—western branch.

Mr. Hard's report, select committee, on proposed removal of gate; Doc. 65, vol. 2, Senate Docs. 1843.

Report of Messrs. A. G. Smith and J. Burdick, a select committee of the Assembly of examination; Doc. 103, vol. 4, Ass'y Docs. 1845.

Report of Messrs. C. Drake, and E. Marshall, a select committee as above; Doc. 37, vol. 2, Ass'y Docs. 1846.

Mr. Gay's report as to power of court of common pleas to remove; Doc. 134, vol. 5, Ass'y Docs. 1848.

Thomas R. Danforth's report of tolls collected; Doc. 113, vol. 3, Ass'y Docs. 1848.

LIVINGSTON SCHUYLER.

Mr. J. A. Lott's report on divorce bill; Doc. 130, vol. 4, Senate Docs. 1846.

JACOB SCRAMLING.

Mr. Allen's report, judiciary, on his petition for a divorce; Doc. 199, vol. 7, Ass'y Docs. 1844.

Mr. T. R. Lee's report, judiciary, on his petition for divorce; Doc. 139, vol. 4, Ass'y Docs. 1845.

AMOS W. SCRIVEN

Report of Canal Board; Doc. 29, vol. 1, Ass'y Docs. 1844.

SEAMENS' RETREAT.

Annual report; Doc. 28, vol. 1, Senate Docs. 1845.
do do 182, do 5, Ass'y Docs. 1846.
do do 34, do 1, Senate Docs. 1847.

SEAMENS' FRIEND SOCIETY.

Mr. Lawrence's report, as to release of loan; Doc. 52, vol. 2, Senate Docs. 1843.

ELIPHALET SERBS, HORACE ADAMS.

Mr. W. A. Gilbert's report, claims; Doc. 29, vol. 2, Ass'y Docs. 1852.

Mr. E. Ward's report, claims; Doc. 44, vol. 2, Senate Docs. 1853.

SENATE OF 1842.

Official list, with districts, counties and nearest post-office; Doc. 3, vol. 1, Senate Docs. 1842.

Classified list; Doc. 4, vol. 1, Senate Docs. 1842.

List of committees; Doc. 5, vol. 1, Senate Docs. 1842.

Report of Sergeant-at-Arms, relative to books in library; Doc. 24, vol. 2, Senate Docs. 1842.

SENATE OF 1843.

Standing committees; Doc. 4, vol. 1, Senate Docs. 1843.

List of members and officers; Doc. 5, vol. 1, Senate Docs. 1843.

Official list; Doc. 6, vol. 1, Senate Docs. 1843.

SENATE OF 1844.

List of members; Doc. 1, vol. 1, Senate Docs. 1844.

Standing committees; Doc. 6, vol. Senate Docs. 1844.

List of members and officers; Doc. 7, vol. 1, Senate Docs. 1844.

SENATE OF 1845.

Members and residence; Doc. 1, vol. 1, Senate Docs. 1845.

Standing committees; Doc. 3, vol. 1, Senate Docs. 1845.

List of, with residences in Albany; Doc. 5, vol. 1, Senate Docs.

SENATE OF 1846.

List of members and post offices; Doc. 1, vol. 1, Senate Docs. 1846.

List with city residences; Doc. 3, vol. 1, Senate Docs. 1846.

Standing committees; Doc. 5, vol. 1, Senate Docs. 1846.

SENATE OF 1847.

Official list; Doc. 1, vol. 1, Senate Docs. 1847.

Residence list; Doc. 3, vol. 1, Senate Docs. 1847.

Post office list; Doc. 6, vol, 1, Senate Docs. 1847.

Standing committees; Doc. 7, vol. 1, Senate Docs. 1847.

Rules and orders; Doc. 25, vol. 1, Senate Docs. 1847.

Rules and orders as amended; Doc. 26, vol. 1, Senate Docs. 1847.

SENATE OF 1848.

Rules and orders; Doc. 1, vol. 1, Senate Docs. 1848.

Standing committees; Doc. 7, vol. 1, Senate Docs. 1848.

Residence list; Doc. 8, vol. 1, Senate Docs. 1848.

Post office list; Doc. 9, vol. 1, Senate Docs. 1848.

Rules 40 and 45; Doc. 10, vol. 1, Senate Docs. 1848.

SENATE OF 1849.

Rules and orders; Doc. 1, vol. 1, Senate Docs. 1849.

List of members and officers; Doc. 3, vol. 1, Senate Docs. 1849.

Standing committees; Doc. 4, vol. 1, Senate Docs. 1849.

SENATE OF 1850.

Official list; Doc. 1, vol. 1, Senate Docs. 1850.

Rules and orders; Doc. 2, vol. 1, Senate Docs. 1850.

Post office list; Doc. 4, vol. 1, Senate Docs. 1850.

Standing committees; Doc. 5, vol. 1, Senate Docs. 1850.

Revised rules and orders; Doc. 7, vol. 1, Senate Docs. 1850.

Joint rules; Doc. 32, vol. 1, Senate Docs. 1850. Doc. 38, vol. 3, Ass'y Docs. 1850.

Statistical list; Doc. 72, vol. 2, Senate Docs. 1850.

SENATE OF 1851.

Official list; Doc. 1, vol. 1, Senate Docs. 1851.

Rules and orders of last Senate, reprinted; Doc. 3, vol. 1, Senate Docs. 1851.

Joint rules; Doc. 4, vol. 1, Senate Docs. 1851.

Rules as adopted; Doc. 6, vol. 1, Senate Docs. 1851.

Mr. Skinner's minority report on rules; Doc. 7, vol. 1, Senate Docs. 1851.

Residence list; Doc. 10, vol. 1, Senate Docs. 1851.

Standing committees; Doc. 11, vol. 1, Senate Docs. 1851.

Official list at extra session; Doc. 76, vol. 3, Senate Docs. 1851.

Standing committees at extra session; Doc. 78, vol. 3, Senate Docs. 1851.

Residence list; Doc. 80, vol. 3, Senate Docs. 1851.

Rules and orders; Doc. 79, vol. 3, Senate Docs. 1851.

SENATE OF 1852.

Rules and orders of 1851, reprinted; Doc. 1, vol. 1, Senate Docs. 1852.

Standing committees; Doc. 3, vol. 1, Senate Docs. 1852.

Joint rules; Doc. 4, vol. 1, Senate Docs. 1852.

Mr. Cooley's report; Doc. 7, vol. 1, Senate Docs. 1852.

Residence list; Doc. 9, vol. 1, Senate Docs. 1852.

Mr. Cooley's report; Doc. 10, vol. 1, Senate Docs. 1852.

Rules and orders; Doc. 27, vol. 1, Senate Docs. 1852.

SENATE OF 1853.

Annual message; Doc. 1, vol. 1, Senate Docs. 1853.

Rules and orders; Doc. 2, vol. 1, Senate Docs. 1853.

Standing committees; Doc. 3, vol. 1, Senate Docs. 1852.

Mr. Conger's report in relation to the rules; Doc. 5, vol. 1, Senate Docs. 1853.

Residence list; Doc. 8, vol. 1, Senate Docs. 1853.

Joint rules; Doc. 9, vol. 1, Senate Docs. 1853.

Further joint rules; Doc. 15, vol. 1, Senate Docs. 1853.

SENATE OF 1854.

Official list; Doc. 1, vol. 1, Senate Docs. 1854.

Rules and orders of 1853, reprint; Doc. 2, vol. 1, Senate Docs. 1854.

Post office list; Doc. 6, vol. 1, Senate Docs. 1854.

Standing committees; Doc. 7, vol. 1, Senate Docs. 1854.

Rules and orders; Doc. 11, vol. 1, Senate Docs. 1854.

Joint rules; Doc. 11, vol. 1, Senate Docs. 1854.

SENATORS OF UNITED STATES.

Governor Wright's message in respect to existing vacancies; Doc. 8, vol. 1, Ass'y Docs. 1845.

SENECA COUNTY.

General view and agricultural survey, by John Delafield; Doc. 150, vol. 6, Ass'y Docs. 1851.

SENECA INDIANS.

Mr. Dixon's report of attendance on council; Doc. 84, vol. 3, Senate Docs. 1843.

Mr. Hard's report, on the act for their protection and improvement; Doc. 93, vol. 3, Senate Docs. 1845.

Memorial of R. L. Tilotson, one of the Massachusetts grantees, in relation to the above act; Doc. 94, vol. 3, Senate Docs. 1845.

Remonstrance of George Jemison, and other warriors, against the above bill; Doc. 104, vol. 3, Senate Docs. 1845.

Governor Wright's communication concerning; Doc. 57, vol. 2, Senate Docs. 1846, with letters of Indians, and Mr. Schoolcraft and Mr. Leland, annexed.

Governor Wright's communication, with their memorial; Doc. 197, vol. 5, Ass'y Docs. 1846.

Reports of removals of white persons for tresspass; Doc. 207, vol. 7, Ass'y Docs. 1847.

Gov. Fish's message in relation to new form of government; Doc. 108, vol. 3, Ass'y Docs. 1849.

Mr. Prescott's minority report; Doc. 189, vol. 3, Ass'y Docs. 1849.

Mr. Curtis's report; Doc. 191, vol. 3, Ass'y Docs. 1849.

Letter of W. L. Marcy, Secretary of War, to Mr. B. Peirce, on subject of paying annuities; Doc. 105, vol. 5, Ass'y Docs. 1849.

Memorial from Wm. Jemerson, and other chiefs; Doc. 21, vol. 1, Senate Docs. 1850.

Communication from N. T. Strong, in behalf of Indian chiefs; Doc. 59, vol. 2, Senate Docs. 1850.

Peter Wilson's memorial for aid to the boarding school on the Cattaraugus Reservation; Doc. 164, vol. 6, Ass'y Docs. 1850.

Mr. Owen's majority report; Doc. 108, vol. 3, Senate Docs. 1850.

SENECA LAKE AND RIVER.

Report of Canal Board, as to water power; Doc. 144, vol. 5, Ass'y Docs. 1846.

Report of Canal Board, as to regulating wiers at the outlet of the lake; Doc. 166, vol. 5, Ass'y Docs. 1846.

Mr. Bishop Perkins' report; Doc. 177, vol. 5, Ass'y Docs. 1846.

Report of Canal Commissioners in relation to obstructions in outlet; Doc. 64, vol. 3, Ass'y Docs. 1848.

SERPENTS.

S. F. Baird's communication to the Regents of the University, concerning varieties in city of New-York, page 97 of Doc. 50, vol. 1, Senate Docs. 1854.

SESSION LAWS.

Communication from Secretary of State, Samuel Young, in relation to publication; Doc. 81, vol. 3, Senate Docs. 1842.

Communication from acting Secretary of State, Archibald Campbell, in relation to publication; Doc. 9, vol. 1, Senate Doc. 1842.

Mr. Snow's report, in relation to publication; Doc. 124, vol. 5, Ass'y Docs. 1844.

Report in relation to publication; Doc. 11, vol. 1, Ass'y Docs. 1852.

SEVENTH-DAY BAPTISTS AND JEWS.

Mr. Joshua A. Spencer's report as to their day of worship; Doc. 131, vol. 4, Senate Docs. 1847.

WILLIAM H. SEWARD.

Annual message, 1842; Doc. 1, vol. 1, Senate Docs, 1842. Doc. 1, vol. 1, Ass'y Docs. 1842.

Correspondence between, and the Governor of Virginia, on the subject of delivery of fugitives from justice, and documents illustrating; Doc. A. in Doc. 2, vol. 1, Senate Docs. 1842. Doc. A. in Doc. 2, vol. 1, Ass'y Docs. 1842.

Letter from, to Secretary of War, John C. Spencer, concerning the propriety of the Government of the United States, purchasing a right of use of the State road; Doc. K, of Doc. 2, vol. 1, Senate Docs. 1842. Doc. D. of Doc. 2, vol. 1, Ass'y Docs. 1842.

Communication accompanying Mr. Bowen, president of Erie railroad report; Doc. 113, vol. 5, Ass'y Docs. 1842.

Message communicating approval of repeal of registry law; Doc. 87, vol. 5, Ass'y Docs. 1842.

Communication in relation to account for arms and military stores, with government United States; Doc. 27, vol. 2, Senate Docs. 1842.

Message in relation to views taken by South Carolina, in respect to controversy with Virginia, concerning fugitives from justice; Docs. 62, vol. 4, Ass'y Docs. 1842.

Communication from, respecting resolutions on same subject; Doc. 41, vol. 2, Senate Docs. 1842.

Communication from South Carolina, in relation to the public lands; Doc. 52, vol 3. Senate Doc. 1842.

Message vetoing bill changing mode of appointing bank commissioners; Doc. 83, vol. 4, Senate Docs. 1842.

Message recommending appropriation for Colonial History; Doc. 85, vol. 4, Senate Docs. 1842.

Message vetoing the bill repealing the New-York Criminal Court bill; Doc. 90, vol. 4, Senate Docs. 1842.

Message in relation to action of South Carolina and Virginia, concerning act giving trial by jury to fugitive slaves; Doc. 96, vol. 4, Senate Docs. 1842.

Message dissenting from action of Legislature respecting refusal to surrender certain persons; Doc. 102, vol. 4, Senate Docs. 1842.

Message at extra session; Doc. 106, vol. 4, Senate Docs. 1842. Doc. 195, vol. 7, Ass'y Docs. 1842.

Message in relation to sending reports of Regents of the University to the government of Holland; Doc. 108, vol. 4, Senate Docs. 1842.

Veto message of State Printer bill; Doc. 172, vol. 7, Ass'y Docs. 1842.

SEWARD, (town of)

Mr. Woodruff's report on town meeting; Doc. 49, vol. 2, Ass'y Docs. 1849.

SENATE DISTRICTS.

Mr. N. K. Hall's minority report on organization; Doc. 203, vol. 6, Senate Docs. 1846.

ASAPH SEYMOUR, WILLIAM COFFIN, RICHARD SAVAGE, WILLIAM S. HARRISON.

Comptroller Flagg's report in relation to their contract for cast iron valve gates; Doc. 205, vol. 7, Ass'y Docs. 1844.

Mr. Tefft's report, claims; Doc. 121, vol. 4, Ass'y Docs. 1845.

Mr. Dean's minority report, claims; Doc. 126, vol. 4, Ass'y Docs. 1846.

Mr. J. E. Beer's report, claims; Doc. 54, vol. 2, Ass'y Docs. 1847.

Mr. Van Valkenburgh's report, claims; Doc. 41, vol. 2, Ass'y Docs. 1852.

HORATIO SEYMOUR.

Report on canals; Doc. 177, vol. 7, Ass'y Docs. 1844.

Annual message; Doc. 1, vol. 1, Senate Docs. 1853. Doc. 1, vol. 1, Ass'y Docs. 1853.

Message relative to appropriations for the Erie and Oswego canals; Doc. 67, vol. 2, Senate Docs. 1853. Doc. 91, vol. 4, Ass'y Docs. 1853.

Message at extra session; Doc. 69, vol. 2, Senate Docs. 1853. Doc. 106, vol. 4, Ass'y Docs. 1853.

Message in relation to the erection of a monument in Independence square at Philadelphia; Doc. 89, vol. 4, Ass'y Docs. 1853.

Message returning with objections the bill in relation to admitting city stocks as basis for banking; Doc. 113, vol. 6, Ass'y Docs. 1853.

Communication in relation to resistance of service of process; Doc. 119, vol. 6, Ass'y Docs. 1853.

Annual message; Doc. 3, vol. 1, Senate Docs. 1854. Doc. 3, vol. 1, Ass'y Docs. 1854.

JAMES SEYMOUR.

Mr. Wheeler's report, claims; Doc. 21, vol. 2 Ass'y Docs. 1843.

LAUREN SEYMOUR.

Mr. Wood's report, claims; Doc. 40, vol. 2, Ass'y Docs. 1853.

Mr. Hitchcock's report, claims; Doc. 38, vol. 1, Senate Docs. 1854.

SHAKERS.

Mr. Taylor's report relative to rescinding trusts; Doc. 198, vol. 3, Ass'y Docs. 1849.

Report of condition of society at New Lebanon, Columbia co. New-York.

WILLIAM SHEPARD.

Mr. John A. Dix's report; Doc. 17, vol. 7, Ass'y Docs. 1842.

SHERBURNE UNION SEMINARY.

Mr. Folsom's report; Doc. 127, vol. 4, Senate Docs. 1847.

WILLIAM SHERMAN, URIAL SHERMAN.

Mr. Hale's report, claims; Doc. 22, vol. 1, Ass'y Docs. 1849.

Mr Wakeman's report, claims; Doc. 142, vol. 6, Ass'y Docs. 1850.

SHERIFFS.

Mr. Kingsley's report on fees; Doc. 62, vol. 4, Ass'y Docs. 1850.

SHERIFF OF NEW-YORK.

Report of fees; Doc. 35, vol. 2, Ass'y Docs. 1848.

Report of Sheriff Westervelt, in answer to a resolution of enquiry, concerning amount of mortgage sale and fees; Doc. 56, vol. 2, Ass'y Docs. 1849.

JAMES H. SHERRILL.

Mr. Johnson's report, claims; Doc. 72, vol. 2, Senate Docs. 1847.

SHIPS AND VESSELS.

Report of committee on judiciary, on the bill relative to the collection of demands; Doc. 77, vol. 2, Ass'y Docs. 1847.

JANNOT C. SHIPPEY, WOODMAN KIMBALL.

Report of Canal Commissioners; Doc. 40, vol. 1, Senate Docs. 1846.

Mr. Johnson's report, claims; Doc. 60, vol. 2, Senate Docs. 1846.

Mr. McCarty's report, claims; Doc. 151, vol. 5, Ass'y Docs. 1848.

HENRY SHOWDY.

Mr. N. Jones' report, claims; Doc. 85, vol. 2, Senate Docs. 1852.

Mr. Delos Bradley's report, claims; Doc. 86, vol. 2, Ass'y Docs. 1852.

SILK MANUFACTURE.

Report in relation to manufacture of silk in Auburn State prison; Doc. I, of Doc. 2, vol. 1, Senate Docs. 1842.

Same in vol. 1, Ass'y Docs. 1842.

Report of Inspectors of Auburn State prison; Doc. 23, vol. 1, Senate Docs. 1843.

Hector Jaquet's memorial respecting culture; Doc. 82, vol. 3, Senate Docs. 1843.

JOHN SIMSON.

Report of Canal Board; Doc. 151, vol. 6, Ass'y Docs. 1844.

SINGLE DISTRICTS.

Mr. B. F. Hall's proposition of constitutional amendment; Doc. 61, vol. 3, Ass'y Docs. 1844.

SING SING STATE PRISON.

Annual report of Inspectors; Doc. 39, vol. 2, Senate Docs. 1842.

Annual report; Doc. 10, vol. 1, Senate Docs. 1843.

Mr. Bockee's report concerning the payment of a judgment Doc. 83, vol. 3, Senate Docs. 1843.

Memorial of John W. Edmonds, one of the Inspectors, concerning financial condition; Doc. 176, vol. 5, Ass'y Docs. 1843.

Annual report; Doc. 20, vol. 1, Senate Docs. 1844.

Report of Inspectors in relation to the labor contracts; Doc. 113, vol. 5, Ass'y Docs. 1844.

Annual report of Inspectors; Doc. 9, vol. 1, Senate Docs. 1845.

Annual report; Doc. 16, vol. 1, Senate Docs. 1845.

Report of the Commissioners of the Land Office, in relation to an armory for a military guard at the prison; Doc. 103, vol. 5, Ass'y Docs. 1846.

Mr. Hand's report on financial condition; Doc. 111, vol. 4, Senate Docs. 1846.

Report of Inspectors on subject of punishments; Doc. 139, vol. 4, Ass'y Docs. 1846.

Annual report; Doc. 5, vol. 1, Senate Docs. 1847.

Mr. Backus' report of investigation; Doc. 153, vol. 4, Senate Docs. 1847.

Mr. J. E. Beers', claims, report on appropriation to Radford claim; Doc. 243, vol. 8, Ass'y Docs. 1847.

Report of Inspectors in relation to contracts; Doc. 258, vol. 8, Ass'y Docs. 1847.

Report of minority of Inspectors, on financial condition; Doc. 17, vol. 1, Senate Docs. 1848.

Report of Inspectors in relation to debt of prison; Doc. 22, vol. 1, Senate Docs. 1848.

Mr. Cornwell's report of investigation; Doc. 51, vol. 2, Senate Docs. 1848.

Attorney-General Jordan's report in relation to location of Hudson river railroad: Doc. 64, vol. 2, Senate Docs. 1848.

Annual report of Inspectors; Doc. 10, vol. 1, Ass'y Docs. 1848.

Mr. Cornwell's report in relation to investigation; Doc. 69, vol. 2, Senate Docs. 1849.

Remonstrance of Inspector Wells, against the Chauncey Smith bill; Doc. 57, vol. 2, Senate Docs. 1851.

Report of committee on claims, in the case of Chauncey Smith, late agent; Doc. 105, vol. 4, Ass'y Docs. 1851.

Mr. S. L. Macomber's report, on wall; Doc. 89, vol. 3, Ass'y Docs. 1851.

Report of the Inspector, relative to an assault and battery on Henry Hagan; Doc. 95, vol. 3, Senate Docs. 1852.

Annual report; Doc. 30, vol. 1, Senate Docs. 1853.

Inspector Darius Clark's report, as to indebtedness; Doc. 66, vol. 2, Senate Docs. 1854.

Inspector Henry Storms' report as to indebtedness; Doc. 70, vol. 2, Senate Docs. 1854.

SLAVERY.

Mr. S. H. P. Hall's resolution, in relation to the extension of slavery; Doc. 5, vol. 1, Senate Docs. 1848.

Report of the judiciary committee on the bill entitled "An act for the protection of personal liberty;" Doc. 14, vol. 1, Senate Docs. 1848.

Mr. Bowen's report; Doc. 139, vol. 3, Ass'y Docs. 1849.

Mr. Geddes' report, on so much of Gov. Fish's message, as relates to subject; Doc. 8, vol. 1, Senate Docs. 1850.

Mr. Henry J. Raymond's minority report; Doc. 29, vol. 3, Ass'y Docs. 1850.

PELEG SLOCUM,

Mr. Schoonmaker's report, claims; Doc. 33, vol. 2, Senate Docs. 1851.

DAVID P. SMALLEY.

Comptroller Flagg's report; Doc. 97, vol. 3, Senate Docs. 1846.

SMITH & Co., of Canajoharie.

Mr. J. Benedict's report, claims; Doc. 104, vol. 5, Ass'y Docs. 1852.

ASA P. SMITH.

Report of the committee on claims, Mr. Sherwood, on claims; Doc. 70, vol. 3, Senate Docs. 1842.

Report of Canal Board; Doc. 31, vol. 2, Senate Docs. 1842.

Report of Canal Board; Doc. 108, vol. 4, Ass'y Docs. 1843.

Mr. Murray's report, canals; Doc. 118, vol. 4, Ass'y Docs. 1843.

Mr. Porter's report, claims; Doc. 28, vol. 1, Senate Docs. 1844.

Mr. Tefft's report, claims; Doc. 95, vol. 4, Ass'y Docs. 1845.

BENJAMIN SMITH.

Report of Attorney General Barker, in reference to escheat of land; Doc. 20, vol. 1, Senate Docs. 1845.

CHAUNCEY SMITH.

Report of Comptroller Fillmore, as to his accounts, as agent of the Sing Sing prison; Doc. 99, vol. 2, Ass'y Docs. 1849.

Report of committee on claims, on his claim as agent of Sing Sing State prison; Doc. 105, vol. 4, Ass'y Docs. 1851.

Mr. Johnson's report, claims; Doc. 83, vol. 3, Senate Docs. 1846.

Report of Canal Board; Doc. 49, vol. 2, Ass'y Docs. 1846.

Mr. J. E. Beers' report, claims; Doc. 69, vol. 2, Ass'y Docs. 1847.

E. DARWIN SMITH.

Report as clerk in chancery for 8th circuit, of office expenses; Doc. 48, vol. 2, Senate Docs. 1846.

E. G. RAWSON SMITH.

Mr. A. C. Hand's report. (This examines the question of change of name.) Doc. 114, vol. 4, Senate Docs. 1846.

JOHN C. SMITH, WARREN NORTON.

Mr. N. Jones' report, claims; Doc. 57, vol. 4, Senate Docs. 1842.

JOHN P. SMITH.

Mr. J. T. Pierce's report; Doc. 18, vol. 1, Senate Docs. 1852.

NOAH SMITH.

Mr. Schoonmaker's report, claims; Doc. 50, vol. 2, Senate Docs. 1850.

OTIS SMITH.

Mr. Barrow's report; Doc. 35, vol. 1, Ass'y Docs. 1854.

WILLIAM SMITH.

Mr. Carpenter's report; Doc. 244, vol. 7, Ass'y Docs. 1845.

Mr. E. G. Spaulding's report; Doc. 85, vol. 3, Ass'y Docs. 1848.

WILLIAM SMITH, JR.

Report of Secretary of State, N. S. Benton, and Surveyor General, H. Halsey, to land purchased of Indians; Doc. 212, vol. 6, Ass'y Docs. 1845.

Report of Secretary of State, N. S. Benton; Doc. 149, vol. 5, Ass'y Docs. 1846.

SODUS BAY CANAL.

Report of Canal Board, as to probable effect on the water power at Oswego, and of the supply from the surplus waters of the Erie canal; Doc. 151, vol. 6, Ass'y Docs. 1850.

Mr. J. J. Townsend's report; Doc. 64, vol. 3, Ass'y Docs. 1851.

Mr. S. M. Burrough's report; Doc. 65, vol. 3, Ass'y Docs. 1851.

SOLE LEATHER.

Mr. H. Putnam's report concerning the inspection; Doc. 75, vol. 3, Senate Docs. 1843.

SONS OF TEMPERANCE, in the town of North East, Putnam county.

Report of committee on judiciary, against special incorporation; Doc. 20, vol. 2, Ass'y Docs. 1852.

SOUTH CAROLINA.

Resolutions of Legislature relative to public lands; Doc. 52, vol. 3, Senate Docs. 1842.

Law report on resolutions of Legislature concerning controversy between New-York and Virginia, on the subject of alleged fugitives from justice; Doc. 62, vol. 4, Ass'y Docs. 1842.

Resolutions of Legislature concerning State debts and annexation of Texas; Doc. 15, vol. 1, Ass'y Docs. 1844.

Mr. Van Schoonhoven's resolutions relative to the expulsion of Mr. Hoar, of Massachusetts; Doc. 26, vol. 1, Ass'y Docs. 1845.

SOUTHFIELD.

Mr. Lott's report, judiciary, as to election of town officers; Doc. 112, vol. 4, Senate Docs. 1846.

SOUTHPORT.

Mr. Philo Jones' report in relation to plankroad; Doc. 161, vol. 6, Ass'y Docs. 1850.

SPAFFORD.

Mr. Haight's report, grievances, in relation to law requiring the town of Marcellus, to remunerate Spafford for support of poor; Doc. 165, vol. 5, Ass'y Docs. 1843.

F. A. SPALDING.

Report of Canal Commissioners; Doc. 85, vol. 3, Senate Docs. 1847.

HARRISON SPALDING.

Mr. Pettingill's report, claims; Doc. 84, vol. 4, Ass'y Docs 1853.

AMBROSE SPENCER.

Report of the arrangements for the celebration of his funeral obsequies by the Legislature; Doc. 131, vol. 2, Ass'y Docs. 1848.

JOHN C. SPENCER.

Communication from, resigning the office of Secretary of State; Doc. 11, vol. 1, Senate Docs. 1842.

Communication respecting W. W. Niles; Doc. 82, vol. 3, Senate Docs. 1850.

Opinion in relation to the Canal Law of 1851; Doc. 102, vol. 4, Ass'y Docs. 1851.

SPENCERPORT.

Report of Canal Board in relation to a nuisance; Doc. 139, vol. 5, Ass'y Docs. 1850.

ROBERT SPOOR.

Report of Canal Board; Doc. 128, vol. 5, Ass'y Docs. 1844.

JAMES SPRAKER.

Report of Canal Commissioners; Doc. 42, vol. 3, Ass'y Docs. 1845.

JAMES SPRAKER, JOSEPH SPRAKER.

Mr. E. Ward's report, claims; Doc. 65, vol. 2, Senate Docs. 1852.

JENKS S. SPRAGUE.

Annual address before State Medical Society; Doc. 33, (page 5,) vol. 4, Ass'y Docs. 1854.

SQUAW ISLAND.

Report of Canal Board upon removal of bar in Niagara river; Doc. 213, vol. 7, Ass'y Docs. 1847.

Report of Canal Board in relation to improvement of harbors connected therewith; Doc. 57, vol. 2, Senate Docs. 1848.

MARY STAFFORD.

Mr. W. S. Smith's report; Doc. 32, vol. 2, Ass'y Docs. 1848.

FREDERICK STARR.

Mr. D. R. F. Jones' report; Doc. 47, vol. 2, Ass'y Docs. 1842.

CHARLES N. ST. CLAIR, JAMES ST. CLAIR.

Mr. Johnson's report, claims; Doc. 75, vol. 2, Senate Docs. 1847.

STATE HALL, NEW.

Report of Comptroller Flagg, in relation to expenditures thereon; Doc. 134, vol. 7, Ass'y Docs. 1842.

Mr. Swackhamer's report, concerning expenditures; Doc. 184, vol. 7, Ass'y Docs. 1842.

Report of trustees; Doc. 20, vol. 1, Senate Docs. 1843.

STATE HALL, OLD.

Mr. Wilson's report upon proposed improvement; Doc. 69, vol. 3, Ass'y Docs. 1853.

Report of Commissioners of Land Office, in relation to proper repairs; Doc. 89, Ass'y Docs. 1854.

STATE PRISONS.

Attorney General Barker's report in relation to contracts; Doc. 169, vol. 5, Ass'y Docs. 1843.

Mr. Suydam's report; Doc. 41, vol. 3, Ass'y Docs. 1844.

Mr. J. T. Rathbun's report on the subject of the connexion of the New-York Prison Association with the prisons; Doc. 222, vol. 7, Ass'y Docs. 1847.

Mr. J. T. Rathbun's report on the better regulation; Doc. 241, vol. 8, Ass'y Docs. 1847.

Comptroller Fillmore's report relative to convicts transported; Doc. 124, vol. 3, Ass'y Docs. 1848.

Report of Inspectors in relation to William Radford's claim; Doc. 23, vol. 1, Senate Docs. 1849.

Annual report; Doc. 30, vol. 1, Senate Docs. 1844.

Annual report; Doc. 16, vol. 1, Senate Docs. 1850. Doc. 198, vol. 8, Ass'y Docs. 1850.

Communication from A. H. Wells, Inspector, concerning lights in cells; Doc. 134, vol. 5, Ass'y Docs. 1850.

Annual report of Inspectors Wells, D. Clark and Spencer; Doc. 13, vol. 1, Senate Docs. 1851.

Mr. A. Rowe's report in relation to a committee of investigation of the State prisons and jails; Doc. 114, vol. 5, Ass'y Docs. 1852.

Dommunication from Darius Clark and Wm. P. Angel, Inspectors, in relation to the action of the committee of investigation; Doc. 33, vol. 1, Senate Docs. 1852.

Annual report of Inspectors Wells, Clark, Angel; Doc. 35, vol. 1, Senate Docs. 1852.

Mr. George Underwood's report, from a committee of investigation; Doc. 20, vol. 1, Ass'y Docs. 1852.

Opinion of Attorney General Ogden Hoffman, in relation to the responsibilities of State prison agents; Doc. 121, vol. 3, Ass'y Docs. 1854.

STATIONERY.

Report of Comptroller J. M. Cook, as to account paid by J. C. Wright; Doc. 55, vol. 1, Senate Docs. 1854.

Report of investigation into stationery account of 1853; Doc. 9, vol. 1, Ass'y Docs. 1854.

STEAM SHIP COMPANY,

(U. S. Mail, New-York and Chagres.)

Mr. C. A. Mann's majority report against incorporation; Doc. 79, vol. 3, Senate Docs. 1850.

Mr. Schoonmaker's minority report in favor of the incorporation; Doc. 79, vol. 3, Senate Docs. 1850.

ENOS STEELE.

Mr. Jerome Fuller's report; Doc. 19, vol. 1, Senate Docs. 1849.

WILLIAM STERNBERGH.

Mr. Ruger's report, claims; Doc. 75, vol. 3, Senate Docs. 1842.

Report of Canal Board; Doc. 55, vol. 3, Ass'y Docs. 1842.

Mr. Lawyer's report, claims; Doc. 106, vol. 4, Ass'y Docs. 1846.

Mr. McCarty's report, claims; Doc. 43, vol. 2, Ass'y Docs. 1848.

Mr. Lewis' report; Doc. 71, vol. 4, Ass'y Docs. 1850.

Report of committee on claims; Doc. 10, vol. 2, Ass'y Docs. 1851.

Mr. Van Valkenburgh's report, claims; Doc. 30, vol. 2, Ass'y Docs. 1852.

ALEXANDER H. STEVENS.

Address as President of State Medical Society, at Albany, Feb. 1850; Doc. 174, vol. 6, Ass'y Docs. 1850.

JOHN L. STEVENSON.

Report of Commissioners of Land Office; Doc. 63, vol. 2, Ass'y Docs. 1847.

JAMES STEWART.

Report of Canal Board; Doc. 125, vol. 4, Ass'y Docs. 1845. (Testimony accompanying.)

Mr. Tefft's report, claims; Doc. 173, vol. 5, Ass'y Docs. 1845.

Mr. Shelton's report, grievances; Doc. 165, vol. 5, Ass'y Docs. 1846.

JOHN STEWART, & Co.

Mr. Hale's report claims; Doc. 180, vol. 3, Ass'y Docs. 1849.

Mr. Schoonmaker's report, claims; Doc. 64, vol. 2, Senate Docs. 1850.

ELIAS STILWELL and B. SMITH.

Mr. N. Jones' report, claims; Doc. 22, vol. 1, Senate Docs. 1853.

ST. JOHN'S COLLEGE. at Fordham.

Report of condition made to Regents of the University; Doc. 77, (page 124) vol. 2, Senate Docs. 1854.

D. B. ST. JOHN,
(Superintendent of Banking Department.)

Annnual report; Doc 9, vol. 1, Ass'y Docs. 1852.
do do 6, do 1, do 1853.

Report as to Merchants' and Mechanics' banks, Oswego; Doc. 68, vol. 2, Senate Docs. 1854.

Annual report; Doc. 15, vol. 1, Ass'y Docs. 1854.

ST. LAWRENCE ACADEMY.

Report of Regents of the University; Doc. 158, vol. 5, Ass'y Docs. 1845.

M. Button's report; Doc. 34, vol. 1, Ass'y Docs. 1849.

STOCKBRIDGE INDIANS.

Report of Commissioners of Land Office, as to relief of purchasers under sales of land by State, Wm. Page, and others; Doc. 18, vol. 1, Ass'y Docs. 1845.

Report of Commissioners of Land Office, as to an appropriation; Doc. 158, vol. 5, Ass'y Docs. 1846.

Report of the Commissioners of the Land Office, on the petition of Eli Hinman, and others, residents on the Stockbridge land; Doc. 18, vol. 2, Ass'y Docs. 1848.

Memorial of head men and sachems, asking for participation in profits made by the State of New-York, in the sale ot their lands ; Doc. 81, vol. 3, Ass'y Docs. 1848.

Report of the sales of land made to State; Doc. 53, vol. 2, Ass'y Docs. 1848.

Mr. W. S. Johnson's report on petition of John Metogen, and other head men and sachems; Doc. 43, vol. 2, Senate Docs. 1849.

Mr. Folger's report in case of Eli Hinman; Doc. 23, vol. 1, Ass'y Docs. 1844.

Mr. Stewart's report in relation to their title to land in Columbia, Rensselaer, Albany and Montgomery counties; Doc. 79, vol. 3, Ass'y Docs. 1853.

AUGUSTUS STOCKWELL.

Mr. Schoonmaker's report, claims; Doc. 49, vol. 2, Senate Docs. 1850.

HIRAM STONE.

Mr. Curtis's report in relation to Erieville reservoir; Doc. 15, vol. 1, Senate Docs. 1851.

SAMUEL H. STONE.

Report of committee on judiciary, on application for confirmation of official acts as treasurer of Oswego county; Doc. 104, vol. 3, Ass'y Docs. 1849.

WM. A. STONE.

Mr. S. C. Johnson's report, claims, as to dealings with the Oneida Indians; Doc. 6, vol. 1, Senate Docs. 1845.

HENRY STORMS.

Mr. J. E. Beers' report, claims, extra services as Commissary General; Doc. 249, vol. 8, Ass'y Docs. 1847.

STOCKS OF THE STATE.

Report of Comptroller Flagg, in relation to interest paid and payable; Doc. , vol. , Docs 1842.

Report of Comptroller Collier, in relation to interest paid and payable; Doc. 98, vol. 4, Senate Docs. 1842.

Comptroller Fillmore's report as to amount issued and where held; Doc. 29, vol. 1, Senate Docs. 1849.

EDWIN B. STRANGE.

Mr. Hand's report, grievances; Doc. 100, vol. 3, Senate Docs. 1846.

FRANCIS J. STRATTON.

Report of Comptroller Flagg, in respect to services for apprehension of fugitives from justice; Doc. 97, vol. 3, Senate Docs. 1847.

STREET CHILDREN in New-York city.

Mr. G. W. Holley's report; Doc. 94, vol. 4, Ass'y Docs. 1853.

St. REGIS INDIANS.

Communication from, to Governor, in relation to their land and money; Doc. H. of Doc. 2, vol. 1, Senate Docs. 1842. Same in vol. 1, Ass'y Docs. 1842.

Report of Commissioners of Land Office; Doc. 136, vol. 5, Ass'y Docs. 1843.

Report of Commissioners of Land Office; Doc. 102, vol. 3, Senate Docs. 1844.

Report of committee on public land, relative to a lease of land in the reservation; Doc. 168, vol. 5, Ass'y Docs. 1845.

Communication from Secretary of State, C. Morgan, in respect to schools; Doc. 27, vol. 3, Ass'y Docs. 1850.

Report of Commissioners of Land Office, in relation to their lands; Doc. 32, vol. 2, Ass'y Docs. 1851.

Report of Mr. P. W. Rose, in relation to compensation for islands in the St. Lawrence river; Doc. 39, vol. 2, Ass'y Docs. 1853.

Mr. Baldwin's report, claims; Doc. 27, vol. 1, Ass'y Docs. 1854.

CHARLES STROUD, OSCAR GRANGER, LESTER HITCHCOCK, WALTER S. TODD.

Mr. Alvord's report, claims; Doc. 148, vol. 6, Ass'y Docs. 1844.

Report of Canal Commissioners; Doc. 14, vol. 1, Senate Docs. 1845.

Mr. Feeter's report, claims; Doc. 127, vol. 5, Ass'y Docs. 1848.

THOMAS J. STRONG, GEORGE W. CHENEY.

Mr. Wheeler's report; Doc. 18, vol. 1, Ass'y Docs. 1850.

SUBMISSION TO THE PEOPLE.

Attorney General Chatfield's opinion, on the question of the constitutionality of a law, dependent upon the approval of a popular vote; Doc. 107, vol. 5. Ass'y Docs. 1850.

SUFFRAGE IN CITY OF NEW-YORK.

Mr. Morrison's report as to the proper regulation of suffrage in the city and county of New-York; Doc. 69, vol. 3, Ass'y Docs. 1845. (This report deems restriction necessary.)

Mr. Nivens' report; Doc. 71, vol. 3, Ass'y Docs. 1845. (This report deems the present laws sufficient.)

SUNDAY CLOSING OF CANAL LOCKS.

Report of Canal Commissioners; Doc. 66, vol. 2, Senate Docs. 1844.

Mr. Denniston's report, canals; Doc. 119, vol. 3, Senate Docs. 1844.

Mr. Howard's report, canals; Doc. 148, vol, 4, Ass'y Docs. 1845.

Mr. T. E. Clark's report on petition of Timothy Stillman; Doc. 61, vol. 2, Senate Docs. 1849.

SUPERINTENDENTS OF CANAL.

Report of Canal Commissioners as to their compensation; Doc. 221, vol. 6, Ass'y Docs. 1846.

SUPERINTENDENT OF COMMON SCHOOLS.

Annual report, Samuel S. Randall, Acting Superintendent; Doc. 12, vol. 1, Ass'y Docs. 1842.

Annual report, Samuel Young, Doc. 14, vol. 1, Ass'y Docs. 1843.

Annual Report, Samuel Young; Doc. 34, vol. 2, Ass'y Docs. 1844.

Annual Report, Samuel Young, Doc. 30, vol. 2, Ass'y Docs. 1845.

Annual report, N. S. Benton; Doc. 30, vol. 2, Ass'y Docs. 1846.

do do do 10, do 1, do 1847.

do do do 5, do 1, do 1848.

Report of Christopher Morgan, in relation to district 19, Lewis county; Doc. 98, vol. 3, Ass'y Docs. 1848.

Report of Christopher Morgan, in relation to distribution of school moneys; Doc. 14, vol. 1, Ass'y Docs. 1849.

Annual report, Christopher Morgan; Doc. 20, vol. 1, Ass'y Docs. 1849.

Report of Christopher Morgan, as to money paid to town superintendents of common schools; Doc. 202, vol. 5, Ass'y Docs. 1849.

Annual report, Christopher Morgan; Doc. 50, vol. 4, Ass'y Docs. 1850. (Free schools.)

Annual report, Christopher Morgan; Doc. 21, vol. 1, Ass'y Docs. 1851.

Annual report, Henry S. Randall; Doc. 25, vol. 1, Ass'y Docs. 1852.

Report, H. S. Randall, in relation to school moneys of the city of New-York; Doc. 63, vol. 3, Ass'y Docs. 1853. Doc. 127, vol. 6, Ass'y Docs. 1853.

Annual report, Henry S. Randall; Doc. 4, vol. 1, Ass'y Docs. 1853.

Annual report, H. S. Randall; Doc. 7, vol. 1, Ass'y Docs. 1854.

SUPERINTENDENT OF PUBLIC INSTRUCTION.

(Victor M. Rice.)

Report as to deaf mutes; Doc. 29, vol. 1, Senate Docs. 1854.

Mr. P. H. Robertson's report on the subject of the separation of the office of Secretary of State; Doc. 39, vol. 1, Senate Docs. 1842.

SUPERIOR COURT, (New-York city.)

Mr. D. R. F. Jones' report; Doc. 130, vol. 5, Ass'y Docs. 1843.

SUPERVISORS.

Reports of clerks of Boards, in answer to resolution of enquiry as to expenses of the Board; Doc. 65, vol. 2, Senate Docs. 1847.

Mr. Barlow's report on the above reports; Doc. 103, vol. 3, Senate Docs. 1847.

Memorial of citizens of Westchester county, asking for a more equal representation; Doc. 74, vol. 2, Ass'y Docs. 1849.

Mr. Corser's report in relation to the power to erect new towns; Doc. 107, vol. 5, Ass'y Docs. 1852.

SUPREME COURT.

Mr. Palmer's report, judiciary, in relation to the place of holding the terms of the court; Doc. 89, vol. 3, Ass'y Docs. 1844. (This is accompanied by a letter from Justices Nelson, Bronson and Cowen, giving their views.)

Report of judiciary committee, as to decision of causes on written arguments; Doc. 64, vol. 3, Ass'y Docs. 1846.

Report of the Justices, on the convention act apportionment; Doc. 181, vol. 5, Ass'y Docs. 1846.

SUPREME COURT CLERKS.

Report of Comptroller as to fees to clerks; Doc. 20, vol. 2, Senate Docs. 1842.

Mr. Haight's report, select committee; Doc. 112, vol. 4, Ass'y Docs. 1843.

Report of Comptroller Flagg, as to fees paid; Doc. 48, vol. 2, Senate Docs. 1845.

Further report; Doc. 49, vol. 2, Senate Docs. 1845.
do do 50, do 2, do 1845.
do do 10, do 1, do 1846.

Mr. Chas. Humphrey's report of clerk hire for 1845; Doc. 34, vol. 1, Senate Docs. 1846.

SURROGATES.

Mr. Porter's minority report, as to printing notices; Doc. 96, vol. 5, Senate Docs. 1844.

Further report, as to returns of fees received; Doc. 100, vol. 3, Senate Docs. 1844.

Report of Secretary of State, N. S. Benton, as to default in making reports to his office; Doc. 78, vol. 2, Senate Docs. 1845.

Mr. Porter's report on fees and disbursements; Doc. 106, vol. 3, Senate Docs. 1845.

Mr. Porter's report respecting fees; Doc. 143, vol. 4, Senate Docs. 1846.

Report of Secretary of State, C. Morgan, in relation to returns of fees; Doc. 57, vol. 3, Ass'y Docs. 1848.

JACOB SUTHERLAND.

Report of fees as clerk of Supreme court; Doc. 44, vol. 1, Senate Docs. 1843.

Report; Doc. 96, vol. 4, Ass'y Docs. 1843.

SWALLOW STEAMBOAT.

Mr. T. Barlow's report from a select committee, on the causes of her wreck, April 7, 1845; Doc. 102, vol. 3, Senate Docs. 1845.

GERRIT C. SWEET.

Report of Canal Board; Doc. 137, vol. 5, Ass'y Docs. 1844.

ROSSEAU SWEET, ERASTUS B. BROWER.

Report of Canal Board; Doc. 114, vol. 5, Ass'y Docs. 1844.

HENRY C. SWIFT.

Report of Canal Board; Doc. 105, vol. 3, Senate Docs. 1847.

Mr. J. E. Beers' report, claims; Doc. 58, vol. 2, Ass'y Docs. 1847.

JOHN SWIFT.

Report of Canal Commissioners; Doc. 67, vol. 2, Senate Docs. 1847.

SYRACUSE.

Report of committee on public lands, on coarse salt lands; Doc. 106, vol. 5, Ass'y Docs. 1842.

Mr. McCarty's report in relation to improvement on State lands; Doc. 160, vol. 5, Ass'y Docs. 1848.

Report of Canal Board in relation to improvement on State lands; Doc. 171, vol. 5, Ass'y Docs. 1848.

Mr. J. L. Lawrence's report on sale of salt lands; Doc. 81, vol. 3, Senate Docs. 1849.

Mr. Fuller's report on the abatement of a nuisance on State lands at Syracuse; Doc. 11, vol. 1, Senate Docs. 1849.

SYRACUSE COARSE SALT COMPANY.

Mr. Schoonmaker's report, claims; Doc. 76, vol. 3, Senate Docs. 1850.

TAX OF STATE.

Comptroller Flagg's report respecting amount of State tax and valuation of real estate; Doc. 64, vol. 3, Ass'y Docs. 1845.

Comptroller Fillmore's report, of sale of land for taxes in counties where situated; Doc. 63, vol. 3, Ass'y Docs. 1848.

Further report; Doc. 8, vol 1, Ass'y Docs. 1849.

Mr. L. Ward Smith's report; Doc. 107, vol. 3, Ass'y Docs. 1849.

Mr. Bagley's report in relation to deeds for lands sold by taxes; Doc. 160, vol. 3, Ass'y Docs. 1849.

Mr. Charles Colt's report on so much of Gov. Fish's message as relates to the subject; Doc. 19, vol. 1, Senate Docs. 1850.

Mr. Charles Colt's report; Doc. 44, vol. 2, Senate Docs. 1851.

Mr. Bristol's report; Doc. 28, vol. 1, Senate Docs. 1852.

Comptroller Wright's report as to time of sale; Doc. 103, vol. 5, Ass'y Docs. 1852.

Comptroller Wright's report as to unpaid taxes; Doc. 49, vol. 2, Senate Docs. 1853.

Further report of Comptroller Wright; Doc. 79, vol. 3, Senate Docs. 1853.

Comptroller Wright's report in relation to proceeds of tax sales; Doc. 25, vol. 2, Ass'y Docs. 1853.

Comptroller Wright's report; Doc. 61, vol. 3, Ass'y Docs. 1853.

Mr. Barret's report in relation to tax of Clinton county; Doc. 122, vol. 3, Ass'y Docs. 1854.

TAXES IN THE CITY OF NEW-YORK.

Mr. Morris Franklin's report; Doc. 77, vol. 3, Senate Docs. 1842.

Mr. John Porter's report on the subject of the taxation of personal property of non-residents, in the city of New-York; Doc. 109, vol. 4, Senate Docs. 1846.

Report of Harvey Hart, receiver; Doc. 103, vol. 3, Ass'y Docs. 1854.

ZACHARY TAYLOR.

Letter from, to the Legislature; Doc. 212, vol. 6, Ass'y Docs. 1848.

OLIVER TEAL, HENRY GREGORY, C. P. LONGSTREET,

Mr. Chamberlain's report; Doc. 51, vol. 2, Ass'y Docs. 1853.

Mr. Barrow's report, claims; Doc. 94, vol. 3, Ass'y Docs. 1854.

TEACHERS' INSTITUTES.

Mr. Burchard's report; Doc. 71, vol. 2, Ass'y Docs. 1847.

Mr. Conger's report; Doc. 82, vol. 2, Senate Docs. 1852.

TEN GOVERNORS OF ALMS HOUSE, (city of New-York.)

Report in relation to charges made; Doc. 35, vol. 2, Ass'y Docs. 1853.

ASA C. TEFFT, JOHN W. BASSETT, HOSEA NICHOLS.

Report of Canal Commissioners, as to exchange of land on canals; Doc. 106, vol. 3, Senate Docs. 1844.

Further report; Doc. 121, vol. 4, Senate Docs. 1844.

Attorney General Barker's report; Doc. 125, vol. 4, Senate Docs. 1844.

HERMAN TERWILLIGER.

Mr. Hopkins' report, claims; Doc. 101, vol. 3, Senate Docs. 1843.

Mr. Porter's report, claims; Doc. 97, vol. 3, Senate Docs. 1844.

Mr. Case's report; Doc. 83, vol. 3, Ass'y Docs. 1848.

TEXAS.

Mr. Rhodes' resolutions; Doc. 107, vol. 3, Senate Docs. 1844.

Mr. Worden's resolutions; Doc. 33, vol. 3, Ass'y Docs. 1845.

Mr. Van Valkenburgh's majority report; Doc. 83, vol. 4, Ass'y Docs. 1845.

Mr. Frisbee's minority report; Doc. 84, vol. 4, Ass'y Docs. 1845.

Resolution of Legislature concerning slavery; Doc. 193, vol. Ass'y Docs. 1850.

GEORGE TIBBETTS.

Mr. McLean's report, claims, in relation to hydraulic privileges; Doc. 106, vol. 3, Ass'y Docs. 1849.

GEORGE TIBBETTS, JAMES STEVENS.

Mr. Jackson's report claims; Doc. 143, vol. 5, Ass'y Docs. 1843.

JOHN TICE, SAMUEL SHELDON, ALFRED WHITE, PETER HYNDS.

Mr. Beach's report; Doc. 102, vol. 3, Ass'y Docs. 1848.

NANCY BLACKWOOD THAYER.

Report of committee on judiciary, on subject of divorce from David Thayer; Doc. 45, vol. 2, Senate Docs. 1842.

Further report; Doc. 103, vol. 4, Senate Docs. 1842.

BRIGGS THOMAS, EBEN WORDEN.

Mr. Johnson's report, claims; Doc. 31, vol. 1, Senate Docs. 1846.

Report of Canal Board; Doc. 34, vol. 1, Ass'y Docs. 1847.

Mr. Schoonmaker's report, claims; Doc. 29, vol. 2, Senate Docs. 1851.

MARY THOMAS, ANN SMALDEN.

Mr. G. R. Babcock's report; Doc. 23, vol. 1, Senate Docs. 1850.

ALEXANDER THOMPSON

Address, as President of the State Medical Society; Doc. 125, vol. 4, Ass'y Docs. 1851.

ANSON THOMPSON.

Mr. Sherwood's report, claims; Doc. 67, vol. 3, Senate Docs. 1842.

ISAAC THOMPSON, LEWIS BEEBE, JAMES L. BEEBE, WILLIAM THOMPSON.

Report of Canal Commissioners; Doc. 26, vol. 1, Senate Docs. 1846.

Mr. Johnson's minority report, claims; Doc. 66, vol. 2, Senate Docs. 1846.

THOMSONIAN PHYSICIANS.

Report of select committee—Mr. Kelly, on their relief from disabilities; Doc. 42, vol. 2, Ass'y Docs. 1842.

Mr. Ely's report, medical societies committee; Doc. 105, vol. 4, Senate Docs. 1842.

Mr. Taylor's report, medical societies committee; Doc. 142, vol. 7, Ass'y Docs. 1842.

Mr Carpenter's report; Doc. 60, vol. 3, Ass'y Docs. 1844.

WASHINGTON THURMAN, WARREN MILLS, BENJAMIN A. TOWNER.

Mr. McCarty's report, claims, on loss of boat in canal; Doc. 150, vol. 5, Ass'y Docs. 1848.

Mr. Ward's report, claims; Doc. 24, vol. 1, Ass'y Docs. 1849.

Further report on same subject; Doc. 59, vol. 2, Ass'y Docs. 1849.

Mr. J. C. Curtis's report; Doc. 45, vol. 2, Senate Docs. 1850.

Mr. N. Jones' report, claims; Doc. 54, vol. 2, Senate Docs. 1852.

Report of committee on claims; Doc. 17, vol. 1, Ass'y Docs. 1852.

Mr. S. Baldwin's report, claims; Doc. 82, Ass'y Docs. 1854.

WALTER S. TODD.

Report of Canal Commissioner; Doc. 13, vol. 1, Senate Docs. 1854.

TOLLS, TRADE AND TONNAGE OF CANALS.

1841.

Doc. 33, vol. 2, Senate Docs. 1842.

1842.

Doc. 100, vol. 3, Senate Docs. 1843.

Comptroller Flagg's report as to passenger tolls; Doc. 21, vol. 1, Senate Docs. 1843.

1843.

Doc. 118, vol. 4, Senate Docs. 1844.

1844.

Doc. 115, vol. 3, Senate Docs. 1845.

1845.

Doc. 59, vol. 2, Senate Docs. 1846.

1846.

Doc. 90, vol. 3, Senate Docs. 1847.

1847.

Comptroller Flagg's report; Doc. 40, vol. 1, Senate Docs. 1847.
Doc. 40, vol. 2, Senate Docs. 1848.

1848.

Doc. 170, vol. 3, Ass'y Docs. 1849.

1849.

Doc. 140, vol. 6, Ass'y Docs. 1850.

1850.

Doc. 56, vol. 3, Ass'y Docs. 1851.

1851.

Doc. 94, vol. 3, Senate Docs. 1852.

1852.

Doc. 107, vol. 4, Ass'y Docs. 1853.

1853.

Doc. 145, vol. 5, Ass'y Docs. 1854.

TONAWANDA.

Report of condition; Doc. 152, vol. 7, Ass'y Docs. 1842.
Further report; Doc. 161, vol. 7, Ass'y Docs. 1842.

TOPOGRAPHICAL SOCIETY.

Mr. Patterson's report; Doc. 32, vol. 2, Ass'y Docs. 1843.
Mr. S. S. Smith's report; Doc. 33, vol. 2, Ass'y Docs. 1853.

TORONTO, SIMCOE, UNION RAILROAD COMPANY, Canada West.

Mr. John J. Townsend's minority adverse report on the application for authority to dispose of the shares, by lot, in this State Doc. 98, vol. 5, Ass'y Docs. 1850.

TOWNS.

Mr. Corser's report, as to the power to erect a new town from parts of Shawangunk, New Paltz, Rochester, in Ulster county; Doc. 107, vol. 5, Ass'y Docs. 1852.

TOWN MEETINGS BY DISTRICTS.

Mr. Ruger's report; Doc. 30, vol. 1, Senate Docs. 1843.

TOWN OFFICERS.

Mr. Lott's report, judiciary, as to Ellenburgh. The same as to Clinton. The same as to Ossinsing; Doc. 90, vol 3, Senate Docs. 1846.

The same as to Southfield, Doc. 112, vol. 4, Senate Docs. 1846.

TRACT SOCIETY, American.

Report of condition; Doc. 75, vol. 2, Ass'y Docs. 1847.

JAMES D. TREAT, HIRAM ALLEN, JOHN BARSE.

Report of Canal Board on petition; Doc. 132, vol. 7, Ass'y Docs. 1842.

Mr. Alvord's report, claims; Doc. 19, vol. 1, Ass'y Docs. 1844.

Report of Canal Commissioners; Doc. 87, vol. 3, Senate Docs. 1845.

TREASURER.

Annual report; Doc. 32, vol. 2, Ass'y Docs. 1842.

Annual report, Thomas Farrington; Doc. 4, vol. 1, Ass'y Docs. 1843.

Annual report, Thomas Farrington; Doc. 12, vol. 1, Ass'y Docs. 1844.

Annual report, T. Farrington; Doc. 6, vol. 1, Ass'y Docs. 1845.

Annual report, Benjamin Enos; Doc. 10, vol. 1, Ass'y Docs. 1846.

Annual report, T. Farrington; Doc. 26, vol. 1, Ass'y Docs. 1847.

Annual report, Thomas Farrington; Doc. 22, vol. 2, Ass'y Docs. 1848.

Annual report, Alvah Hunt; Doc. 6, vol. 1, Ass'y Docs. 1849.
do do do 20, do 3, do 1850.
do do do 5, do 1, do 1851.
do do do 6, do 1, do 1852.

Report of B. Welch, Jr., in relation to clerical force; Doc. 7, vol. 1, Senate Docs. 1853.

Annual report, B. Welch, Jr., Doc. 13, vol. 1, Ass'y Docs. 1853.

Report, B. Welch, Jr., in relation to fees paid by Attorney General; Doc. 16, vol. 2, Ass'y Docs. 1853.

Annual report, B. Welch, Jr., Doc. 14, vol. 1, Ass'y Docs. 1854.

TRINITY CHURCH CORPORATION.

Report of rector, church wardens and vestrymen, of property; Doc. 86, vol. 3, Senate Docs. 1846.

Mr. Orville Clark's majority report on the rights of the corporation; Doc. 117, vol 4, Senate Docs. 1846.

Mr. Emmons' minority report on same; Doc. 118, vol. 4, Senate Docs. 1846.

Mr. Burnell's report, judiciary committee, on the same subject; Doc. 114, vol. 4, Ass'y Docs. 1847.

Memorial in relation to Christopher C. Kiersted, suit; Doc. 63, vol. 2, Senate Docs. 1853.

Mr. W. Clark's report as to title to real estate; Doc. 67, vol. 2, Senate Docs. 1854.

Report of real and personal estate; Doc. 130, vol. 4, Ass'y Docs. 1854.

TROY.

Report of Canal Commissioners relative to the side cut from the Erie canal into the Hudson; Doc. 57, vol. 3, Ass'y Docs. 1845.

Memorial of city authorities against the bridge at Albany; Doc. 72, vol. 3, Ass'y Docs. 1845.

Mr. Porter's report, finance, on the petition of the authorities of Troy, relative to the stock of the Troy and Schenectady railroad; Doc. 74, vol. 3, Senate Docs. 1846.

TROY ART UNION.

Mr. A. Greene's report against special incorporation; Doc. 125, vol. 5, Ass'y Docs. 1850.

TRUST COMPANY, NEW-YORK LIFE INSURANCE AND

Communication of Chancellor Walworth, with annual report of company; Doc. 37, vol. 2, Ass'y Docs. 1843.

Annual report to Chancellor; Doc. 53, vol. 3, Ass'y Docs. 1843.

TRUST AND SAVINGS BANK OF BUFFALO.

Mr. Cooley's report, on special corporation; Doc. 40, vol. 1, Senate Docs. 1852.

AMOS S. TRYON.

Comptroller Flagg's report; Doc. 35, vol. 1, Senate Docs. 1847.

BENJAMIN TURNER.

Mr. N. Jones' report, claims; Doc. 74, vol. 2, Senate Docs. 1852.

WILLIAM TURNER.

Mr. McLean's report, claims; Doc. 153, vol. 3, Ass'y Docs. 1849.

TURNOUTS AND SWITCHES.

Report of W. J. McAlpine, State Engineer; Doc. 21, vol. 1, Senate Docs. 1853.

TUSCARORA INDIANS.

Memorials of chiefs in relation to taxation and citizenship; Doc. 65, vol. 2, Senate Docs.

WHITING TUTTLE.

Mr. Lewis' report; Doc. 40, vol. 3, Ass'y Docs. 1850.

TWO-THIRD BILLS.

Report of committee on two-third bills, Mr. Humphrey, as to question whether Attica and Buffalo railroad company organization bill requires a vote of two-thirds; Doc. 67, vol. 4, Ass'y Docs. 1843.

Report of Attorney General Barker, as to whether the act "concerning escheats," required a two-third vote; Doc. 48, vol. 3, Ass'y Docs. 1844.

Mr. J. R. DePuy's minority report, as to the bill amending the Long Island railway company charter; Doc. 242, vol. 7, Ass'y Docs. 1845.

Mr. Ansel Bascom's report as to the bill authorising the commissioners of the Land Office, to permit the supervisors of Erie, to take stone from the public land in Black Rock; Doc. 44, vol. 1, Ass'y Docs. 1847.

ABRAHAM L. UNDERHILL.

Mr. T. R. Lee's report, judiciary, as to escheat of Jacob G. Tybrant; Doc. 61, vol. 3, Ass'y Docs. 1845.

UNITED STATES GOVERNMENT.

Resolutions in relation to their expenses; Doc. 4, vol. 1, Senate Docs. 1844.

UNION COLLEGE.

Annual report; Doc. 56, vol. 3, Senate Docs. 1842.

Annual report;	Doc.	77,	vol. 4,	Ass'y Docs.	1843.
do	do	80,	do 3,	do	1844.
do	do	188,	do 5,	do	1845.
do	do	129,	do 4,	do	1846.
do	do	232,	do 5,	do	1849.

Report in relation to property; Doc. 213, vol. 5, Ass'y Docs. 1849.

Annual report; Doc. 190, vol. 8, Ass'y Docs. 1850.

Mr. J. W. Beekman's majority report of investigation; Doc. 146, vol. 6, Ass'y Docs. 1850.

Mr. Pruyn's minority report; Doc. 147, vol. 6, Ass'y Docs. 1850.

Comptroller Fuller's report; Doc. 26, vol. 2, Senate Docs. 1851.

Mr. J. W. Beekman's report on the affairs of the College; Doc. 71, vol. 3, Senate Docs. 1851.

Annual report; Doc. 143, vol. 5, Ass'y Docs. 1851.

Report of Comptroller Wright, Attorney General Chatfield, David Buel and John N. Campbell, Regents of the University, commissioners, on funds and affairs; Doc. 58, vol. 2, Senate Docs. 1852.

Report of John N. Campbell, one of the Regents of the University, John C. Wright, Comptroller, L. S. Chatfield, Attorney General, a majority of Commissioners, on the affairs and finances; Doc. 41, vol 3, Senate Docs. 1853. (To this are appended the schedules and inventory and balances of the accountant, L. Vanderheyden.)

Minority report of Phillip S. Van Rensselaer and David Buel, commissioners, on the same; Doc. 41, (page 3,) vol. 2, Senate Docs. 1853.

Memorial of Alexander Holland, treasurer of the college; Doc. 41, (page 233,) vol. 2, Senate Docs. 1853.

Memorial of Eliphalet Nott; Doc. 41, (page 236,) vol. 2, Senate Docs. 1853.

Mr. Beekman's resolution; Doc. 68, vol. 2, Senate Docs. 1853. (To this are appended statements of Levinus Vanderheyden, Neziah Bliss, and accounts of Eliphalet Nott.)

Mr. N. Jones' majority report from committee of investigation; Doc. 5, vol. 1, Senate Docs. 1854.

Roport of condition of college, made to Regents of University; Doc. 77, (page 39,) vol. 2, Senate Docs. 1854. (To this are appended the papers of Dr. Nott's trust deed.

Annual report of trustees; Doc. 134, vol. 6, Ass'y Docs. 1853.
do do do 143, do 4, do 1854.

UNION HALL ACADEMY,

Reports of Regents of the University; Doc. 141, vol. 5, Ass'y Docs. 1846.

UNIVERSITY OF BUFFALO.

Mr. Pratt's report on appropriation; Doc. 74, vol. 4, Ass'y Docs. 1850.

UNIVERSITY of New-York.

Report of committee on medical societies and colleges, in relation to endowment of medical department; Doc. 125, vol. 5, Ass'y Docs. 1842.

Communication from Chancellor, of Doc. C., accompanying Doc. 2, Senate Docs. 1842. Doc. C., Doc. 2, vol. 1, Ass'y Docs. 1843.

Mr. T. H. Bond's report on appropriation; Doc. 23, vol. 1, Senate Docs. 1848.

Mr. Pruyn's report on investigation; Doc. 104, vol. 3, Ass'y Docs. 1849.

Report of condition made to Regents of the University; Doc. 77, (page 102) vol. 2, Senate Docs. 1854.

Report of medical department, is page 113, same document.

UTICA CITY.

Report of Canal Board, on memorial of city relative to canal bridge; Doc. 30, vol. 1, Ass'y Docs. 1844.

Report of Canal Board in relation to Court street and Fayette street bridge; Doc. 204, vol. 7, Ass'y Docs. 1844.

USURY.

Mr. Hand's report, judiciary; Doc. 42, vol. 2, Senate Docs. 1847.

Mr. G. R. Babcock's report; Doc. 30, vol. 1, Senate Docs. 1850.

Mr. John D. White's report; Doc. 66, vol. 4, Ass'y Docs. 1850.

Mr. G. R. Babcock's report on bill prohibiting corporations from interposing the plea of usury; Doc. 112, vol. 3, Senate Docs. 1850.

Mr. E. D. Morgan's report; Doc. 40, vol. 2, Senate Docs. 1851.

Mr. H. C. Cady's report; Doc. 86, vol. 3, Ass'y Docs. 1851.

CORNELIUS VAN ALSTINE and ALBERT MABIN.

Mr. S. Baldwin's report, claims; Doc. 98, vol. 3, Ass'y Docs. 1854.

CHARITY VAN ALSTINE.

Mr. Gilbert's report, claims; Doc. 19, vol. 1, Ass'y Docs. 1852.

Mr. W. A. Gilbert's report, claims; Doc. 78, vol. 2, Ass'y Docs. 1852.

DAVID VAN ALSTINE.

Mr. McCarty's report, claims; Doc. 87, vol. 3, Ass'y Docs. 1848.

Mr. Fitzhugh's report; Doc. 96, vol. 2, Ass'y Docs. 1844.

JOHN C VAN ALSTINE.

Mr. Richard's report; Doc. 43, vol. 2, Ass'y Docs. 1849.

Mr. Barrow's report; Doc. 23, Doc. 29, vol. 1, Ass'y Docs. 1854.

JOHN VAN BUREN.

Report of Comptroller Flagg, as to moneys paid for services as Attorney-General, in attending the trials in Columbia and Delaware, in 1845, with Gov. Wright's letters; Doc. 28, vol. 1, Senate Docs. 1846.

Report of receipts for services, other than from his salary; Doc. 36, vol. 1, Senate Docs. 1846.

Mr. Lott's report, judiciary, as to the extra compensation paid; Doc. 63, vol. 2, Senate Docs. 1846.

Report as to his attendance before Supreme Court of United States, in arguing passenger tax case; Doc. 95, vol. 3, Senate Docs. 1846.

Report as to statement of all emoluments of his office, as Attorney General; Doc. 28, vol. 1, Senate Docs. 1847.

Report as to payments made him by State, other than salary, from , to January 1, 1847; Doc. , vol. , Ass'y Docs. 1847.

Communication respecting power of Legislature over the banks under the general banking law; Doc. 106, vol. 4, Ass'y Docs. 1847.

Communication as to power of the Legislature to dissolve such banks; Doc. 145, vol. 4, Ass'y Docs. 1847.

MARTIN VAN BUREN.

Communication from, declining the appointment of Regent of the University; Doc. 196, vol. 5, Ass'y Docs. 1845.

JAOCB VANDEMARK, JOHN VANDEWERKER, OSCAR GRANGER, LESTER HITCHCOCK, CHARLES STROUD, WALTER S. TODD.

Mr. Putnam's report, claims; Doc. 95, vol. 3, Senate Docs. 1843.

Report of Canal Commissioners; Doc. 15, vol. 1, Senate Docs. 1845.

Mr. Soper's report, claims; Doc. 76, vol. 2, Ass'y Docs. 1847.

JOSHUA B. VAN DEUSEN, FRANCIS BATES.

Mr. Hale's report; Doc. 18, vol. 1, Ass'y Docs. 1849.

JOHN E. VAN EPS.

Mr. Skelton's report, grievances; Doc. 43, vol. 2, Ass'y Docs. 1846.

Mr. Beach's report; Doc. 45, vol. 2, Ass'y Docs. 1848.

Mr. Ward Smith's report; Doc. 21, vol. 1, Ass'y Docs. 1849.

Mr. Ward's report, claims; Doc. 39, vol. 1, Senate Docs. 1852.

Mr. E. Ward's report, claims; Doc. 12, vol. 1, Senate Docs. 1853.

ANTHONY VAN INWAGEN

Mr. N. Jones' report, claims, for loss of canal boat; Doc. 79, vol. 2, Senate Docs. 1852.

Mr. Van Valkenburgh's report, claims; Doc. 49, vol. 2, Ass'y Docs. 1852.

MARY ANN VAN RIPER.

Mr. D. E. Wheeler's report in favor of the petition for divorce; Doc. 237, vol. 6, Ass'y Docs. 1845.

ANTHONY VAN SCHAICK, JOHN S. VAN SCHAICK, ALBERT C. GUNNISON, ELIZA V. S. GUNNISON.

Mr. Sherman's report; Doc. 107, vol. 4, Ass'y Docs. 1851.

JOHN VAN STEENBURGH, EDWARD O'CONNOR.

Governor Wright's commutation of sentence for the murder of Orman N. Steele; appendix to Doc. 2, vol. 1, Senate Docs. 1846.

CORNELIUS C. VAN VRANKEN.

Mr. Haight's report; Doc. 151, vol. 5, Ass'y Docs. 1843.

Report of Canal Board; Doc. 157, vol. 5, Ass'y Docs. 1845.

ALEXANDER VATTEMARE.

Communication to Gov. Wright; Doc. 185, vol. 5, Ass'y Docs. 1845.

Communication to Gov. Young; Doc. 128, vol. 4, Senate Docs. 1847.

Address delivered in Assembly chamber, at the request of both Houses of the Legislature, October 20, 1847; Doc. 226, vol. 7, Ass'y Docs. 1847. (In appendix, are instructions for collecting, preserving and transporting objects of Natural History, by the professors, administrators of the Museum of Natural History at Paris, and Arthur Young, jr., botanist, to the State of Maine.)

Letter suggesting a statistical document; Doc. 288, vol. 5, Ass'y Docs. 1849.

Letter from, in relation to loss by shipwreck; Doc. 93, vol. 3, Senate Docs. 1850.

Letter to Governor Fish; Doc. 192, vol. 8, Ass'y Docs. 1850.

do do do 201, do 5, do 1850.

JOHN H. VEDDER, and associates.

(Harrison Rouse, David Ruger, G. M. Smith, John A. Rouse, Conrad Forbes, William Cramer.)

Report of the Commissioners of the Land Office; Doc. 7, vol. 1, Senate Docs. 1846.

Report of Canal Board; Doc. 135, vol. 4, Ass'y Docs. 1846.

VENTILATION.

State Engineer, H. C. Seymour's report; Doc. 63, vol. 4, Ass'y Docs. 1850.

VERMONT.

Resolutions relative to time of holding Presidential election; Doc. 14, vol. 1, Ass'y Docs. 1842.

Resolutions relative to franking privilege; Doc. 15, vol. 2, Ass'y Docs. 1843.

Resolution of Legislature, concerning slavery; Doc. 181, vol. 8, Ass'y Docs. 1850.

VIRGINIA.

Gov. Seward's message, dissenting from action of Legislature, relative to his refusal to surrender certain persons to Gov. of Virginia; Doc. 102, vol. 4, Senate Docs. 1842.

Documents illustrating the effect of Inspection laws of Virginia, on New-York commerce; Document D. accompanying Governor Seward's extra session message; Doc. 106, vol. 4, Senate Docs. 1842.

Document D. accompanying, and Doc. 195, vol. 7, Ass'y Docs. 1842.

Mr. Loomis' report on the questions at issue concerning apprehension of alleged fugitives, between New-York and Virginia; Doc. 185, vol. 7, Ass'y Docs. 1842.

Memorial of owners of shipping at Richmond county, in relation to the effect of the Virginia restriction laws upon the commerce of New-York; Doc. 25, vol. 2, Ass'y Docs. 1843.

Mr. Jones' report, judiciary, on the controversy between New-York and Virginia; Doc. 49, vol. 3, Ass'y Docs. 1843.

Gov. Bouck's message concerning said controversy; Doc. 140, vol. 5, Ass'y Docs. 1843.

Resolutions of State concerning certain resolutions of Massachusetts, as to free representation; Doc. 190, vol. 7, Ass'y Docs. 1844.

Resolutions of Legislature, concerning the Wilmot Proviso; Doc. 111, vol. 4, Ass'y Docs. 1847.

VOLUNTEER REGIMENTS, (War with Mexico.)

Mr. Small's report on outfit; Doc. 13, vol. 1, Ass'y Docs. 1847.

Communications and correspondence relative to organization; Doc. 80, vol. 2, Ass'y Docs. 1847.

Report of Adjutant General, Samuel Stevens, as to the filling of vacancies; Doc. 154, vol. 6, Ass'y Docs. 1847.

Mr. Bower's report on compensation; Doc. 93, vol. 3, Ass'y Docs. 1848.

Adjutant General Steven's report, on memorial of Titus Gazynski; Doc. 177, vol. 5, Ass'y Docs. 1848.

Mr. Pruyn's report on petition of Titus Felix Gazynski; Doc. 178, vol. 5, Ass'y Docs. 1848.

Mr. Yard's report on their services; Doc. 163, vol. 6, Ass'y Docs. 1850.

Report of select committee on bill for the relief of; Doc. 58, vol. 3, Ass'y Docs. 1851.

Mr. Reily's report; Doc. 48, vol. 1, Senate Docs. 1852.

GEORGE FRANCIS VON BECK.

Mr. Strong's report on legality of marriage; Doc. 62, vol. 2, Senate Docs. 1844.

CHARLES VROOMAN, LEVI HURLBURT.

Mr. Van Valkenburgh's report, claims; Doc. 58, vol. 2, Ass'y Docs. 1852.

Mr. E. Ward's report, claims; Doc. 19, vol. 1, Senate Docs. 1852.

BENJAMIN WADSWORTH.

Mr. Hale's report, claims; Doc. 48, vol. 2, Ass'y Docs. 1849.

JAMES WADSWORTH.

Report of the committee on literature, in relation to his donation of the Bishop Alonzo Potter's work, "The School and the Schoolmaster," to the schools of the State; Doc. 34, vol. 1, Senate Docs. 1843.

LEONARD WAGER, FRANCIS SMITH.

Mr. Udell's report, on their claim for compensation for injuries received by the discharge of a cannon at parade; Doc. 108, vol. 4, Ass'y Docs. 1846.

PETER J. WAGNER.

Report of Canal Commissioners; Doc. 84, vol. 3, Senate Docs. 1846.

Mr. S. C. Johnson's report, claims; Doc. 99, vol. 3, Senate Docs. 1846.

SILAS WALLACE.

Mr. J. A. Dix's report; Doc. 175, vol. 7, Ass'y Docs. 1842.

JOHN J. WALRATH, DANIEL WALRATH.

Mr. Nicoll's report, claims; Doc. 71, vol. 3, Ass'y Docs. 1843.

Mr. Porter's report, claims; Doc. 21, vol. 1, Senate Docs. 1844.

Mr. Porter's report, claims; Doc. 92, vol. 3, Senate Docs. 1845.

Mr. Newkirk's majority report, claims; Doc. 66, vol. 3, Ass'y Docs. 1845.

Mr. Tefft's minority report; Doc. 67, vol. 3, Ass'y Docs. 1845.

Mr. A. Coe's report, claims; Doc. 67, vol. 3, Ass'y Docs. 1848.

Mr. Curtis' report; Doc. 37, vol. 2, Senate Docs. 1851.

CLINTON WALWORTH.

Mr. Dix's report, canals, on petition; Doc. 158, vol. 7, Ass'y Docs. 1842.

HIRAM WALWORTH.

Report of fees and salary as Assistant Register in Chancery; Docs. 81 and 119, vol. 3, Senate Docs. 1843.

WAPPINGER'S CREEK.

Mr. S. Ely's report; Doc. 79, vol. 3, Senate Docs. 1842.

WARDS OF NEW-YORK CITY.

Mr. Ketchum's majority report as to more equal division; Doc. 146, vol. 5, Ass'y Docs. 1843.

Mr. E. Baldwin's minority report; Doc. 164, vol. 5, Ass'y Docs. 1843.

WAR OF 1812.

Comptroller Wright's report as to pay of soldiers; Doc. 52, vol. 2, Senate Docs. 1853.

ALEXIS WARD, THOMAS WILSON.

Mr. Pettingill's report, claims; Doc. 75, vol. 3, Ass'y Docs. 1853.

WAREHOUSING SYSTEM.

Mr. Wheeler's resolutions; Doc. 90, vol. 4, Ass'y Docs. 1845.

WARRENSBURGH AND JOHNSBURGH BRIDGE.

Mr. Bockee's report, finance, in relation to an appropriation; Doc. 70, vol. 2, Senate Docs. 1844.

WARDENS OF THE PORT, NEW-YORK.

Petition of masters and wardens; Doc. 64, vol. 2, Senate Docs. 1844.

Report of compensation; Doc. 38, vol. 1, Senate Docs. 1847.

WASHINGTON COUNTY.

Historical, Topographical and Agricultural survey, Asa Fitch; Doc. 175, vol. 7, Ass'y Docs. 1850.

WASHINGTON NATIONAL MONUMENT.

Gov. Hunt's message relative to the transmission of a block of marble, as the gift of the State; Doc. 144, vol. 5, Ass'y Docs. 1851.

WASHINGTON'S HEAD QUARTERS, AT NEWBURGH.

Mr. Leland's report on so much of Governor Fish's message, as relates to the preservation and ownership by the State; Doc. 122, vol. 5, Ass'y Docs. 1850.

Mr. C. Lyon's report, on petition of Jonathan Hasbrouck; Doc. 57, vol. 3, Ass'y Docs. 1851.

WATERVLIET AND PORT SCHUYLER AND WEST TROY CANAL INVESTIGATION.

Resolution of Mr. Dickinson; Doc. 24, vol. 1, Senate Docs. 1843.

Mr. Flagg's report as to expenditures; Doc. 35, vol. 1, Senate Docs. 1843.

Mr. Flagg's report concerning David Hamilton; Doc. 39, vol. 1, Senate Docs. 1843.

Report of select committee, Messrs. Ely, Franklin and Mitchell; Doc. 118, vol. 3, Senate Docs. 1843.

SMITH A. WATERMAN.

Proceedings of Canal Board, and testimony on investigation; Doc. 71, vol. 3, Senate Docs. 1853.

THOMAS P. WATERS.

Report of committee on canals, on petition; Doc. 169, vol. 3, Ass'y Docs. 1849.

JOHN WATKINS.

Report of Canal Appraisers; Doc. 41, vol. 3, Ass'y Docs. 1845.

Report of Canal Board; Doc. 63, vol. 2, Senate Docs. 1850.

WATERLOO VILLAGE.

Mr. Chamberlain's report in relation to drainage; Doc. 95, vol. 4, Ass'y Docs. 1853.

WAYNE COUNTY.

Report of minority of committee on erection and division of towns and counties, on division of county; Doc. 135, vol. 5, Ass'y Docs. 1851. (Opinions of T. R. Strong, J. K. Porter, Alvah Worden, Nicholas Hill, jr., L. S. Chatfield, Ira Harris.)

Mr. Wooster's majority report; Doc. 127, vol. 4, Ass'y Docs. 1851.

Mr. Corser's majority report against division; Doc. 55, vol 2, Ass'y Docs. 1852.

Mr. Gallup's minority report in favor of division; Doc. 67, vol. 2, Ass'y Docs. 1852.

Mr. Rose's report in relation to the removal of county buildings; Doc. 53, vol. 2, Ass'y Docs. 1853.

WEIGHING OF MERCHANDIZE.

Report of minority of committee on trade and manufactures, (Mr. Ross) on proposed repeal of law, as regards the city of New-York; Doc. 36, vol. 3, Ass'y Docs. 1844.

WEIGHTS AND MEASURES.

Report of Secretary of State, S. Young, as to condition of the State weights and measures, with a list; Doc. 22, vol. 1, Ass'y Docs. 1845.

Report of W. H. Clark, of Normal school, on system; Doc. 241, vol. 5, Ass'y Docs. 1849.

Memorial of John Paterson, superintendent; Doc. 4, vol. 1, Ass'y Docs. 1854.

WEBSTER'S DICTIONARY.

Mr. S. Miller's majority report, favorable to the bill to authorise its purchase for the school districts; Doc. 81, vol. 3, Senate Docs. 1851.

Mr. J. W. Beekman's minority report adverse to the same bill; Doc. 89, vol. 3, Senate Docs. 1850.

CHRISTINA WEBBER.

Mr. N. Jones' report claims; Doc. 11, vol. 1, Senate Docs. 1853.

JOSHUA WEBSTER.

Mr. Martin's report, claims; Doc. 141, vol. 5, Ass'y Docs. 1848.

P. G. WEBSTER.

Mr. Gorham's report, claims; Doc. 200, vol. 7, Ass'y Docs. 1844.

ALBERT WELLS.

Mr. T. J. Wheeler's report, claims; Doc. 27, vol. 1, Senate Docs. 1847.

WEST TROY.

Report of Canal Commmissioners, as to bridge across the canal; Doc. 149, vol. 6, Ass'y Docs. 1844.

WHARFAGE—(New-York and Brooklyn.)

Mr. Williams' minority report; Doc. 91, vol. 3, Senate Docs. 1850.

Mr. J. B. Varnum, jr's. report; Doc. 162, vol. 6, Ass'y Docs. 1850. (With statistics of property.)

Mr. Wakeman's report; Doc. 112, vol. 4, Ass'y Docs. 1851.

Mr. J. B. Varnum's report; Doc. 123, vol. 4, Ass'y Docs. 1851.

WHEATLAND.

Report relative to damages of town; Doc. 210, vol. 5, Ass'y Docs. 1849.

ALVAH WORDEN.

Giles Hawley, Edward Dickinson, Abraham E. Culver, William Fort.

Mr. Mitchell's report, claims; Doc. 83, Ass'y Docs. 1854.

JOHN G. WHEELOCK, and associates.

Report of Canal Board; Doc. 27, vol. 1, Ass'y Docs. 1844.
do do do 203, do 7, do 1844.

Mr. Cornwell's report, grievances; Doc. 76, vol. 3, Ass'y Docs. 1846.

Mr. Hammond's report; Doc. 127, vol. 4, Ass'y Docs. 1847.

GEEORG WHEELER, STEPHEN ADAMS, JOHN McWHORTER, LEVI SANFORD, JUSTICE CRANDALL, DAVID SMITH.

Mr. Skelton's report, grievances; Doc. 102, vol. 4, Ass'y Docs. 1846.

Mr. J. E. Beers' report, claims; Doc. 92, vol. 2, Ass'y Docs. 1847.

HENRY WHITE, JOHN WILLIAMS

Report of committee on claims, Mr. Tupper, on petition; Doc. 72, vol. 4, Ass'y Docs. 1842.

Mr. Tower's report, claims; Doc. 35, vol. 2, Ass'y Docs. 1843.

Mr. Lawrence's report, claims; Doc. 23, vol. 1, Senate Docs. 1844.

HENRY H. WHITE.

Mr. H. W. Strong's report in relation to imprisonment for non-payment of costs; Doc. 34, vol. 1, Senate Docs. 1844.

JOHN WHITEHEAD, as to payment for revolutionary services of William Whitehead.

Mr. Sweeny's report; Doc. 93, vol. 4, Ass'y Docs. 1845.

Mr. Hubbard's report; Doc. 30, vol. 1, Ass'y Docs. 1847.

WHITEHALL AND PLATTSBURGH ROAD.

Mr. Cuthbert's report; Doc. 186, vol. 3, Ass'y Docs. 1849.

JAMES F. WHITNEY.

Report of Commissioners of Land Office; Doc. 186, vol. 7, Ass'y Docs. 1847.

Mr. J. E. Beer's report, claims; Doc. 239, vol. 8, Ass'y Docs. 1847.

HENRY WILKINS, DARIUS TALLMAN.

Mr. J. E. Beers' report, claims; Doc. 49, vol. 2, Ass'y Docs. 1847.

EMMA WILLARD,
(Troy Female Seminary.)

Report of committee on literature, on application for aid; Doc. 117, vol. 5, Ass'y Docs. 1852. Appendix contains letters to Mrs. Willard, from Bishop A. Potter, W. H. Seward, Lewis Cass, Henry Clay.

Memorial in relation to female education; Doc. 74, vol. 2, Ass'y Docs. 1852. Appendix contains letters to Mrs. Willard, from DeWitt Clinton, John Adams, George Combe.

GEORGE W. WILLARD.

Mr. Barrow's report, claims; Doc. 92, vol. 3, Ass'y Docs. 1854.

MARIA H. WILLIAMSON, R. COLDEN, MARIA BLEAKLEY, Devisees.

Mr. Shumway's report in relation to proof of will; Doc. 94, vol. 2, Ass'y Docs. 1847.

WILLIAMS, (town of.)

Report in relation to lost papers; Doc. 214, vol 6, Ass'y Docs. 1848.

WILLIAM H. WILLIAMS.

Mr. H. G. Root's report, claims; Doc. 114, vol. 5, Ass'y Docs. 1850.

Mr. Bradley's report, claims; Doc. 81, vol. 2, Ass'y Docs. 1852.

WILLIAMSBURGH.

Mr. John N. Cross' report on consolidation with New-York and Brooklyn; Doc. 74, vol. 3, Senate Docs. 1851.

WILLIAMSBURGH AND CYPRESS HILLS PLANK ROAD CO.

Report; Doc. 14, vol. 1, Senate Docs. 1854.

DAVID WILLIAMS,
(One of the captors of Major Andre.)

Mr. Willett's report on monument; Doc. 76, vol. 3, Ass'y Docs. 1848.

ELEAZER WILLIAMS,
(The claimant to the Dauphin.)

Report of Commissioners of Land Office, on conveyance of land to him (an Indian); Doc. 7, vol. 1, Senate Docs. 1845.

JAMES WILLIAMS.

Mr. Reamer's report; Doc. 155, vol. 5, Ass'y Docs. 1848.

PLATT WILLIAMS.

Report of Canal Commissioners; Doc. 74, vol. 3, Ass'y Docs. 1846.

Report of committee on claims; Doc. 46, vol. 2, Senate Docs. 1847.

Mr. Orlando Allen's report; Doc. 109, vol. 5, Ass'y Docs. 1850.

JOSEPH WILLIS.

Mr. N. Jones' report, claims; Doc. 75, vol. 2, Senate Docs. 1852.

Mr. W. A. Gilbert's report, claims; Doc. 4, vol. 1, Ass'y Docs. 1852.

Mr. Barrow's report; Doc. 22, vol. 1, Ass'y Docs. 1854.

PETER WILSON.

Memorial in behalf of the Cayuga Indians; Doc. 56, vol. 2, Senate Docs. 1853.

Mr. Bristol's report; Doc. 81, vol. 3, Senate Docs. 1853.

ROBERT WILSON.

Mr. Glass' report; Doc. 199, vol. 3, Ass'y Docs. 1849.

DANIEL W. WING.

Mr. Johnson's report, claims; Doc. 81, vol. 2, Senate Docs. 1845.

JOEL A. WING.

Biographical notice; Doc. 67, (page 345,) vol. 3, Ass'y Docs. 1843.

WITNESSES IN CRIMINAL CASES.

Mr. C. G. Myers' report on compensation; Doc. 95, vol. 3, Ass'y Docs. 1848.

WOMEN'S RIGHTS.

Report of select committee; Doc. 129, vol. 4, Ass'y Docs. 1854.

Further report; Doc. 149, vol. 5, Ass'y Docs. 1854.

ASA D. WOOD.

Mr. Severance's report, claims; Doc. 80, vol. 3, Ass'y Docs. 1851.

Mr. J. B. William's report, claims; Doc. 21, vol. 1, Senate Docs. 1852.

EDWARD WOOD.

Mr. Remer's report; Doc. 138, vol. 5, Ass'y Docs. 1848.

EZRA WOOD.

Mr. McCarty's report, claims; Doc. 49, vol. 2, Ass'y Docs. 1848.

GEORGE WOOD.

Report of Regents of the University in relation to catalogue; Doc. 89, vol. 3, Senate Docs. 1847.

SEYMOUR S. WOOD.

Mr. Chamberlain's report; Doc. 35, vol. 2, Ass'y Docs. 1852.

JAMES WOODWARD, EBENEZER HUMPHREY.

Mr. Severance's report, claims; Doc. 19, vol. 1, Ass'y Docs. 1851.

WOODWORTH PLANING MACHINE.

Mr. G. Van Santvord's minority report, that it is not expedient to take legislative action on the subject of the patent; Doc. 64, vol. 2, Ass'y Docs. 1852.

WILLIAM E. WORDEN, MORGAN D. WORDEN.

Rrport of Commissioners of the Land Office; Doc. 53, vol. 3, Ass'y Docs. 1851.

JOSHUA WCRRELL.

Mr. W. A. Gilbert's report, claims; Doc. 22, vol. 1, Ass'y Docs. 1852.

ELEANOR F. WORS.

Mr. S. A. Brown's report, aliens; Doc. 35, vol. 3, Ass'y Docs. 1845.

ELIHU C. WRIGHT.

Mr. Backhouse's report; Doc. 104, vol. 4, Ass'y Docs. 1851.

JOHN C. WRIGHT, (Comptroller.)

Report of cost of printing and engraving Documentary History; Doc. 5, vol. 1, Senate Docs. 1852.

Report of expenses of government from 1817 to 1851; Doc. 31, vol. 1, Senate Docs. 1852.

Report of expenditures of clerical department of Legislature; Doc. 42, vol. 1, Senate Docs. 1851.

Report as to Union College; Doc. 58, vol. 2, Senate Docs. 1852.

Report as to General Fund debt; Doc. 68, vol. 2, Senate Docs. 1852.

Annual report; Doc. 10, vol. 1, Ass'y Docs. 1852.

Report as to amount of State debt on June 1, 1846; Doc. 87, vol. 2, Senate Docs. 1852.

Report in relation to the receipts from general fund; Doc. 103, vol. 5, Ass'y Docs. 1852.

Report in relation to contingent expenses of the Legislature; Doc. 124, vol. 5, Ass'y Docs. 1852.

Report in relation to the clerical force in his office; Doc. 36, vol. 2, Senate Docs. 1853.

Report in relation to expenses of colonial history; Doc. 24, vol. 1, Senate Docs. 1853.

Report as to unpaid taxes; Doc. 49, vol. 2, Senate Docs. 1853.

Report in relation to expenses of State government; Doc. 76, vol. 3, Senate Docs. 1853.

Report in relation to unpaid taxes; Doc. 78, vol. 3, Senate Docs. 1857.

Annual report; Doc. 5, vol. 1, Ass'y Docs. 1853.

Opinion as to the rule of taxation of railroads; Doc. 5, (page 107) vol. 1, Ass'y Docs. 1853.

Report of State debts, from 1835 to 1852; Doc. 24, vol. 2, Ass'y Docs. 1853.

Report of proceeds of tax sales; Doc. 25, vol. 2, Ass'y Docs. 1853.

Report in relation to State tax; Doc. 61, vol. 3, Ass'y Docs. 1853. Doc. 114, vol. 5, Ass'y Docs. 1853.

Annual report; Doc. 5, vol. 1, Ass'y Docs. 1854.

SILAS WRIGHT.

Annual message; Doc. 2, vol. 1, Senate Docs. 1845. Doc. 2, vol 1, Ass'y Docs. 1845.

Message relating to New-York pilot laws; Doc. 25, vol. 1, Senate Docs. 1845.

Proclamation concerning disturbances in the county of Delaware; Appendix to Doc. 2, vol. 1, Ass'y Docs. 1846.

Message concerning vacancies existing in office of United States Senator; Doc. 8, vol 1, Ass'y Docs. 1845.

Message transmitting the report of the Commissary General for 1845, and with suggestions concerning the arsenal at New-York, the fortifications on Staten Island, and the sale of arms.

Message giving his views as to the propriety of the acceptance by the State, of the last instalment of $10,000 of money accruing from the proceeds of the public lands; Doc. 88, vol. 4, Ass'y Docs. 1845.

Message returning the canal bills, with objections; Doc. 251, vol. 7, Ass'y Docs. 1845.

Annual message; Doc. 2, vol. 1, Senate Docs. 1846. Doc. 3, vol. 1, Ass'y Docs. 1846.

(Proclamation of Delaware county in insurrection. Commutation of John Van Sternburgh, Edward O'Connor, for the murder of Orman N. Steele. Proclamation declaring the insurrection in Delaware quelled, are appended.)

Letters to Comptroller Flagg, concerning payments to Attorney General, J. Van Buren, for attending trials in Columbia and Delaware, in 1845; appended to Doc. 28, vol. 1, Senate Docs. 1846.

Communication respecting the Seneca Indians; Doc. 57, vol. 2, Senate Docs. 1846; with letters from Indians and H. R. Schoolcraft, and G. C. Leland, annexed.

Communication transmitting the report of the Commissary General; Doc. 59, vol. 2, Ass'y Docs. 1846.

Message concerning cession of land to United States, at Buffalo, Sacketts Harbor, Charlotte, on the St. Lawrence; Doc. 164, vol. 5, Ass'y Docs. 1846.

Communication, with memorial from the Seneca Indians; Doc. 197, vol. 5, Ass'y Docs. 1846.

Communication respecting restoration of Marcus Aylesworth, to citizenship; Doc. 208, vol. 6, Ass'y Docs. 1846.

Communication from, respecting an examination of Clinton prison; Doc. 18, vol. 1, Senate Docs. 1847.

EVERT YATES.

Report of Canal Board; Doc. 73, vol. 3, Ass'y Docs. 1844.

ISAAC J. YATES.

Mr. D. S. Howard's report; Doc. 221, vol. 6, Ass'y Docs. 1845.

JOHN P. YATES.

Report of Canal Board; Doc. 214, vol. 6, Ass'y Docs. 1845.

YATES and VANDERBOGART.

Report of Canal Board; Doc. 108, vol. 5, Ass'y Docs. 1844.

Mr. Gorham's report, claims; Doc. 129, vol 5, Ass'y Docs. 1844.

Mr. Boughton's report, grievances; Doc. 65, vol. 3, Ass'y Docs. 1846.

ANDREW J. YATES.

Report of Canal Board; Doc. 191, vol. 5, Ass'y Docs. 1845.

Mr. Babcock's report; Doc. 28, vol 1, Senate Docs. 1850.

NEAL H. YOUELLS.

Mr. J. E. Beers' report, claims; Doc. 229, vol. 8, Ass'y Docs. 1847.

Mr. McCarty's report, claims; Doc. 101, vol. 3, Ass'y Docs. 1848.

JOHN YOUNG.

Annual message; Doc. 2, vol. 1, Senate Docs. 1847. Doc. 3, vol. 1, Ass'y Docs. 1847.

Mr. Wright's resolutions of reference of message; Doc. 12, vol. 1, Ass'y Docs. 1847.

Communication in respect to international exchanges; Doc. 128, vol. 4, Senate Docs. 1847.

Annual message; Doc. 2, vol. 1, Senate Docs. 1848. Doc. 3, vol. 1, Ass'y Docs. 1848.

WILLIAM YOUNG, JAMES DANA, DAVID A. RICHTMEYER.

Report of committee on grievances; Doc. 97, vol. 2, Ass'y Docs. 1847.

SAMUEL YOUNG,
(Secretary of State.)

The entries will be found at length under the head of the different subjects.

SCHOOLS.

Doc. 14, vol. 1, Ass'y Docs. 1843. Doc. 34, vol. 2, Ass'y Docs. 1844. Doc. 30, vol. 2, Ass'y Docs. 1845.

CRIME.

Doc. 51, vol. 3, Senate Docs. 1842. Doc. 110, vol. 4, Ass'y Docs. 1843. Doc. 92, vol. 2, Senate Docs. 1844.

DISTRICT ATTORNEY.

Doc. 89, vol. 5, Ass'y Docs. 1842.

DIGEST OF PATENTS.

Doc. 122, vol. 5, Ass'y Docs. 1842.

POOR.

Doc. 121, vol. 5, Ass'y Docs. 1842. Doc. 38, vol. 2, Ass'y Docs. 1843. Doc. 73, vol. 2, Senate Docs. 1844.

PRINTING.

Doc. 79, vol. 2, Senate Docs. 1844.

RAILROADS.

Doc. 123, vol. 5, Ass'y Docs. 1844.

WEIGHTS AND MEASURES.

Doc. 22, vol. 1, Senate Docs. 1845.

DISTRIBUTION OF BOOKS.

(Geological Survey.)

Doc. 67, vol. 2, Senate Docs. 1842. Doc. 72, vol. 3, Senate Docs. 1843.

INSPECTION RETURNS.

Doc. 131, vol. 5, Ass'y Docs. 1843. Doc. 81, vol. 2, Senate Docs. 1844.

NATURAL HISTORY.

Doc. 87, vol. 3, Ass'y Docs. 1843. Doc. 6, vol. 1, Senate Docs. 1845.

NORMAL SCHOOL.

Doc. 24, vol. 1, Senate Docs. 1845.

www.ingramcontent.com/pod-product-compliance
Lightning Source LLC
LaVergne TN
LVHW010231110826
845151LV00004B/1261
9781425525583